Municipal Officials, Their Public, and the Negotiation of Justice in Medieval Languedoc

Later Medieval Europe

VOLUME 10

The titles published in this series are listed at brill.com/lme

Municipal Officials, Their Public, and the Negotiation of Justice in Medieval Languedoc

Fear Not the Madness of the Raging Mob

By

Patricia Turning

BRILL

LEIDEN · BOSTON
2013

Cover illustration: The Capitole (built in the 18th century) marks the very heart of the 'Ville rose' (Pink city.) It has a superb facade using brick, stone and marble. The eight columns symbolize the eight « capitols », or governors who administered the city from the middle ages to the revolution. Today it houses the town hall and the Théâtre du Capitole of the city of Toulouse.
©Photograph by Patricia Turning

Library of Congress Cataloging-in-Publication Data

Turning, Patricia.
Municipal officials, their public, and the negotiation of justice in medieval Languedoc : fear not the madness of the raging mob / by Patricia Turning.
p. cm. -- (Later medieval Europe, ISSN 1872-7875 ; v. 10)
Includes bibliographical references and index.
ISBN 978-90-04-23464-2 (hbk. : alk. paper)
1. Criminal justice, Administration of--France--Toulouse--History--To 1500. 2. Public administration--France--Toulouse--History--To 1500. 3. Municipal officials and employees--France--Toulouse--History--To 1500. 4. Toulouse (France)--Politics and government. I. Title.

HV9960.F72T688 2012
364.944'73670902--dc23

2012027134

This publication has been typeset in the multilingual "Brill" typeface. With over 5,100 characters covering Latin, IPA, Greek, and Cyrillic, this typeface is especially suitable for use in the humanities. For more information, please see www.brill.com/brill-typeface.

ISSN 1872-7875
ISBN 978 90 04 23464 2 (hardback)
ISBN 978 90 04 23465 9 (e-book)

This book is printed on acid-free paper.

CONTENTS

A Note about Abbreviations and Citations vii

Introduction 1

1 From Count to King: The Capitols' Struggle to Maintain Control over the Legal Structure of Toulouse 17

2 The Spatial Distribution of Crime in Toulouse 43

3 "With an Angry Face and Teeth Clenched:" Personal Conflict and Public Resolution 73

4 Forces of Order, Forces of Disorder: Corrupt Officers and the Confusion of Authority 103

5 The Power to Punish in Medieval Toulouse 137

Conclusion 177
Selected Bibliography 185
Index 195

A NOTE ABOUT ABBREVIATIONS AND CITATIONS

AMA – The *Archives municipales* of Albi
AMM – The *Archives municipales* of Moissac
AMT – The *Archives municipales* of Toulouse
ADHG – The *Archives départementales de la Haute Garonne* in Toulouse
BN – The *Bibliothèque nationale de France* in Paris
BMT – The *Bibliothèque municipale* of Toulouse
CR – *Comptes royaux (1314-1328)*, ed. François Maillard (Paris: Imprimerie nationale, 1961)
DRT – *Dictionnaire des rues de Toulouse: voies publiques, quartiers, lieux-dits, enseignes, organisation urbaine*, 2 vols., ed. Pierre Salies (Toulouse: Éditions Milan, 1989)
HGL – Claude Devic and Joseph Vaissète, *Histoire générale du Languedoc*, ed. Auguste Molinier, 16 vols. (Toulouse: Privat, 1872-1904)
Statuts – Marcel Fournier, ed. *Les statuts et privilèges des universités françaises, depuis leur foundation jusqu'en 1789*, vol. 1 (Aalen, Italy: Scientia Verlag, 1970)

INTRODUCTION

"[Toulouse is] another promised land, flowing in milk and honey, where prolific herbs flourish, where fruit trees bud, where Bacchus reigns over vineyards and Ceres rules over the fields... and so fear not the malice of the raging mob or the tyranny of an injurious prince...here it is seen that courtly good humor has struck a covenant with knighthood and clergy."[1]

Jean de Garland, 1230

In 1230, the scholar Jean de Garland attempted to lure Parisian masters to join him at the newly instituted university in the southern city of Toulouse. Just a year earlier in Paris, a deadly town and gown row led to a student strike, which effectively disbanded the university. As the above quote suggests, Jean de Garland needed to assure the newly displaced masters and students that they would not suffer at the hands of the people, or the exploitation of local officials. He insisted Toulouse was a stable and flourishing environment where they would enjoy their proper legal privileges. In the same year of 1229, Toulouse and the surrounding region of Languedoc surrendered to the Capetian kings, thus ending the decades long and arduously fought Albigensian Crusade against the Cathar heretics. The peace treaty ordered the elected officials of Toulouse, known as capitols, to destroy the city walls and defensive garrisons, and stipulated that with the cooperation of their citizens, they would support and protect university scholars so as to ensure that heresy would not return to the region. In addition, the peace agreement extended royal judicial control over the local court system. The papacy also sent Dominican inquisitors into Toulouse, where they established their tribunal headquarters for the persecution of the lingering numbers of suspected Cathars in the area. But despite the best efforts of royal and papal authorities to set up institutions of order and orthodoxy in the city, the administrators and citizens of Toulouse simply did not correspond with the portrait presented by Jean

[1] *Statuts*, 440, no. 504 no. 72, 129–131. "Et ut libentius Tholose gloriam simul cum studio studiosi dinoscant, sciant hanc alteram esse terram promissionis fluentem lac et mel, ubi fetose pascue virent, ubi arbores pomifere frondent, ubi Bacchus regnat in vineis, ubi Ceres imperat in arvis, ubi temperatur aër antiquis philosophis fuerat consideratis terre stadiis preelectus...An timetis malitiam populi sevientis vel tyrannidem principis injuriosi? Ne timeatis...videtur enim hic facetia curialis cum militia simul et cum clero federa pepigisse."

de Garland. Instead, violent eruptions of protest from the citizens and capitols alike targeted the scholars, friars, and royal officials as the representatives of outside oppression and occupation, and drove them from the city on numerous occasions. Jean de Garland himself became so fearful of the urban population that within three years of his boasts about the civility and security of Toulouse, he fled the city by boat just barely escaping an angry mob.[2]

The process, then, of incorporating Languedoc into the broader Capetian kingdom was not removed from the consciousness of the local population. Indeed, at times the administrators seemed to collaborate with their citizens in their resistance to royal authorities well into the later Middle Ages, and this ultimately is the argument of the following book. In order to elucidate the premise, this study explores the participatory nature of the medieval urban public in shaping and engaging in local political and judicial developments in thirteenth- and fourteenth-century Toulouse. By the end of the Middle Ages, city streets and public squares, buildings and landmarks, all served as a forum for judicial discourse between the local administration and urban inhabitants. Municipal officers (including messengers, trumpeters, sergeants, and night guards) patrolled the neighborhoods, pronounced and enforced laws, and interacted with people through daily social activity. Elected officials and notaries presided over courts in the town hall, where citizens brought forth complaints and sought restitution for various illicit infractions. Through these points of contact, urban administrators and their residents constantly negotiated notions of law and order through both dramatic and subtle ways. Much like today, disgruntled citizens flocked to the streets of Toulouse in violent demonstrations against local practices or new taxes. In fact, only Paris hosted more insurrections than Toulouse in medieval France.[3] But citizens also took more formal and peaceful measures like filing criminal charges against the city's officers for issues like police brutality.

The details of these incidents, preserved in criminal records and jurisdictional disputes from Toulouse, suggest that the people living in the late medieval city had a vested interest in their local judicial systems because it permeated so many facets of their lives. For example, elected politicians assumed both legislative and judicial responsibilities, so citizens turned to

2 Cyril Eugene Smith, *The University of Toulouse in the Middle Ages: Its Origins and Growth to 1500 AD* (Milwaukee, Wisconsin: The Marquette University Press, 1958), 56.

3 Samuel K. Cohn, *Lust for Liberty: The Politics of Social Revolt in Medieval Europe, 1200–1425* (Cambridge: Harvard University Press, 2006), 161.

them for both protection and justice. As such, medieval municipal officials could not just impose any new policies or pronounce controversial legal decisions without expecting some response from the citizens themselves, whether it was an affirmation or a protest. And similarly, many of the urban populace demanded to be recognized, their opinions to be heard, when there were any changes to the existing local system itself. These exchanges and interactions between municipal officials and their citizens became increasingly complicated as royal and ecclesiastical institutions (as well as universities) sought to extend and to legitimize their own jurisdiction in the urban realm.

In this era, Toulouse serves as an important example in our understanding of how this overlap of authority and changes in a city's judicial system impacted the medieval urban population in the practice of everyday life. Again, after the Albigensian Crusade, the French monarchy established a new judicial hierarchy over the local court system as a means of state building, and sent royal officials to reside and to administer in Toulouse. The Catholic Church intensified its demands for the legal privileges of the clergy and university students, and supported the influx of Dominicans into the city. But the integration of Languedoc into the larger Capetian kingdom was only complete once it had been tested and challenged by the local residents in the public arena of the urban environment. The capitols and their constituents challenged royal changes in the judicial system of Languedoc through both subtle and spectacular displays of protest that encompassed the public arena of Toulouse. As royal representatives became more intrusive in the judicial system and policing of Toulouse, as Dominican inquisitors pursued and imprisoned suspects, and as the university became a better defined institution, the capitols encouraged the citizens to subvert the king's sovereignty in order to maintain the traditions of their office and the region in general. The capitols, however, were politically astute enough to blame the more controversial demonstrations on an unidentified "raging mob" when they were held accountable by the king, or to shroud their real motivations under a more neutral guise.

This last assertion has been touched upon tangentially by David Nirenberg in his *Communities of Violence* (1996), in which he explored cruelty against minorities in the fourteenth century. Although the bulk of his analysis focuses on tension between Muslims, Jews and Christians in Spain, he begins the work with France's Shepherds' Crusade and Lepers' Plot of 1320 and 1321, respectively. The Shepherds' Crusade originated around Paris, as a multitude of lowborn rural workers targeted royal castles and officials, but exerted most of their aggression towards Jews.

As the movement made its way south through Aquitaine and into Languedoc, it culminated in a massacre of Jews in Toulouse on June 12, 1320. Pope John XXII responded to the attacks by imploring both the archbishop and the seneschal of Toulouse to intervene on behalf of the Jews. But it was not until fall of the same year that the royal seneschal of nearby Carcassone defeated the marauding shepherds and drove them from the region. When the French monarch Philip V attempted to punish the individuals who participated in the attacks, this sparked a second rebellion in Languedoc in 1321, and the targets were now Jews and lepers. During the fray, municipal officials of Toulouse, Albi and Carcassone petitioned the king to expel Jews from France, and to segregate the lepers from society. When the king refused, municipal officials took matters into their own hands and arrested, tortured and executed lepers accused of poisoning wells. They only notified the king's agents after the fact. At first glance these movements could be dismissed as 'irrational' medieval violence of first the rural, and then the urban masses. But Nirenberg insists that there were very deliberate political and judicial motives behind these acts. In the Lepers' Plot, for instance, the same petition presented to the king against minorities included an extensive list of complaints about royal justice in Toulouse, including a charge that royal officials claimed jurisdiction over cases that should have been tried in municipal courts.[4] And so the capitols of Toulouse ordered the arrest and execution of lepers as a means of usurping royal judicial authority, under the pretense of broader religious discourse.

Beyond these explosive examples that involved malice towards minorities as an extension of political protest, medieval historians of France rarely have the opportunity to explore how the developments in political and judicial structures affected urban inhabitants after a city was incorporated into the larger Capetian kingdom. Most studies, particularly of Languedoc, rely on documents that do not identify by name any member of public protests and riots. In this respect, the history of Toulouse in the thirteenth and fourteenth century has been an analysis of the political exchanges and correspondence between high ranking officials, removed from the people equally impacted by the city's transition into a royal legal system. Part of the problem is that seventeenth-century amateur scholars chose to publish only charters and chronicles that involved the nobility

[4] David Nirenberg, *Communities of Violence: Persecution of Minorities in the Middle Ages* (Princeton: Princeton University Press, 1996), 53–55.

and which reflected the wealth of the region and its counts. As such, they do not provide much information about the common people living in Toulouse.[5] Historians interested in the municipal political organization relied on these editions and on the positive and customary laws from the turn of the thirteenth century preserved in the municipal archive. Two cartularies (from the *cité* and *bourg*), contain the earliest charters from the administration under the local count of Toulouse, and reveal the economic and judicial privileges of the city before the region was captured by the king.[6] The subject matter of these documents largely concerns the municipal administration's acquisition of land, peace treaties with other territories, and commercial regulations. Once city officials began to correspond with the Capetian king and his representatives, rather than the local counts, scholars had access to a broader range of source material. This has led to numerous studies of the French king's centralization of his sovereignty in the thirteenth century. For example, King Louis VIII appointed his son, Alphonse of Poitiers, as the count of Languedoc after the Albigensian Crusade in order to ensure both the eradication of heretics and the region's compliance with royal law. As an administrator, Alphonse wrote extensive letters of instruction to his vicar, his seneschal and the capitols concerning their judicial and legal policies.[7] After the death of Alphonse in 1271, the king demanded oaths of loyalty from the town's citizens, and a royally approved codification of the city's customary law.[8] Historians have primarily focused upon the legal

---

[5] The two best examples are Guillaume Catel, *Histoire des comtes de Toulouse, avec quelque traitez et chroniques anciennes, concernans la mesme histoire* (Toulouse: P. Bosc, 1623), and Germain de Lafaille, *Annales de la ville de Toulouse depuis la réunion de la compté de Toulouse à la couronne*, 2 vols. (Toulouse: Guillaume-Louis Colomyez, 1687–1701). Both works have fundamental flaws in their accuracy, but are invaluable because they include transcriptions of documents which would otherwise have been lost to historians.

[6] AMT-AA 1, AA 2. The majority of the charters are dated from the 1180s to the 1220s. Both of the cartularies are published, with a summary and bibliographical essay, in Roger Limouzin-Lamothe, *La commune de Toulouse et les sources de son histoire, 1120–1249* (Paris and Toulouse, 1932). See also, John Hine Mundy, *Liberty and Political Power in Toulouse, 1050–1230* (New York: Columbia University Press, 1954).

[7] Auguste Molinier, *Correspondance administrative d'Alphonse de Poitiers*, 2vols. (Paris: Imprimerie Nationale, 1894 and 1900). See also, John W. Baldwin, *The Government of Philip Augustus: Foundations of French Royal Power in the Middle Ages* (Berkeley: The University of California Press, 1986).

[8] The registry of the oaths is published by Yves Dossat, *Saisimentum Comitatus Tholosani* (Paris: Bibliothèque Nationale, 1966). This is a transcription of the extant seventeenth-century copy of the thirteenth-century original. One copy of Toulouse's customary law is found in, BN ms. latin 9187. It is published, along with a commentary found in the manuscript, in Henri Gilles, *Les coutumes de Toulouse (1283) et leur premier commentaire (1296)* (Toulouse: Imprimerie Maurice ESPIC, 1969).

changes and bureaucratic reorganization of Toulouse, and how it was shaped by royal representatives, the capitols, and, later, university legal scholars.[9]

Scholars interested in other issues besides the political evolution of the city have consulted tax records, guild statutes, and various ecclesiastical documents in order to ascertain standards of living, means of economic production, and family structures in medieval Toulouse. In 1335, the capitols began to gather a census of the taxable wealth of each head of household, either male or female.[10] This list of the values of immovable and movable property is important to historians interested in wealth distribution in the city and citizens' ownership of land outside of Toulouse, but unfortunately, the surviving extract from the early fourteenth century contains information for a small portion of the *bourg*.[11] Toulouse's archives contain a large number of guild statutes and regulations from this era, but they have not been fully exploited by scholars beyond transcriptions and brief observations about the production of goods.[12] John Hine Mundy employed church documents, such as matrimonial contracts and testaments, in order to recreate family histories for some of the wealthiest families of the city.[13] Documents from the Dominican inquisitors, stationed in Toulouse as early as 1233, have been exhaustively mined by scholars of heresy and the mechanisms of church repression, partly because inquisitors such as Bernard Gui kept fastidious records of the penalties that they

---

[9] The most recent study is Christopher Gardner, "Negotiating Lordship: Efforts of the Consulat of Toulouse to Retain Autonomy under Capetian Rule (ca. 1229–1315)," (Ph.D. diss, Johns Hopkins University, 2002). Gardner relies heavily on the loyalty oaths of the capitols to explore the political negotiation between capitols and the king.

[10] AMT-CC1 and CC2.

[11] Philippe Wolff has worked with these documents extensively from the later fourteenth- and fifteenth-century in *Les "estimes" Toulousaines des XIVe et XVe siècles* (Toulouse: Centre National de la Recherche Scientifique, 1956), and *Commerces et Marchands de Toulouse (vers 1350–1450)* (Paris: Librairie Pilon, 1954), "Toulouse vers 1400: répartition topographique des fortunes et des professions," *Regards sur le midi* (Toulouse: Private, 1978), 269–278. Jean-Nöel Biraben has also used the tax records to attempt to calculate the city's population, in "La population de Toulouse au XIVe et XVe siècles," *Journal des Savants* (1964): 285–300.

[12] Sister Mary Ambrose Mulholland, *Early Guild Records of Toulouse* (New York: Columbia University Press, 1941). See also her, "Statutes on Clothmaking: Toulouse, 1227." *Essays in Medieval Life and Thought, Presented in Honor of Austin Patterson Evans,* ed. John H. Mundy, Richard W. Emery and Benjamin N. Nelson (New York: Columbia University Press, 1955), 167–180.

[13] See, for example, his *The Repression of Catharism at Toulouse: The Royal Diploma of 1279* (Toronto: Pontifical Institute of Mediaeval Studies, 1985), 129–303, and *Men and Women at Toulouse in the Age of the Cathars* (Toronto: Pontifical Institute of Mediaeval Studies, 1990), 171–194.

administered to the convicted heretics.[14] These studies provide the legal, religious and economic context for the city of Toulouse during this era of political transition into the Capetian kingdom, but they also open the door to new questions about the impact this period had upon society and culture in general.

The overarching aim of the historiography of Toulouse has been to establish when the capitols and the Toulousains fully accepted royal sovereignty, and how the king succeeded in taking over the region of Languedoc. In the nineteenth century, scholars emphasized that the city eagerly embraced the king and his rule throughout the thirteenth century, and it housed complacent subjects by the beginning of the fourteenth century.[15] Although more recent studies have complicated this relationship by tracing the political negotiations between royal officials and the capitols concerning the city's rights and privileges, most agree that the city's smooth integration into the kingdom could be attributed to the king's recruitment of local men to work in his administration.[16] According to these arguments, the capitols and people of Toulouse willingly accepted royal sovereignty by the beginning of the fourteenth century and offered no resistance to changes in the judicial system. As the following pages will show, this general consensus does not take into consideration the increasing importance of criminal justice in the lives of urban inhabitants, and how the capitols depended on their court system to maintain the power over their constituents that royal authority would have superseded. As the judicial structure and practices of Toulouse were becoming better defined and codified due to the influx of university trained lawyers,the capitols realized that maintaining control of the right to pass judgment was the most effective way to preserve the legitimacy of their

---

[14] BMT– MS 388. Bernard Gui's register of sentences is published in Philipp van Limborch, *Historia inquisitionis, cui subjungitur Liber sententiarum inquisitionis Tholosanae ab anno Christi MCCCVII ad annum MCCCXXIII* (Amsterdam: Apud H. Wetstenium, 1692). A register of his sentences and meetings with the capitols is also located in BN, man. lat. 11848 (1307–1323), published in Annette Pales-Gobilliard, *Le Livre des sentences de l'inquisiteur Bernard Gui (1308–1323)*, 2 vols. (Paris: CNRS Éditions, 2002). See also, Célestin Douais, ed. *Documents pour servir à l'histoire de l'inquisition dans le Languedoc* (Paris: H. Champion, 1977). Walter L. Wakefield, *Heresy, Crusade and Inquisition in Southern France* (Berkeley: University of California Press, 1974).

[15] The first editors of the multi-volume series *HGL*, began their endeavor of compiling documents in order to preserve the region's close connection and unique history with the monarchy. See, also, Edgard Boutaric, *La France sous Philip le Bel – Étude sur les institutions politiques et administratives du moyen âge* (Paris: Henri Plon, 1861).

[16] James Given, *State and Society in Medieval Europe: Gwynedd and Languedoc under Outside Rule* (Ithaca: Cornell University Press, 1990). Gardner, "Negotiating Lordship."

office.[17] This work will show that the capitols, with the witting and unwitting cooperation of the people of Toulouse, fought to maintain the autonomy of the city well into the fourteenth century.

Only by exploring the relationship between the capitols and the people of Toulouse is it possible to understand how the changes in the judicial structures were negotiated in daily activity. To accomplish this means examining a series of sources ignored by previous generations of historians. The municipal archives hold a collection of criminal records and jurisdictional disputes between local and royal administrators. They reveal that even though the capitols had conceded to royal authority in the official written statutes, in practice, legitimate sovereignty over Toulouse was challenged and fought for in the streets of the city. The most significant source for this purpose is a criminal register from 1332 containing the transcript of a trial that resulted in the execution of a university student's squire. Dubbed by modern scholars as the "Aimery Berenger Affair," this case provoked years of debate in the 1330s between the king, pope, and capitols concerning the extent of royal jurisdiction over a university student's servant.[18] Most historians have seen this event as an anomaly in the city's otherwise harmonious existence within the royal kingdom.[19] This assessment is contradicted by the records of fifty-one additional cases also contained in the register, that offer remarkable insight into the legal process of Toulouse, and the daily lives, tensions, and concerns of the people who interacted with each other and with the municipal officers in the streets of the city. The cases are certainly not representative of all of the criminal activity in Toulouse. If a clerk committed an infraction, for example, he would be tried in an ecclesiastical court. Aside from jurisdictional limitations to the number of cases heard by the capitols, many lesser offences were never recorded or even made it to trial. Instead, the capitols primarily heard cases that resonated with the populace and invited public performances at trial and punishments.

The criminal register describes the large number of municipal officials involved in the judicial process, both attending the trials, and representing

---

17 Henri Gilles, "L'Enseignement du droit en Languedoc au XIII siècle," *Les Universités du Languedoc au XIIIe siècle* (Toulouse: Privat, 1970), 205–229.

18 AMT-FF 57. A copy of the Aimery Berenger case is found in AMT-FF 58, as well. Chapter 5 treats the details and significance of the case. Each folio in the register is numbered in Roman numerals. A modern archivist has added Arabic numbers as well. I use the modern pagination.

19 For example, Philippe Wolff views the scandal as an embarrassment in the otherwise flourishing era of the *Jeux Floraux*, a troubadour poetry competition founded in 1323. *Histoire de Toulouse* (Toulouse: Édouard Privat, 1958), 177–179.

the capitols in the city streets. The capitols presided over the hearings, although not all twelve were always present at the same time. In especially controversial cases, many other "good men" and officials were present as well, including bureaucrats and legal advisors such as notaries and jurists; but there was also a banker (*campsor*) from Toulouse, and the municipal jailer in attendance at sentencing.[20] The roles of messengers and sergeants at the capitols' disposal, who announced the crimes and arrested the criminals, are well depicted in the records, and the case transcripts recount numerous other night guards conflicting with the inhabitants while patrolling the city for malefactors. The accused defendants employed multiple defense attorneys for their trials.[21] According to local practice, lawyers could stand in place of their clients, and at any point a defendant could have as many as five different attorneys present during the trial. Each lawyer had the authority to act independently of the other attorneys, which undoubtedly led to some confusion. In addition, the capitols called upon at least six medical experts who examined victims of physical assaults, and who offered testimony which established the severity of the wounds. These court cases, then, not only offer insight into the formalities of court proceedings in the determination of guilt or innocence, but also point to the ways in which municipal officers interacted with the citizens in and out of the courtroom.

As municipal capitols, royal representatives, ecclesiastical inquisitors, and their policing officials crowded the streets and courtrooms of Toulouse (along with the other men and women of the city), it is imperative to understand how negotiations of justice flowed from the bottom-up, not just the top-down. In order to accomplish this goal, this book builds upon the works of theorists, such as Michel Foucault and Pierre Bourdieu, who described space as a contested geography and territory, over which groups and individuals try to exert power and control.[22] Bourdieu argues the power of a society's dominant group lies in its ability to control the constructions of reality that reinforce its own status, so that subordinate groups accept the social order and their own place in it.[23] To maintain its

---

20 AMT-FF 57, 18.

21 In the register, Magister Guillelmus de Payranis served as the most commonly employed procurator, whereas other attorneys, such as Magister Johannes de Soloquis, Magister Arnaldus Boneti, Magister Raymundus de Bax, and Magister Bernardus Raymundus Baiuli served less frequently.

22 Michel Foucault, *Power/Knowledge: Selected Interviews and Other Writings, 1972–1977*, ed. and trans. Colin Gordon, et al (New York, 1980), 149.

23 Pierre Bourdieu, *Outline of a Theory of Practice* (Cambridge, 1977), 90–91, 160–163.

advantages, any powerful group must create an ordering of space for subservient groups through symbolic rituals, laws, or the regulation of habitation and work opportunities. Over the past few years, medieval historians such as Barbara Hanawalt and Kathryn Reyerson, editors of *City and Spectacle*, have begun to examine the various ways in which monarchs, popes, and the common man or woman manipulated, perceived, and lived in their urban space in light of spatial theory. They acknowledge that, "to medieval urban inhabitants, space was not neutral. Selection of particular spaces for events speaks to exclusion of some urban inhabitants as well as inclusion of others."[24] People living in medieval cities recognized the symbolic meanings behind civic rituals and ceremonies which were enacted throughout the streets in order to assert municipal authority, legitimize a new monarch, or celebrate pride in a guild's history or achievements. Spectacle used space to show, or refuse, a realignment of sovereignty and control, and social cohesion.

"Fear Not the Madness of the Raging Mob" employs the concept of space as a contested territory to unpack the greater meanings behind the interactions in social communities as preserved in the registers of criminal trials. Even though the available data does not always provide satisfactory answers to questions about the patterns of crime and criminality in medieval cities, more historians have begun to unpack trials as a civic ritual of justice. For example, Robert Bartlett sees the trials themselves as windows into greater meanings of the interactions within social communities and concepts of crimes.[25] In other words, the trial itself served as a "staged event," in which the criminal proceedings were a play of a real life drama.[26] Trials reveal more than the way "crime is defined, disciplined and perceived in the past."[27] The "tales" that are told in the court records bring to light the values of the judges and the judged, and establish the society's

---

24 Barbara A. Hanawalt and Kathryn L. Reyerson, eds. *City and Spectacle in Medieval Europe* (Minneapolis: University of Minnesota Press, 1994), xviii.

25 See, Robert Bartlett, *The Hanged Man: A Story of Miracle, Memory, and Colonialism in the Middle Ages* (Princeton: University of Princeton Press, 2004).

26 Antoine Garapon, *Bien juger: Essai sur le rituel judiciaire* (Paris: Odile Jacob, 1997). Andrée Courtemanche divides one trial into literary categories such as "protagonists" and the "plot" in, "The Judge, The Doctor, and the Prisoner: Medical Expertise in Manosquin Judicial Rituals at the End of the Fourteenth Century," *Medieval and Early Modern Ritual: Formalized Behavior in Europe, China, and Japan*, ed. Joëlle Rollo-Koster (Boston: Brill, 2002), 105–123.

27 Edward Muir and Guido Ruggeiro, "Afterword: Crime and the Writing of History," *History from Crime*, ed. Edward Muir and Guido Ruggiero, trans. Corrada Biazzo Curry, Margaret A. Gallucci and Mary M. Gallucci (Baltimore: The Johns Hopkins University Press, 1994), 226.

system of rules of behavior.[28] Thus, the notary's description of crimes and the witness testimony reveal to historians the boundaries of good and bad behavior, and decided who was included in and excluded from an ordered society.[29] Michel de Certeau asserts that trials are "spatial" stories in a sense, drawing both literal and figurative borders in the city: restrictions of acceptable behavior, communal obligations of conduct, as well as physical boundaries of social interaction in neighborhoods and city streets.[30] The litigants who brought cases before the capitols did not necessarily consider the outcome of the trial as the most important factor of the dispute. Instead, the public nature of the accusation and the spectacle of the social drama involved in taking an enemy to court were just as significant.[31] Medieval people invested in pressing charges against their enemy, not necessarily for the financial outcome, but because they could defame an opponent, or give legitimacy to the hatred or anger they may possess. The records from medieval Toulouse reveal how a wide spectrum of people postured for primacy and negotiated justice not only in the courtroom, but also outside in the city streets.

This methodology allows the nuances of medieval urban violence to be teased out, from interpersonal conflicts to destructive popular protests and demonstrations, to the explosive town and gown rows. By concentrating on Toulouse, where municipal, royal and ecclesiastical officials and representatives struggled for jurisdiction over the city's population during this period of transition from an independent commune (with the local count out of the way) into the Capetian kingdom, this work provides a greater depth to scholarly discussions of urban protests and revolts. Whereas the most recent study of the phenomenon by Samuel K. Cohn takes a broad geographic and chronological perspective of rebellions,

---

[28] Daniel Lord Smail, "Telling Tales in Angevin Courts," *French Historical Studies* 2 vol. 20 (Spring, 1997): 183–215. Natalie Zemon Davis, *Fiction in the Archives: Pardon Tales and their Tellers in Sixteenth-Century France* (Stanford, California: Stanford University Press, 1987).

[29] For example, B. Ann Tlusty examines witness testimony in early modern Augsburg in order to argue that the society had varying levels and standards of acceptable violence, particularly among the artisans who frequented taverns. "Violence and Urban Identity in Early Modern Augsburg: Communication Strategies Between Authorities and Citizens in the Adjudication of Fights," *Cultures of Communication from Reformation to Enlightenment: Constructing Publics in the Early Modern German Lands*, ed. James Van Horn Melton (Burlington, VT: Ashgate Publishing Company, 2002), 10–23.

[30] Michel de Certeau, *The Practice of Everyday Life*, trans. Steven Rendall (Berkeley: The University of California Press, 1984), 123.

[31] Daniel Lord Smail, *The Consumption of Justice: Emotions, Publicity, and Legal Culture in Marseille, 1264–1423* (Ithaca: Cornell University Press, 2003), 23.

uprisings, and riots, the examples from Toulouse are contextualized and individualized.[32] The events in Languedoc can be understood as the urban public's demands to be recognized by their authorities, rather than as senseless or random acts by a "raging mob." The protestors aspired to draw attention to these broader concerns by publicly challenging local officials to improve the current conditions of their community, or to exert notions of justice, even though some individuals took their actions to a destructive extreme. All sectors of the urban space were incorporated into the political discourse between the local administration and urban inhabitants, struggling to accommodate demographic, economic and judicial changes in France.

This study begins with an examination of the changes in the political and legal structures of Toulouse after the Albigensian Crusade. Although many historians of Languedoc have paid this particular subject a lot of attention (especially for the period of the thirteenth century), it is crucial to this study to establish the overlapping jurisdictions which resulted in the city, and to elucidate how the transition from a relatively independent commune to part of a royal kingdom effected the role of the capitols in the lives of the Toulousains. While counts controlled Languedoc, the capitols secured many privileges for the city and power for their office. In this era before the Albigensian Crusade, in the late twelfth and early thirteenth century, the municipal officers held a firm grasp over the enforcement of law and order in Toulouse, because they had their own police force that regulated everything from criminal activity to funeral processions, and they had the sole power to inflict criminal punishments. Once the royal crusaders overcame the city's defenses, royal authority steadily usurped the capitols' supremacy, which included the forfeiture of their right to administer criminal punishments without the approval of a royal representative. In addition, the king sent a large number of sergeants and officers to enforce the new royal law, to patrol the city streets, to manage royal jails, and to serve as the strong arm of the Dominican inquisitors. It was at this time that the University of Toulouse fought as well to establish itself as an island of jurisdiction, protected by the privileges granted by the king and the pope. The ground that was once patrolled and judged by the capitols and their officers alone was rapidly becoming crowded with competitors for jurisdiction. The capitols struggled in this environment to secure their own power, and they relied on their officers and the general public to aid them in this endeavor.

32 Cohn, *Lust for Liberty*.

In Chapter 2, I explore the social and physical topography of the city. The major goal of this section is to assess where most offenses and protests took place in the city. Toulouse was divided into twelve regions, known as *capitoulats*, and the population of each section elected a capitol. But beyond political divisions, economic production and religious affiliation portioned the city space. For example, with the growing power of the church in Toulouse after the crusade, the territory surrounding the city's basilica and cathedral became populated with clerks and university students. After identifying the overlapping social, religious, political and economic regions of the city, I will also map the alleged reported crimes throughout Toulouse, to ascertain whether there was a particular portion or neighborhood of the city which was rife with criminal activity. I discovered that the people in the criminal records were, for the most part, individuals with firmly established ties to the city, and the conflicts occurred in the most populous region of the city. This reveals that the court system was not occupied with bandits or a dark underworld of crime as was the case in Paris; the capitols and their officers engaged with people contributing to the society in general.

This demographic sketch of the alleged offenders and their victims paves the way for the discussion in Chapter 3, which explores the nature of the crimes described in the trial testimony from 1332. The sources reveal that most of the criminal activity transpired in the streets of the city, with a wide range of witnesses and participants. In the neighborhoods throughout Toulouse, men and women announced their disdain for their rivals to whoever would listen, and vowed and plotted to make sure that their threats of violence would come to fruition. When the physical attacks did occur, the perpetrator ensured that an audience was present to acknowledge that dominance over a foe had been displayed through confrontation. But the members of the public did not passively observe these fights. The capitols issued proclamations that encouraged the citizens to intervene if they witnessed crimes, and many people did step forward to stop attacks that erupted in the city streets. Other men and women of Toulouse participated in the crimes in a more conspiratorial manner, serving as accomplices in the event or concealing the plot. As these crimes were not clandestine and private matters, but open events experienced by spectators, the pursuit of justice was also a public ritual so that the victims and their families could believe that the capitols had restored their honor within their community. The capitols and their officers 'performed justice' in the trial through proclamations of the offenses in the various neighborhoods of Toulouse, by opening their courtroom doors to witnesses and spectators, and through their public reading of sentences. In many respects, because the crimes were public events, so too did the trial in order to reestablish a sense of order to the community. Overall, this chapter will emphasize that conflict and resolution between individuals, their families, and the municipal officers, all transpired in the public buildings, squares and streets of Toulouse.

But the capitols and their officers did not always maintain peace in the community, and they did find occasions to advance their own personal agendas during the course of their interactions with the people of Toulouse. Chapter 4 begins with a controversial incident from the late thirteenth century which unfolded on the courtyard in front of the town hall. This scenario complicates the relationship between the capitols, their officers, and the people of Toulouse, and points towards the municipal officials' motivations to subvert royal authority in the city. Because of the uncertain and tumultuous conditions of the medieval urban environment, the capitols had to employ large, aggressive men to serve as their officers. Unfortunately, some of these men tended to be corrupt, and had few qualms unleashing unwarranted brutality when dealing with certain portions of the public. Although the capitols held the most scandalous officers accountable for the crimes in their courtroom, the same sergeants and night guards proved indispensable to the elected officials when they cooperated in plans to subvert the authority of the king and his royal representatives.

The book concludes with a chapter concerning the importance of public punishments in medieval Toulouse. The historiography of medieval punishments is a vast and complex field, with debates surrounding everything from the meaning behind the spectacle of the execution to the actual number of prisoners who suffered corporal punishment. In Toulouse, the sources suggest that the capitols employed a variety of public punishments for criminals, at a fairly consistent rate, incorporating many regions throughout the city. Convicted criminals could suffer the humiliation of running the streets as a trumpeter beckoned witnesses, or they could be ordered to stand in shackles, exposed in a window of the town hall's jail. The capitols used the city space to demonstrate their authority to the citizens, while also satisfying the victims' need for public restitution. When the capitols began to lose autonomy to the royal representative in the determination of criminal sentences, and when they faced competition in the public arena from the Dominican inquisitors who were punishing heretics, they devised new ways to preserve the status of their office. I contend that they accomplished this goal by enlisting the aid of their officers in order to coordinate punitive events which defied royal mandates and displayed sovereignty over the urban space and people. Once the king held the capitols accountable for this boldness, the elected officials denied culpability and placed blame upon their officers and a nameless mob as a means of avoiding charges of treason.

Overall, this book stresses the urban public's role in the formation of political and judicial structures in the thirteenth and fourteenth century. As local officials negotiated issues of dominion with the royal centralized authority in charters and in written correspondence, the people of Toulouse insisted that their opinions and their participation in municipal affairs not be ignored. If a royal representative violated their standards of justice, thousands of the urban inhabitants took to the streets and congregated at the town hall to protest and to demonstrate their discontent. The capitols learned to manipulate this outpouring of public sentiment to undermine the king's power in Toulouse, and to preserve the legitimate authority of their office well into the fourteenth century. The most dramatic and powerful way they demonstrated this power to the public was through the organization of spectacular punishments, which incorporated a wide range of the city space. The capitols and their officers performed their control of the judicial system, the urban space and their people by orchestrating the elaborate chastisements which defied royal mandates. The integration of Toulouse into the Capetian kingdom, then, was only complete once it had been tested and challenged by the municipal authorities and the citizens in the public arena of the urban environment.

CHAPTER ONE

FROM COUNT TO KING: THE CAPITOLS' STRUGGLE TO MAINTAIN CONTROL OVER THE LEGAL STRUCTURE OF TOULOUSE

In August, 1226, the municipal patrol of Toulouse discovered two men's bodies lying outside of the city's walls. The victims, identified as Willelmus Petrus de Flurento and Geraldus de Vaquiriis, inhabitants of Toulouse, not only were murdered, but horribly mutilated and torn to pieces.[1] Relatives and friends of the men suspected that Raymond VII, Count of Toulouse, had granted the alleged murderer asylum in his home or court. Shortly thereafter, a large crowd of infuriated Toulousains took turns guarding Willelmus and Geraldus's dismembered bodies in front of the town hall, to admonish the count's protection of the man they believed guilty of the murders. During the demonstration, protesters prevented the twelve elected capitols and their officers from entering the building, begged for justice and threatened the administrators with violence if they did not fulfill the obligations of their office and seek restitution for the victims and their families. Either convinced or shamed by the public outcry, the capitols quickly summoned Count Raymond and several thousand Toulousains to gather in a large patch of grass on the right bank of the Garonne River known as the Carbonelli field. At the capitols' request, Raymond declared publically that he would not provide refuge in his home or in his court to a criminal accused of killing anyone from the city of Toulouse or its vicinity. The count agreed to uphold the capitols' sentences in all criminal cases including punishments which involved the seizure of a prisoner's property from then on. Count Raymond not only made this oath orally to the capitols and before the people of Toulouse, but signed a notarized charter to be confirmed by his successors.

On the rare occasions when scholars discuss this incident, it is nearly always in the context of the resolution of the capitols' jurisdictional

[1] This *procès-verbal* is found in the cartulary of the cité, preserved among the oldest extant series of charters, privileges granted to the city, in addition to peace treaties and the capitols' early judgments. The date range for the documents begins in 1120 and ends in 1249. AMT-AA 2:83, fol. 107v–fol. 111v. August 2, 1226. Published in Limouzin-Lamothe, *La commune de Toulouse*, 470–471.

authority.[2] This case has much more significance to the history of Toulouse than one of jurisdiction alone because it demonstrates the layers of the relationship between the municipal administrators and their citizens. To begin with, it shows that the capitols had to fight for the ability to pass judgment and to punish criminals in their local arena. From the early thirteenth century well into the fourteenth, the twelve elected officials constantly negotiated, cajoled, and even defied outside authority's attempts to regulate or to interfere with their right to render criminal justice for the citizens of Toulouse. Secondly, the public showed that it supported the capitols' authority when it protested the count's intervention in the case. They took over the center of the city and held their capitols accountable for this injustice. The pressure they brought to bear on the capitols resulted in the increase of the capitols' authority. From this point on, the capitols could use public protest as an effective political tool to obtain power from, first, the local counts, and then, Capetian royal authority. The capitols invoked the public's protests to draw outside authority into a debate concerning the liberties of their office, which allowed them to maintain a sense of reverence and deference to the administrative hierarchy. In other words, the gathering in 1226 reveals that the jurisdictional framework and organization of authority in medieval Toulouse was not resolved solely through negotiations between the twelve elected officials and the count, or later, royal representatives. Instead, the authorities had to take into consideration the reaction and the participation of the public when formulating policies concerning issues of law and order, or crime and punishment, which were then announced and enforced in the streets of the city. The efficacy of the city's governors depended on it.

For several decades in the late twelfth century, a council of twelve elected men governed Toulouse under the fairly light supervision of the Raymondine counts of Languedoc. At this same time period, the increasing number of Cathars, a peaceful sect who lived in the territory, attracted the attention of the papacy and French royalty.[3] Beginning with the Third Lateran Council in 1179, much of the papal enmity was directed against these heretics in Albi and Toulouse. Shortly thereafter, Pope Innocent III sent several of his representatives and preachers into Languedoc, hoping to convince Count Raymond to eradicate the belief in his realm. When the

[2] See, for example, Mundy, *Liberty and Political Power in Toulouse*, 98. Wolff, *Histoire de Toulouse*, 114.

[3] For a good survey of the doctrinal elements of Catharism, see Christine Thouzellier, *Catharisme et valdéisme en Languedoc a la fin du XIIe et au début du XIIIe siècle* (Paris, 1966).

count ignored the pope's threats of excommunication, and to make matters worse, a papal legate was murdered in Languedoc, the pope launched a crusade against the Cathars with the help of the French king. The pope needed the king's military strength to conquer the heresy, and the king aspired to gain the land which would provide him direct access to the Mediterranean Sea. As more outside religious and military pressure was placed upon the walled community of Toulouse, the capitols' political control and economic stability weakened. Inevitably, the public confidence in the elected city councilors declined, and the people expressed a desire to return to the jurisdiction of the count. The inhabitants of Toulouse hoped that a reunion with the count would provide them with greater military protection against the invading forces of the French king.[4] However, even the wealthy and knightly count could not protect the citizens of Toulouse against the Capetian army, and in 1229, the king forced him to submit to royal control and to sign a peace treaty in front of the gates of Notre Dame Cathedral. After the Crusade, the number of royal representatives positioned in the city grew, and Pope Gregory IX began to appoint men to serve as inquisitors in the region. All three administrators, the royal component, the church (and by extension, the university), and the elected local capitols, eventually began to seek control over the judicial system and the policing officers of the city, because it was an extremely effective way to demonstrate authority to the residential Toulousains.

The city's archives contain extant cartularies concerning issues of jurisdiction and appeals to the king from both municipal and ecclesiastical authorities which offer an opportunity to explore how the judicial process developed in medieval Toulouse. Throughout the following discussion, the ways in which the various administrations created laws and instructed their officers to approach the Toulousains in the city streets will be an underlying theme in the analysis. For example, the capitols lived among their neighbors who elected them to office. As such, the capitols could employ their intimate knowledge of their neighbors to their advantage in order to bolster their position as the most important administrators of the city. In many ways, the capitols remained the first line of defense and the first resort for justice for the Toulousains because they all shared the same history, civic space, and customs that the royal and ecclesiastical men simply did not. This is best evidenced by the fact that the individuals who utilized and depended upon the municipal court system were very much

[4] Mundy, *Liberty and Political Power*, 160.

part of the local social fabric. Even though the political landscape of the city changed from autonomous to royal, the capitols and their constituents maintained a very distinct relationship that would enable civic leaders of Toulouse to subvert royal and ecclesiastical authority well into the fourteenth century.

In order to develop the notion that all three major administrations attempted to exercise power and to establish a legitimate authority over Toulouse through control of the judicial system, this chapter begins with an introduction to the political relationship between the capitols and the local counts in the early thirteenth century. This will present the organization of the communal court system and early laws which regulated and punished criminal behavior, orchestrated largely by the capitols and their officers alone. Not surprisingly, this structure became much more complicated when the counts of Toulouse conceded defeat to the Capetian kings, and the bishop found renewed political strength with the influx of Dominicans friars into the city. The second segment explores how the emergence of new ecclesiastical and royal courts confused jurisdictional issues, leaving the capitols struggling to maintain their constituents' faith in the office. This discussion includes an assessment of how the king and pope granted so many legal privileges to the university that the scholars became virtually untouchable by any local administration. The capitols' connection to the local urban public in the judicial realm served as an impetus for their insistence upon their primacy in all matters legal. The capitols had to walk a fine line between elevating their status to remain competitive with the royal, university and ecclesiastical agents, and still being regarded as the first line of defense for their constituents.

The Capitols and the Count: The Early Political Structure of Toulouse

The shape and identity of Toulouse dates back to its foundation during the Roman Empire.[5] Situated upon the banks of the Garonne River at the crossroads of prominent commercial thoroughfares, the ancient city was surrounded by fortified walls that protected its inhabitants from barbarian attacks. As the centuries passed, and the Roman and Carolingian Empires came and went, the surrounding region eventually fell into the hands of a prominent family of the counts Toulouse and Saint-Giles. By the eleventh

[5] Jean Coppolani, *Toulouse: étude de géographie urbaine* (Toulouse: Privat-Didier, 1954), 3–35.

century, the family held the town and much of Occitania, from modern day Provence to west of Moissac, an area sixty kilometers down the Garonne River from Toulouse.[6] The resourceful inhabitants took advantage of its geographical location, and the city grew in size and population as merchants and artisans migrated into the city.[7] Later on pilgrims flocked to Toulouse in order to worship the relics of local saints preserved in the great basilica of Saint Sernin, which served as a resting point for these devout travelers on their way to Compostella, Spain.[8] From an early date, its size and commerce made the city an ideal administrative capitol for the counts, but they enjoyed adventure too much to spend significant time in Toulouse. When on crusade or campaign, the counts ruled the city through vicars, who exercised comital justice and managed all of the count's property and finances. As result, over time the people of the city acquired a considerable amount of political and economic autonomy, and developed strategies to preserve the community through their own cooperation and customary traditions of law and order.

Before the thirteenth century, Toulouse was divided into two parts, the *cité* and the *bourg*, each an independent community, with their own administrators, and separate financial organizations until they united politically in 1215. The *cité* was the oldest portion of the town, enclosed by the ancient Roman walls, and held the count's palace, the Château-Narbonnais, and the city's cathedral, Saint-Étienne. The early counts built the Château Narbonnais as a symbol of their authority in the region. It was meant to serve as a permanent reminder of the count's presence in the city, looming over the physical space and its inhabitants from the southeastern side of the city.[9] Originally, the *bourg* began as a small grouping of merchants' homes and canons' residents built around the basilica of Saint Sernin. Inn keepers, tavern owners, and sellers of souvenirs and religious keepsakes moved to the area to cater to the pilgrims attracted to the basilica's famous relics. Eventually, the walls of the *cité* expanded to include the *bourg* as well.[10] A second château, purchased by the city in the early thirteenth century, protected both the Bazacle Bridge over the Garonne River and one of

[6] Jean Raynal, *Histoire de la ville de Toulouse, avec une notice des hommes illustres, une suite chronologique et historique, et une table génénerale des capitouls* (Toulouse: Jean-François Forest, 1759).

[7] Mulholland, *Early Guild Records of Toulouse*, ix-li.

[8] Wolff, *Histoire de Toulouse*, 78–94.

[9] Maurice Prin and Jean Rocacher, *Le Château Narbonnais: Le Parlement et le Palais de Justice de Toulouse* (Toulouse: Éditions-Privat, 1991), 46.

[10] Coppolani, *Toulouse*, 41.

the most important gates of the city.[11] Once the two parts of the city merged, the municipal officials divided the city into twelve administrative districts, called *capitoulats*, each based around a civic landmark. In the *cité*, three districts (La Daurade, Le Pont-Vieux, La Dalbade) were situated close to the Garonne River, while the other three (Saint-Pierre and Saint-Géraud, Saint-Étienne, and Saint-Romain), included the areas around the Château Narbonnais, the cathedral, and town hall respectively. In the *bourg*, the divisions took their names from the main gates into Toulouse (Las Crosses, Arnaud Bernard, Pousonville, Matabovis, and Villeneuve), and the ancient church of Saint-Pierre-des-Cuisines. Each district elected representatives who ran the local government and served on a council to protect the interests of the men and women who lived in these neighborhoods.

A sign of the growing prestige of the capitols during the early years of the thirteenth century was the construction of the town hall, which housed their courtroom and all of the important charters and documents of the city. Until then, the capitols had no fixed place where they met. They gathered either at the ancient church of Saint Pierre des Cuisines, or in an open field that could accommodate large groups of spectators. Once the municipal government became better organized in the thirteenth century, the capitols wanted a home that represented their sovereignty in the city just as the Château Narbonnais represented comital power. They deliberately chose a location at a distance from the château, in a different part of the city, so as not to be dwarfed by the fortress and to be more accessible to the populace.[12] Around 1190 they began to buy property and homes in a central location in the city. As representatives of the people of Toulouse, it was only proper for the capitols to locate the town hall at the heart of the city, to meet the needs of their constituents.

Although Count Raymond V first approved the formation of any municipal council of men in 1152,[13] subsequent counts of Toulouse conceded control of the election process of the capitols to the citizens, and vowed that they would not influence or interfere in the results of who became a capitol. As each count assumed authority, he confirmed the organization of the institution, and later clarified the notion that six men from the *cité* and six men from the *bourg* should direct the administration. By 1223

[11] AMT-AA 1: 75, AA 1: 37. The capitols purchased this property from Arnaldus Guilabertus in 1205.

[12] Jules Chalande, "Histoire Monumentale de L'Hôtel de Ville de Toulouse," *Extrait de la Revue Historique de Toulouse* (Toulouse: Imprimerie Saint-Cyprien, 1922).

[13] *HGL*, vol. V. no. 596, col. 1165.

Count Raymond VII announced in "the presence and audience of all of the population who had gathered there," that he had no say in the election of the capitols and that he only had the right to intervene in municipal policies if the people wanted him to do so.[14] Even after the defeat to the Capetian kings in 1229, in 1248, the year before his death, Count Raymond again acknowledged in front of an audience in the town hall the freedom of the election process, and granted that the people had the right to change the system if necessary.[15] In these early years, there were no real restrictions upon who could run for or hold office in Toulouse; the only stipulation was that the man had to be over twenty-five years old, and had to be a free citizen. The election process was a fairly open system among an assembled *universitas* of citizens who gathered at large fields or courtyards to voice their vote for the men nominated for the twelve openings. A person officially became a citizen if he served in the militia, vowed to obey the laws and customs of Toulouse, paid taxes, and proclaimed, "I want to enter Toulouse and I want to be made a citizen of Toulouse."[16] Many of these average citizens formed a broader Common Council, which varied in the size throughout the years. The council members offered advice to the capitols when they changed municipal laws, and served as witnesses for the documentation of important decisions or agreements. During the tumultuous Albigensian Crusade, citizens gathered frequently in general assemblies along with the Common Council to plan ways to strengthen the military composition of the city.

The counts of Toulouse granted the community extensive economic and judicial privileges, such as tax exemption for particular citizens. The counts allowed the elected capitols to establish market rules, and maintain the drainage system of the city.[17] By the twelfth century, the capitols sought and secured jurisdictional claims over the city and surrounding territory; the capitols heard all legal cases and could administer punishments for the criminal activity of Toulouse.[18] Even if the capitols

---

[14] AMT-AA 1: 77, April 8, 1223: "in presentia et in audientia tocius illius populi qui ibi erat congregatus." Limouzin-Lamothe, *La Commune de Toulouse*, 426–427.

[15] AMT-AA 1: 103, January 25, 1248. Cited in Limouzin-Lamothe, *La Commune de Toulouse*, 460–463.

[16] Mundy, *Liberty and Political Power in Toulouse*, 149–158. Adolphe François Tardif, *Le droit privé au XIIIe siècle d'après les coutumes de Toulouse et Montpellier* (Paris: A. Picard, 1886), 20–21: "ego volo intrare Tholosam et facere me civem Tholose."

[17] AMT-AA 1:19. November, 1180. Published in Limouzin-Lamothe, *La Commune de Toulouse*, 295–298.

[18] AMT-AA 1:79. September 23, 1222. Published in Limouzin-Lamothe, *La Commune*, 415–416.

could not convene and hear a case because of a scheduling conflict, the counts promised they still would not preside over any cases.[19] Technically, the counts' law was the highest jurisdiction in the land and could hear appeals, but in practice, the capitols rendered justice over all of the immediate disputes and conflicts which transpired between the inhabitants of the city. The customary law established regulations and penalties for settling civil contestations of property ownership, adultery, inheritances, and even banned the practice of accepting clothes from gamblers as payments for debts.[20] Even the count succumbed to the capitols' jurisdiction in his own civil matters: in one scenario his vicar came before the capitols' court to settle a property dispute with the prior of church of la Daurade.[21]

Within the realm of criminal matters, the capitols had a vast array of punitive options, but in some circumstances, they allowed the inhabitants of Toulouse to take justice into their own hands. For example, if a resident found a thief in vineyards, fields, or gardens, he had the right to seize and to detain him. The suspect had to compensate both the owner of property, and the individual who made the arrest, by paying two *sols* of amend to each.[22] Punishment for other violent attacks or criminal activity varied from the municipal administrations' confiscation of goods, monetary fines paid to the victim or the city,[23] banishment,[24] or standing in the pillory.[25] More specifically, the pillory was administered to wandering musicians and players who entered into a respectable citizen's home without the husband, or lord of the house, present. For rape, if the female victim was of a low social status, the man could either marry her or compensate her financially. If the rapist could not provide a dowry, he was subjected to corporal punishment at the judgment of the court.[26] These customary laws, then, allowed the capitols to regulate both civil and criminal disputes in their political structure.

The political and judicial organization of Toulouse changed dramatically when the pope turned his attention to the Cathar heresy in

19 AMT-AA 1: 8. Published in Limouzin-Lamothe, *La commune*, 275.

20 AMT-AA 1:52, AA1:5.

21 AMT-AA 1:22. 1199.

22 AMT-AA 1:4.

23 AMT-AA 4:19. March 23, 1283. Carrying illegal arms during the night or the day warranted the confiscation of the arms and paying sixty *sols tols* as a fine.

24 AMT-AA 1:6, 7, 52. For example, any man or woman who "made war" against the count or inhabitants of Toulouse, would be banned for perpetuity.

25 AMT-AA 1:52.

26 AMT-AA 1:4.

Languedoc.[27] Pope Innocent III sent several missionaries to preach for conversion in the county, and legates to meet with Count Raymond VI in order to demand that he increase his efforts to discipline the heretics. After the count dismissed the legates' threats of excommunication, the pope cajoled King Philip Augustus of France to launch a crusade. After several decades of grueling warfare, the Capetian king and his royal crusaders conquered Toulouse, and in 1229, the count of Toulouse signed a peace treaty in front of Notre Dame Cathedral in Paris. Several of the count's concessions of defeat had direct ramifications for the citizens of Toulouse, including his agreement to establish a university in the city, funded by its inhabitants. The peace treaty stipulated that Count Raymond's daughter, Jeanne, marry the king's brother, Alphonse of Poitiers, and identified the two as the sole heirs to all of the land in Languedoc. If they died without an heir (which they did in 1279), all of the land passed directly to the king.[28] Other studies and collections of his correspondence have demonstrated how, during his rule, Alphonse of Poitiers aspired to curtail the privileges and autonomy of the capitols in Toulouse and to consolidate royal sovereignty in the region.[29] For the purposes of this study, we know, for example, that he denied the capitols' claims of jurisdictional power over a citizen when the criminal offense occurred outside of the walls of the city.[30] Count Alphonse stationed his vicar and other officers in the Château Narbonnais, and the vicar became the supreme judicial officer in the town who received all appeals in criminal matters and who oversaw the capitols' legal process. Historian John Hine Mundy's research has shown that some of the citizens of Toulouse soon learned to manipulate this appeals process by taking their cases from the capitols' court to that of the count's in the hopes they would receive a more favorable verdict.[31]

---

[27] Studies concerning the Albigensian Crusade and the Cathar heresy abound. See, for example, Elaine Graham-Leigh. *The Southern French Nobility and the Albigensian Crusade* (Woodbridge, Suffolk, England: Boydell Press, 2005); Aubrey Burl, *God's Heretics: The Albigensian Crusade* (Stroud: Sutton, 2002); Jonathan Sumption, *The Albigensian Crusade*, (London and New York: Faber and Faber, 1978); Walter L. Wakefield, *Heresy, Crusade, and Inquisition in Southern France, 1100–1250* (Berkeley: The University of Berkeley Press, 1974); Michael Costen, *The Cathars and the Albigensian Crusade* (New York: St. Martin's Press, 1997).

[28] *HGL*, 8, no. 271, cols. 883–893.

[29] See the many documents of Auguste Molinier, *Correspondance administrative d'Alphonse de Poitiers*. 2vols. (Paris: Imprimerie Nationale, 1894 and 1900), and George Boyer's, "Remarques sur l'administration de Toulouse au temps d'Alphonse de Poiters," *Mélanges I: Mélanges d'histoire du droit occidentale* (Paris: Sirey, 1962), 198–209.

[30] *HGL*, 10, art. 5 and *HGL*, 8, doc. 456, col. 1385.

[31] Mundy, *Society and Government in Toulouse*, 260–261.

Unfortunately for the capitols, it was also at this time that the Catholic Church regained a position of leverage and privilege in the political realm due to the king's financial and military support. Ever since Saint Saturninus achieved martyrdom by being dragged by a bull through the streets of the city in the third century, the church played a large role in the formation of the topography of Toulouse.[32] By the twelfth century, the city boasted numerous parish churches, monasteries, a cathedral and a basilica. The ecclesiastical courts were preoccupied primarily with protecting the church's property rights, and then dealing with issues of debts and dowries. They claimed jurisdiction over the actions of all clerks accused of crimes including blasphemy, rape and murder. In regards to the laity, the church courts held jurisdictional rights over marriage disputes, annulment, wills, and burial of the dead.[33] In Toulouse, the bishop's court in the cathedral of Saint Étienne held the highest importance and closest connection with the pope, although it was in frequent competition with the archdeacon of Saint Sernin, and the prior of the Daurade. However, the bishop and the other ecclesiastical figures did not have much political power in Toulouse throughout the twelfth century, until the pope and king directed their attention towards eradicating heresy in the region.[34] With the pope's determination to combat the Cathars through the king's sergeants and officers, the role of the judicial process in the lives of the citizens of Toulouse became a more pronounced mechanism of authority.

Prior to this development in the early thirteenth century, both the municipal and ecclesiastical courts followed the basic accusatory procedure which prevailed throughout medieval Europe. In this system, the criminal and civil courts served the citizens as an arbitrator between feuding parties in finding compromises to disagreements. The judges were more interested in finding solutions to conflicts than in determining guilt or innocence. In other words, the court room was not a forum where justice was imposed from an impartial judge. In these circumstances, a defendant would bring forth their complaint against an offender to a mediator offering either oral testimony or notarized documents to support their

[32] Saint Saturninus' service and martyrdom as the first bishop of Toulouse is celebrated within the basilica Saint Sernin, built in his honor. L'Abbé Cayre, *Histoire des Évêques et archevêques de Toulouse depuis la foundation du siège jusqu'à nos jours* (Toulouse: Imprimerie Louis & Jean-Matthieu Douladoure, 1875), 11–15.

[33] James A. Brundage, *Medieval Canon Law* (London and New York: Longman, 1995), 71.

[34] The one exception to this generalization is the Bishop Folques, who met with Saint Dominic and his friars in order to coordinate the inquisition in Toulouse. Cayre, *Histoire des Évêques*, 140–152. A biography of Bishop Folques can also be found in *HGL*, X, n. xxxviii, cols. 289–291.

claims. In defense, the accused secured witnesses to swear by their good honor and name, or offered an alibi. Occasionally, particularly in cases heard by the ecclesiastical authorities, the conflicts could be settled through judicial ordeals as the medium for mediation.[35] In the municipal system, judges first received litigants' complaints and decided whether or not it warranted the officials' attention for arbitration. If the capitols heard both sides of the dispute in civil cases, they frequently called upon an outside legal expert or jurist for advice in rendering their decisions.[36] In this judicial structure, the capitols became involved in civil and criminal matters only if an individual requested a neutral environment to resolve disputes through compromise.

But this practice was soon bypassed when the Dominican friars standardized and institutionalized new practices of inquest to eliminate heresy in Toulouse. The Fourth Lateran Council in 1215 forbade the use of ordeals in ecclesiastical courts, and systematically outlined provisions of an inquisitorial procedure in tribunals to prosecute suspects.[37] In this new judicial process, the ecclesiastical inquisitors no longer had to wait for accusations against malefactors to be brought to their attention; instead, they could actively pursue and prosecute suspected heretics or other deviants by the power of their office. The Dominicans proved to be tremendously effective in formulating new methods of interrogation and ways to extract confessions from people in their custody. As the universities of Europe trained more men in canon and civil law, many of these techniques of the inquisition carried over into the civic judicial procedures in France.[38] By the end of the thirteenth century, a variety of officials (ecclesiastical and civil), regulated the behavior of the citizens of Toulouse, and investigated suspected crimes through interrogation, detainment, and in some circumstances, torture.

While the counts ruled Toulouse, the capitols and their officers had enjoyed a considerable amount of judicial autonomy. The community elected capitols from each of the twelve districts, and the men who held the office strove to protect the citizens' economic interests and overall

[35] Brundage, *Medieval Canon Law*, 120–153. Robert Bartlett, *Trial by Fire and Water: The Medieval Judicial Ordeal* (Oxford: Oxford University Press, 1986).

[36] Mundy, *Liberty*, 144–47. Given, *State and Society*, 80–82.

[37] James B. Given, *Inquisition in Mediveal Society: Power, Discipline and Resistance in Languedoc* (Ithaca: Cornell University Press, 1997), 13–22.

[38] Frederic L. Cheyette, "Inquest, Canonical and French," *Dictionary of the Middle Ages*, vol. 6 (New York: Scribner, 1985), 478–480. A. Esmein, *A History of Continental Criminal Procedure with Special Reference to France*, trans. John Simpson (Boston: Little, Brown, 1913), 88–93.

well-being. Conflicts and disputes between neighbors were brought to the capitols' courtroom in the town hall, so that the officials could mediate disputes, and issue punishments when necessary. When the pope and the king of France became involved in the region, pursuing heretics with unprecedented vigor, the municipal government became immersed in the broader political and judicial structure of the Capetian kingdom. The capitols steadily began to lose many of their privileges to pass judgment upon their citizens, and they faced increasing competition from royal and ecclesiastical representatives advancing their own agendas in the city. The greatest struggle for the municipal authority, then, became maintaining control over the legal and policing structures of Toulouse, especially because judicial systems were becoming one of the most effective ways that political power was legitimized in the thirteenth century.

The King and the Capitols: The New Inquisitorial Procedure

In 1279, the local comital authority that had served as a buffer between the Capetian king and the capitols of Toulouse disappeared with the death of Alphonse of Poitiers. The steps towards centralization of authority under the king's sovereignty continued with the installation of a royal court structure over the already existing overlapping jurisdictions in the city. Languedoc was divided into regions, *sénséchaussées*; each administered by a seneschal, a royal officer, who oversaw the military, economic and political interests of the king in the territory. The seneschal had a judicial court, which served as the last court of appeals in matters before the Parlement in Paris.[39] The *sénséchaussées* were then further subdivided into *viguerie*, or *jugerie*, with a royal vicar presiding over a court with a variety of lesser officers and bureaucrats. In Toulouse, these officials resided and worked in the Château Narbonnais. Between 1280 and 1320, King Philip the Fair sent large numbers of officers trained in Roman law to serve in the royal administration in Languedoc as judges, or as royal procurers.[40] Some became professors and instructors at the University of

[39] This political organization of France is best described in John W. Baldwin, *The Government of Philip Augustus: Foundations of French Royal Power in the Middle Ages* (Berekely: The University of California Press, 1986), and more recently, Elizabeth M. Hallam, *Capetian France, 987–1328* (New York : Longman, 2001).

[40] See Joseph R. Strayer's *Les Gens de Justice du Languedoc sous Philippe le Bel* (Toulouse: Association Marc Bloch, 1970), and *The Reign of Philip the Fair* (Princeton, N.J.: Princeton University Press, 1980). Marie-Martin Chague "Contribution à l'étude du recrutement des agents royaux en Languedoc aux XIVe et XVe siècles," *France du Nord et France du*

Toulouse, although there are great lacunas in the records of who was there at any given time.[41] These royal officials, whose duty was to protect the will and interests of the king, advanced their own personal agendas of securing power and profit from the capitols and citizens of Toulouse.

Historian Harold Berman attributed the Capetian monarchs' success in territorial expansion to the blending of local custom with legal learning.[42] The kings realized the importance of maintaining customary law in the regions that they acquired to the royal domain, and assigned scholars the task of codifying and writing laws to follow a formal and standardized legal procedure. The capitols of Toulouse sent the king their proposed privileges and laws, which were either accepted or rejected by the king, and then a notary recorded the final approved set.[43] One of the most contested issues for the capitols concerned who had legitimate custody of the town, and who held jurisdiction over its inhabitants.[44] In October, 1283, Philip III addressed this debate and worked out a compromise between the capitols and the royal vicar.[45] He proclaimed that the capitols had the right to hear all criminal cases for offenses committed in Toulouse and the surrounding vicariate (most of Languedoc), either brought to their attention in the form of an official complaint, or if sergeants seized the defendant in the process of committing the crime. If a royal sergeant caught the suspect, he was expected to hand the prisoner over to municipal authorities. During the trial, the vicar or his lieutenant would sit in on the proceedings, and approve the capitols' recommendation for corporal sentences. With this royal mandate, the capitols continued in the role as the first resource for justice for the people of Toulouse, enforcing the

Midi: Contacts et influences réciproques vol. 1 (Toulouse: Actes du 96e Congrès National des Sociétés Savantes, 1971), 359–378.

[41] Eduard M. Meijers offers a list of these men who served as professors and were later appointed as judges in Languedoc from 1280–1330 in his *Responsa doctorum tholosanorum*.

[42] Harold J. Berman, *Law and Revolution: The Formation of the Western Legal Traidtion* (Cambridge: Harvard University Press, 1983), 467–477.

[43] Many of the exchanges and rejected statutes are preserved in AMT-AA 3:2, from 1274–1275, and ATM-AA 3:3, lists the ones that are rejected. The codification of the customary law is preserved in a variety of locations, including BN man. lat. 9187, and has been analyzed and discussed in great detail by Gilles, *Les coutumes de Toulouse*.

[44] *HGL*, X, doc. 26, art. IV, col. 154. "Item super eo, quod dicti consules supplicabant quod inhiberetur dicto vicario, ne de cetero villam Tholose custodiat, set permittat dicte ville custodiam dictis consulibus, cum ad eos solos, ut dicunt, spectet dicta custodia, quod eis negatur per vicarium, ut eis contrarium asseratur. Responsum est, quod dicti consules custodiant villam, prout consueverunt, et nichilominus vicarius vel subvicarius et servientes ipsorum eam custodiant, cum viderint expedire."

[45] AMT-AA 3:4 and AMT AA 4:1, dated October 1283.

customary law of their predecessors. The capitols' judicial autonomy, however, had been compromised by the vicar's presence in the courtroom, and in the determination of corporal punishment.

The king held a considerable amount of influence and authority over the bishop's court in Toulouse as well. The royal administration granted the bishop the right to oversee cases and litigation relevant to church interests, and to hear appropriate appeals before they were brought to the king's court. The ecclesiastical court of Toulouse apparently had a reputation for treating its wayward clerks a bit leniently. And so the royal vicar decided to resolve this issue by apprehending clerks who were breaking local laws. He ordered his officers to arrest clerks roaming the city with illegal arms, and to detain them in the Château Narbonnais. The bishop protested vehemently this action, and when the vicar refused to surrender the men to the ecclesiastical authorities, he appealed to the Parlement, which decided in 1275 that he alone had the authority to determine clerical status, and to punish the offenders according to canon law.[46] By 1289, Philip IV issued correspondence to Toulouse which encouraged the bishop to seek out murderous clerks aggressively, and to punish the evildoers of the church.[47] The king had granted ecclesiastical authorities and their men the privilege of a protected status, but he still expected the clergy to be held accountable when they committed crimes.

The royal provision that members of the church could only be seized and tried in ecclesiastical courts caused some frustration for the capitols and the people of Toulouse. As more men claiming clerical status moved into Toulouse, in order to serve as faculty of the university or with the Dominican inquisition, it became more difficult for the municipal officers to identify clergy by sight alone. The king reprimanded the capitols on several occasions for the arrests of men without confirming the individual's clerical status. In accordance with royal mandates, the capitols had to release any suspect who claimed clerical status to the ecclesiastical authorities, even if the claims were dubious. In 1279, the capitols arrested a man named Poncius Amati and held him in custody, despite his insistence that he was a clerk.[48] They questioned his affiliation with the church because he was wearing lay clothes. Poncius Amati, however, appealed his case all the way to the Parlement in Paris. The royal authorities demanded his release and a financial compensation from the municipal government.

---

46 *HGL*, X, doc. 18, cols. 133–134.
47 Ibid., doc. 64, cols. 241–242, art. V.
48 Ibid., col. 156, art. XVI.

The Parlement also heard the appeals of a clerk Arnaude de Cossac, who claimed that the capitols' officers arrested him, convicted him of a crime and then confiscated his goods as punishment.[49] The capitols became so aggravated by this impingement of royal power that by 1292, the bishop claimed that they arrested clerks indiscriminately, detained them in their prisons, tortured them, and finished by throwing the suspects into the Garonne River during the night.[50] The Capetian king not only had to resolve the jurisdictional tensions between the ecclesiastical and municipal officials concerning the determination of clerical status, but he also had to monitor the behavior of officers in Toulouse.

This point can be elaborated further with regard to the issue of asylum in the city. According to the canonical law of asylum, anyone seeking refuge from a public authority could be protected in any church or monastery, where they could not be removed.[51] In the cartulary of Toulouse's *bourg*, however, the capitols offered their own interpretation of asylum. The capitols decreed that no accused murderer could seek shelter in a church or cloister, especially if the criminal had broken into a home and committed theft at night. As early as 1152, municipal statutes declared there would never be asylum in Toulouse for someone who had kidnapped for ransom, mutilated, or stolen from a Toulousain.[52] And by 1193, people could not take malefactors under their protection or their authority, nor could they contract marriage with them without the consent of their victim.[53] But the notion of asylum was important to the church, as it was a means of continuing a physical presence and authority in the secular legal component of Toulouse: the ecclesiastical authorities wanted to keep churches as recognizably protected spaces in order to maintain power in municipal jurisdiction.[54] The capitols and their officers challenged this stipulation in 1288, which caused the archbishop of Toulouse to issue a complaint to King Philip IV.[55] Earlier that year, a criminal had fled from

---

[49] The appeal to the Parlement is found in AMT-AA 4:28. June 19, 1290. Printed in *HGL*, X, doc. 69, col. 254.

[50] ADHG-1G 347, fol. 64. Printed in *HGL*, X, doc. 77, col. 281.

[51] Jacques Ellul, *Histoire des Institutions, vol. 3: Le Moyen Âge*, (Paris, Presses Universitaires de France, 1962), 243.

[52] AMT-AA 1: 4 (1152). Limouzin-Lamothe, *La Commune de Toulouse*, 267–268.

[53] AMT-AA 1:16 (1193). Limouzin-Lamothe, *La Commune de Toulouse*, 290.

[54] See, for example, an example of the negotiations between the church and municipal authorities in Montpellier in 1332, in Katheryn L. Reyerson's "Flight from Prosecution: The Search for Religious Asylum in Medieval Montpellier." *French Historical Studies* 17, No. 3 (Spring, 1992): 603–626. J. Charles Cox, *The Sanctuaries and Sanctuary Seekers in Mediaeval England* (London: G. Allen and Sons, 1911).

[55] ADHG-1 G 345, fol. 42–43.

the capitols to the church of Nazareth, immediately evoking the privilege of asylum. A messenger of the capitols disregarded the safeguard of the religious site, broke into the church and dragged the accused to the town hall. Horrified to learn that capitols submitted the man to interrogation and to the torture of "questioning" in order to hear a confession, the archbishop beseeched the king to enforce the protection of the church's sacred space. The royal Parlement ordered the capitols to return the prisoner to ecclesiastical officials, thus continuing the tradition of asylum and rendering the capitols impotent once again against the royal protection of the church. This is a very different outcome from a scenario concerning asylum which unfolded in Montpellier decades later in 1353. In this case, Montpellier's municipal officials forcibly removed six foreigners from their refuge in a local church after they were suspected of attacking and leaving for dead a lawyer. After a rapid trial, four of the defendants confessed to homicide and were later executed on the gallows. But when the lawyer did not die from the wounds of the assault, the relatives of the foreigners protested and appealed to the French monarchy for an inquest into the condemnation, arguing the men died for a crime they did not commit. By this time, however, the royal judicial administration was less interested in protecting the authority of the Catholic Church, and in Montpellier, secular power overshadowed the religious privilege of asylum.[56]

The one institution that benefited the most from both external royal and papal protection in this same era was the struggling University of Toulouse. Since antiquity, governments granted scholars and teachers legal privileges and a protected status. Roman civil law, for example, freed those engaged in the "liberal arts" from compulsory public duties, like performing military service or housing soldiers, and heavily fined anyone causing harm or injury to them.[57] These early mandates of scholarly privilege existed in theory, but as Pearl Kibre has argued, local secular officials constantly tested these immunities and exemptions. Kings, emperors and popes frequently needed to intervene on the behalf of students and their masters. This repeated involvement resulted in further defining and shaping these legal privileges as the years progressed and as the medieval university came into fruition. The oldest and most important privilege of the

[56] Reyerson, "Religious Authority in Medieval Montpellier," 623.

[57] Pearl Kibre, *Scholarly Privileges in the Middle Ages: The Rights, Privileges and Immunities of Scholars and Universities at Bologna, Padua, Paris and Oxford* (Cambridge, Massachusetts: Medieval Academy of America, 1962), 3.

Middle Ages was "the benefit of the clergy," which meant that university affiliates had clerical status, and as such, they were immune from secular jurisdiction, and were only bound by canon law and ecclesiastical courts.[58] But even this protection became realized in Paris after a conflict erupted between the scholars and the urban population, which established the University of Paris as the standard model of the *studium generale* in France. In 1200, after a violent town and gown brawl, King Philip Augustus issued a Charter of Privileges which acknowledged that scholars were exempt from secular jurisdiction, prohibited municipal officials from arresting or imprisoning scholars for any reason, and insisted that the urban bourgeoisie vow to respect and to protect the scholars in all circumstances.[59] This famous charter served to render local magistrates with very little legal recourse when dealing with the university community. Even if secular authority caught a student in the middle of committing a heinous crime, officials needed to handle him courteously, to refrain from injuring him, and to hand him over to ecclesiastical judges as soon as possible. As if that was not enough, the papacy also wanted scholars to be exempt and to be protected from local ecclesiastical authorities. In the twelfth century, Pope Alexander III ordered that no clergy, including bishops and archbishops, could lay hands on a student, and that only the pope and he alone, could punish a scholar with excommunication. Although this premise was challenged and reasserted for Parisian masters in 1219, 1222, and 1231, it became another valuable way in which the University of Paris was becoming a virtually autonomous, self-governing judicial entity, fully supported by the king and the pope.[60]

Bolstered by these provisions, many Parisian university masters and students brazenly defied local authority, which indirectly resulted in the extension of these same royal and papal privileges to scholars working at the University of Toulouse, founded in 1229. Despite the papal encouragement to the students and masters to be well-mannered and moderate, conflicts still erupted between scholars and local townsmen, with justice usually falling on the side of the university. But during the carnival of 1228–1229, several students from The University of Paris were drinking in a suburban tavern, when a fight broke out between the bar owner and several locals over the amount of the bill and the quality of the wine.[61]

---

[58] Ibid., 85.

[59] Ibid., 86–87.

[60] Ibid., 88.

[61] Henrich Denifle and Emile Chatelain, ed., *Chartularium universitatis Parisiensis* (Paris, 1889–1897), vol. I, no. 62, 118.

Seeking revenge for the brawl, Parisian soldiers targeted and attacked a random group of innocent students who were engaged in holiday games outside of the city walls, killing several of the young men. The masters declared that their privileges had been impeded upon, demanded immediate justice within three months, and accordingly, a mass of the scholars left Paris and headed towards cities like Toulouse in 1229.[62] It was not until 1231 that the Parisian masters resumed their work and lectures, with their legal security even further reinforced by yet another papal decree, Pope Gregory IX's "Parens scientiarum." This charter granted university masters an enormous amount of liberty in the city, including a reaffirmation of all of the previous stated legal immunities and added the right of scholars to cease lectures (effectively, this was the right to strike) if they felt their privileges threatened in any way.[63]

Toulouse, however, was hesitant to accept its *universitas* of scholars with open arms, despite the reassurances of men like Jean de Garland that the city was "flowing in milk and honey." Many of the locals resented the fact that this was one of the first occasions where the papacy and the king decided that they could command the inception of a university.[64] And when Count Raymond of Toulouse signed the peace treaty with King Louis IX on April 12, 1229, he agreed to pay the salaries of a set number of scholars brought into the city.[65] By this time, Pope Honorius III had sent letters to Parisian theologians, where he invited them to venture south to teach. He promised them ample pay and even more generous privileges in Toulouse than those obtained at The University of Paris.[66] But because Count Raymond refused to pay the foreign scholars and the capitols expressed equal disdain for Dominicans coming into their city (who administered the inquisition against the Cathars),[67] Pope Gregory IX had to issue threats of excommunication before the count finally agreed to make the payments which ensured some type of stability to the university.[68] Each pope who came to office granted the university scholars of Toulouse the same privileges as obtained at The University of Paris, which

62 Ibid., no. 79, 80–81.

63 Kibre, *Scholarly Privileges in the Middle Ages*, 95.

64 Verger, *Les universités*, 44–45.

65 *Statuts*, vol. I, no. 505, 441. "Item quator milia marcarum deputabuntur a nobis quatuor magistris theologie, duobus decretistis, sex magistris artium liberalium et duobus grammaticis regentibus Tholose."

66 Ibid., no. 502, 437–438.

67 Ibid., nos. 510–516, 443–447.

68 Ibid., no. 514, p. 447. Interestingly, the count begs the pope to lift the excommunication, and expresses his willingness to concede to his demands in no. 515, 447.

continued to recognize the scholar as a member of the clergy protected under ecclesiastical jurisdiction.[69] In 1245, Innocent IV decreed that Gregory IX's "Parens scientiarum" should apply to the masters of Toulouse, and issued a confirmation of the university as a permanent entity in the city.[70] Around the same time, Innocent IV reminded the count, capitols, and citizens of Toulouse to respect the privileges of the university and to not harm the unarmed scholars.[71] In practice, though, Toulouse's scholars did not receive all of the immunities of their Parisian counterparts: in 1266, the bishop of Toulouse found he was incapable of handling the multitude of clergy affiliated with the university, especially those who carried weapons night and day. He thereby authorized the vicar and the capitols to arrest armed scholars, and later, scholars caught committing serious crimes, with the understanding that the secular authority would hand the offender over to the bishop's court for judgment.[72] After the Avignon split of the papacy, and partially due to the growing trends of secularism, the Capetian king became the dominant protector of the university affiliates. This meant that by the fourteenth century, the full arm of royal authority was behind the university scholar, and anyone who dared to violate it was subject to serious repercussions in Paris and beyond. By 1324, the University of Toulouse had grown to the point where it received royal privileges from King Charles the Fair, who commanded his local seneschal to protect the *studium* from violence and molestation by townsmen.[73] Once again, the university became an insular institution, surrounded by legal protection from both the king and the pope. These legal privileges created a symbolic protected space around the student and master. As the scholar ventured out into town, he was exempt from the municipal legal and social hierarchy in which the individual townsman and capitol had so much invested.

When Alphonse of Poitiers died in 1279, the capitols surrendered much of their judicial control to the royal vicar who lived in Toulouse. Their judicial decisions, which were once the primary and immediate legal recourse for the urban residents, were now subject to scrutiny and to appeal up the

---

[69] Ibid., no. 509, 442. no. 518, 449. In 1316, Pope John XXII released the same bull, no., 546, 495–496.

[70] Ibid., no. 518, 449. In 1316, Pope John XXII released the same bull, no., 546, 495–496.

[71] Ibid., no. 522, 450–451. "Si grex parvulus imbecillis viribus, dum non sit qui pro illis murum defensionis opponat, opprimentium injuriis pateat infensus, universitatem vestram rogandam duximus et monendam, per apostolica vobis scripta mandantes."

[72] Ibid., nos. 526–527, 453.

[73] Ibid., no. 552, 497.

chain of the royal court hierarchy. But even if the Parlement in Paris did not consider a case from Languedoc, the royal vicar was a looming presence in the capitols' courtroom. The capitols also had to adjust to the fact that the King legally and diligently protected the church and its members, and the university masters and students. The capitols, their officers and the Toulousains constantly tested and challenged all of these prescriptive privileges and immunities. After all, we can only surmise how difficult it must have been in the heat of the moment for a municipal officer to identify a royal protected figure like a cleric or a scholar in the midst of a crime, and to restrain from taking action. Likewise, we can imagine the capitols' struggle to remain relevant in this expanding judicial realm of Toulouse. As the thirteenth century closed, the evidence suggests that the capitols were looking for new ways to ensure that their office continued to be a respected agent in the social, political and judicial landscape.

Building Status: Protecting the Office of the Capitols

The capitols of Toulouse suffered yet another set back in 1283, when King Philip III made the stipulation that the royal vicar had the right to oversee the elections for their office. In the new organization of municipal elections, when the capitols finished their terms, they were to choose three candidates as potential successors to their office, and to submit the names to the vicar. The royal official then could select one name from the three, and, if none were suitable, he could reject them all and choose whomever he liked. The vicar then expected the new elected capitols to swear the vows of their office and to pledge loyalty to the king on the steps of the Château Narbonnais.[74] By this era, the château symbolized the royal power which lurked continuously on the outer limits of the city. This was a significant change from the congregations of concerned citizens in the beginning of the thirteenth century, who met in fields and open courtyards to select their representatives who were later sworn in at the communal town hall.[75] Because of this shift in the election process and the continuation of the imposition of royal power into local politics, we start to see the capitols employing subtle and not-so-subtle efforts to enhance the prestige of their office.

---

[74] AMT-AA 3:4 and AA 34, doc. 7.

[75] Jean-Paul Buffelan, *La noblesse des capitouls de Toulouse* (St. Gaudens: L'Adret, 1986), 41–53.

We should keep in mind that the capitols were still relevant and visible figures in the everyday lives of the inhabitants of Toulouse, even as royal administrators curtailed their judicial freedom and legal practices. For example, they did continue to exercise control over the guilds and the economic production of the city. Most of the extant guild statutes from the late thirteenth century confirmed that the capitols had the right to police the exercise of the trades, in order to prevent abuses, and to punish evildoers.[76] The capitols had the privilege to name, or to revoke, the bailiff who regulated the guilds.[77] This official, who swore an oath of loyalty to the capitols, made rounds to the shops to ensure there were no fraudulent practices, and to impose fines if necessary. Still, the capitols had to negotiate with the king in order to secure some exemptions and legal privileges for their office as well. The capitols certainly found ways to work with the royal representatives in the city to accomplish common goals of law and order, but in these first decades of integration into the larger political hierarchy of the royal kingdom, many of the lines of authority were tested, defied, and clarified on the streets of Toulouse and in the reality of everyday life.

One of the most direct ways in which the capitols sought to elevate the status of their office was by securing their exemption from torture. Within the inquisitorial procedure introduced by the Dominicans, legal officials incorporated new and effective ways to gain evidence against the accused, although there were great concerns surrounding the validity of a confession secured under torture.[78] Torture (*quaestio* or *tormentum* in the documents), was considered part of the legal process in the thirteenth and fourteenth centuries, and another element of jurisdiction that was debated between the administrations of Toulouse.[79] In the extant documents, the capitols expressed a determination to convince the king to mandate that they were exempt from torture and to extend that exemption to the office holders' descendants. The inclusion of the capitols' heirs was a new development in this era of the later Middle Ages, and it seems to be an attempt to attach a kind of hereditary privilege and legal immunity to the person of the capitol that transcended the office itself. The thirteenth-century

---

76 See, Mulholland, *Early Guild Records of Toulouse*, 3–4, 19, 25–26.

77 AMT-AA 34:21, (1295).

78 Brundage, *Medieval Canon Law*, 95–95.

79 Edward Peters, *Torture* (New York: Basil Blackwell, Inc., 1985), 40–73. Claude Gauvard, «*De Grace Especial*»: *Crime, état et société en France à la fin du Moyen Âge* (Paris: Publications de la Sorbonne, 1991), 145–189. Berman argues that torture was more likely to be used in secular cases rather than in ecclesiastical courts. *Law and Revolution*, 252–253.

commentator on the *coutumes* of Toulouse argued that because the capitols were so inherently noble, they could not be submitted to torture by their peers. This protection might have worked better in theory than in practice, however, because it restricted the reigning capitols from seeking justice in at least a couple of scenarios. For example, the same commentator of the *coutumes* referred to the case of Ramundus Tholosanus, who was accused of drowning his wife in the Garonne River. In this situation, despite sufficient evidence, the capitols could not administer any type of torture because his father was a former capitol of Toulouse.[80] And again, on May 18, 1308, two of the capitols' criminal investigators appealed to King Philip IV about their pursuit of a man accused of murdering Bernardus Sedasserii, an inhabitant of Toulouse.[81] The capitols sought the king's permission to interrogate the prime suspect, Jean Jourdain, who was incarcerated in the Châtelet of Paris. The criminal investigators wanted to administer the "question" to Jourdain in order to gain his confession. As a counter tactic, Jourdain issued an appeal to the king's court for royal safeguard, claiming that he not only held office at one time as a capitol, but his father was also a capitol. He was thus exempted from municipal torture or imprisonment.[82] Even though Sedasserii's widow doubted the guilt of Jourdain, the capitols patiently waited for the king's verdict. Although the sources are silent on the resolution of this particular case, in 1315, King Louis X settled the broader matter through an ordinance sent to the seneschal of Toulouse and royal judges of the territory, securing the privileges of capitols and of their sons in the matter of torture. The statute decreed that no capitol of Toulouse, or their sons, could be submitted to the "question," except for crimes of treason.[83]

Compared to the vast royal protection extended to the clergy and the university scholars, this immunity feels like a fairly meager gain, especially as many historians have argued that secular administrators applied torture rather sparingly.[84] But it speaks to a broader movement at the end of

---

80 Giles, *Les coutumfes*, 154–155.

81 AMT-AA 3:208.

82 Jourdain held office 1297–1298, and 1304–1305. He was a capitol from the territory of the Bourg, the neighborhood of Villeneuve.

83 AMT-AA 3: 172, article 22 (April 1, 1315). Copied in AMT-AA 34:67.

84 See, Kenneth Pennington, who believes that torture was not practiced as often during the thirteenth and fourteenth centuries as previously suspected. *The Prince and the Law, 1200–1600: Sovereignty and Rights in the Western Legal Tradition* (Berkeley and Los Angeles: University of California Press, 1993), 42–44, 157–160. James Given concurs that the inquisitors in Languedoc rarely used torture to gain confessions. Instead, imprisonment served as a more effective means of converting suspected heretics. *Inquisition and Medieval Society*, 54.

the thirteenth century to affix a sense of regality and history to the office of the capitols in Toulouse. Even the use of the title 'capitol' seems conspicuously deliberate and purposeful in this era. In the earliest municipal documents from the twelfth century, these office holders were called *consules*, a title befitting their role of giving 'council' or advice to the government of the city. But in 1295, the term 'capitol' was introduced in the city's customary law, and the commentator stressed that the administrative title 'capitol' could only be assigned three times in history: to Rome, Constantinople, and Toulouse.[85] A century later, Arnaldus Aginus, a canon of the basilica Saint Sernin, designated Jerusalem, not Constantinople, with this honor, and stressed that only Toulouse was able to still boast of her glory.[86] Although it is impossible to assess with absolute accuracy why the authors made these particular groupings, it suggests that they made a conscious effort to really highlight the longevity and endurance of Toulouse. They ignored Paris, and by extension the Capetian power, and accentuated Toulouse's distinct place in their sense of history because it had survived the perils and invasions of antiquity. The inclusion of Jerusalem also introduces spiritual connotations. But overall, could this reference from the later Middle Ages imply that Toulouse, and the capitols, made it through the conquest from the north as well, and still served as a beacon of a majestic past? Modern scholars of Toulouse have debated if the term was adopted by a broader audience in the fourteenth century, or if it was only circulated in later centuries thanks to a "Renaissance pomposity."[87] Regardless, the title appears in the archival records, including the criminal documents analyzed for the rest of this study.

In addition to their titles, we find other references where the capitols insisted that the town hall was situated upon the very location where the city's patron saint, Saturninus, was martyred in the Roman era. Saint Saturninus was one of the earliest bishops of Toulouse and when he refused to sacrifice to the pagans living in the city, they "tied him to a bull's legs and drove the animal from the highest point of the capitol, precipitating him down the steps to the bottom. Thus Saturninus, with his skull and his brains spilled out, happily consummated his martyrdom."[88]

[85] Gilles, *Les coutumes de Toulouse*, 158. E. Martin-Chabot. "La tradition capitoline à Toulouse à la fin du XIIIe siècle." *Annales du Midi* 29–30 (1917–1918): 345–354.

[86] BMT- MS 874, 11.

[87] Ernest Roschach, "Comment l'hôtel de ville de Toulouse a pris le nom de Capitole," *Revue de Toulouse* 23 (1866): 445–448.

[88] Jacobus de Voragine, *The Golden Legend: Readings on the Saints*, vol. II, trans. William Granger Ryan (Princeton, N.J.; Princeton University Press, 1993), p. 342, no. 173.

The wording from this *vita* has sparked debate from historians and archeologists for centuries concerning the actual location of the mentioned capitol, and whether or not the modern or medieval site corresponds with the Roman.[89] But again, like the emphasis placed upon the title 'capitol,' the connection to the martyr Saturninus conceivably demonstrates some notion that individuals affiliated with Toulouse may be persecuted and tortured, but still persevere in the greater scheme of things. In the years following the bloodshed of the Albigensian Crusade, it may also have been an opportunity to demonstrate that Toulouse had its roots in Catholic orthodoxy, and to establish a physical connection or continuity with the town hall, city space, and the saint who battled against other enemies of the faith. In addition, the *domum communum* steadily became more than the administrative building it was a century before. It now held the responsibility of symbolizing permanence, order, and local authority in the town. It stored all of the important charters, tax records, and beginning in 1296, the *Douze Livres* of Toulouse. The *Douze Livres* are a series of municipal yearbooks that recorded the names of the elected officials, and included portraits of the capitols themselves, wearing magisterial robes of red and black.[90] The inaugural year of the town annals began with the poem:

> Toulouse was free, with full rights, and will be without end;
> If she is just and pious, she will be forever populous.
> Toulouse is proud of its twelve consuls
> Who govern her, fair, pious and powerful.[91]

The capitols thus sought to perpetuate the town's continuity with its past, in an effort to show that the municipal officers, even the town hall itself,

---

89 E. Martin-Chabot. "La tradition capitoline à Toulouse à la fin du XIIIe siècle." *Annales du Midi*, vol. XXIX-XXX (1917–1918): 345–354. Ernest Roschach, "Comment l'hôtel de ville de Toulouse a pris le nom de Capitole." *Revue de Toulouse*, vol. XXIII (1866), 445–448.

90 Buffelan, *La noblesse des capitouls*, 133–134.

91 "Toulouse a été libre, de plein droit, et le sera sans fin; Si elle est juste et pieuse, elle sera toujours populeuse. Toulouse est fière des douze consuls, Qui la gouvernent, justes, pieux et pleins de force." The first sheets of the original thirteenth century manuscript no longer exist, but the Latin text of this poem was conserved in a copy of an eighteenth century manuscript, made during a trial, and carrying the signature of a clerk and secretary of the town hall, named Martin pour Claussolles. The French is published in Ernest Roschach, *Les Douze Livres de l'Histoire de Toulouse Chroniques Municipales Manuscrites du Treizieme au Dix-Huiteme Siecle* (1295–1787). (Toulouse: Douladoure-Privat, n.d.), 5–7, no. 1. He does not reveal the eighteenth century document's location. François Bordes has examined the extant *Douze Livres*, which are located in the Archives Municipales de Toulouse, Toulouse's Musée des Augustines, and one in the Pierpont Morgan Library in New York. See his articles, "Vêtement et functions municipales à Toulouse (XIIIe-XVe siècle): du text à l'image." *Vêture et pouvoir; XIIIe –XXe siècle: actes du colloque des 19 et 20 octobre 2001, Centre universitaire d'Albi*, ed. by Christiane Aribaud and Sylvie Mouysset (Toulouse: n.d.), 125–136.

were steeped in a tradition of endurance, independence and stability which would continue to guide Toulouse with an orthodox and righteous hand.

Conclusion

In the case that opened this chapter, the capitols and the people of Toulouse united against the count in their demands for justice. The two murder victims' families and thousands of protestors insisted that the capitols secure the count's oath that he would not stand in the way of the pursuit of justice for crimes committed against the citizens. The municipal leaders responded to the protests, and negotiated more autonomy and power for their office in all judicial matters. For decades, the capitols and the civic officers enjoyed the freedom of their court structure, and found a cooperative balance with the population in the establishment of law and order in the city. When royal and papal interest turned to the region and the city fell to the crusaders from the north, the political and judicial transition of the late thirteenth and early fourteenth century created profound changes in the jurisdictional framework of Toulouse. The capitols surrendered much of their judicial sovereignty to the royal representatives who were stationed in the Château Narbonnais and walking through the town. The increasing presence of the bishop and papal inquisitors complicated the overlapping competition for jurisdiction in the city, and also influenced the formation of new strategies of inquest into crimes, and the courtroom procedures in general. As the royal and ecclesiastical representatives exerted their claims of authority and privileged status within the municipal judicial structure, the capitols turned to their traditions and connections with the people of Toulouse in order to find means to maintain their control over their customs of law and justice.

CHAPTER TWO

THE SPATIAL DISTRIBUTION OF CRIME IN TOULOUSE

Perhaps one of the reasons that the capitols of Toulouse fought so hard to maintain control of their municipal court and to the distribution of punishment was because they did not frequently hear the types of cases that involved poor and (socially and geographically) marginalized men and women who lived or passed through the city. Instead, the courtroom was an environment where they interacted with established members of the public, and they exerted authority by rendering justice for victims and their families. Not all of the people of Toulouse, therefore, could take advantage of the legal services offered in the town hall. Many of the inhabitants who committed or who were victims of lesser offenses, such as petty theft, rarely had formal hearings. Like many other studies, it is virtually impossible to create a thorough demographic composition of every man and woman accused of crimes in medieval Toulouse. And we cannot necessarily rely upon other sources such as medieval chronicles to fill the lacunae, because contemporary authors like Guillelmus Bardin only recorded spectacular criminal incidents that included large, nameless mobs. The purpose of this chapter, then, is to assess the economic and social status of the citizens who *did* stand trial in the capitols' courtroom in the early fourteenth century, and who *did* rely upon the capitols and the judicial system to deliver verdicts of guilt or innocence. On the basis of the extant criminal register from 1332, we find that these men and women were active contributors to the urban society, and their offenses transpired in populous and central locations. Cases that were brought to trial, in other words, concerned the citizens who had personal and financial interests in the city, and in the functions of the municipal court.

Inherently, the historiography of medieval urban crime reveals the problematic nature of trying to create a universal portrait of the face of criminality, with the vast array of results contingent upon the types of sources being analyzed. In addition, scholars may focus their investigation upon questions such as whether or not criminal activity differed between the classes or between the sexes, and whether or not it transpired in central or marginal locations in the city space. All of these variations indicate that it is virtually impossible to make any generalizations about the history of medieval crime, and instead we must depend upon local findings. For instance, David Nicholas relied upon records of arbitral judgments from the administrative councils of fourteenth-century Ghent to find that elites and the lower class alike were involved in brutal disputes, often based upon familial and personal vendettas.[1] Trevor Dean exploited the criminal registers of the *podestà's* court from Bologna in order to find that the majority of thefts were committed (not surprisingly) out of necessity by the lower classes and that there were many nuanced differences between how and why men and women committed this offense.[2] Violent crimes throughout the rest of northern Italy, however, were scattered over a random social pattern: homicide rates, for example, did not follow any class, guild or other lines.[3] In England, Barbara Hanawalt has referenced both coroners' reports and trial records to show that criminals resorted to physical aggression to solve disputes in both urban and rural settings alike, and across the whole social spectrum.[4] Other scholars have blamed criminal activity upon the influx of displaced transients, soldiers and university students who preyed upon the urban inhabitants. In his study of Oxford, Carl Hammer isolated the majority of the homicides and violent rows to the university's academic term, when the city was full with the student population. However, most of the victims and perpetrators came from the lower class, and thus not necessarily out of the group of scholars.[5]

Scholars of late medieval Paris have been more definitive in identifying the criminal element as the poor and marginal figures living in the Capetian capital. This demographic committed unequivocally most of the recorded offenses. Fourteenth-century France experienced a series of events which led to a rootless population of poor immigrants in the

---

[1] David Nicholas, "Crime and Punishment in Fourteenth Century Ghent," *Revue Belge de philologie et d'histoire,* vol. XLVIII (Brussels: Fondation Universitaire et du Ministère de l'Éducation Nationale et de la Culture, 1970), 289–334, 1141–1176.

[2] Trevor Dean, "Theft and Gender in Late Medieval Bologna," *Gender and History* vol. 20, no. 2, (August, 2008), 399–415.

[3] See, for example, the various articles in *Violence and Disorder in Italian Cities, 1200–1500,* ed. Lauro Martines (Berkeley: The University of California Press, 1972).

[4] Barbara A. Hanawalt, "Violent Death in Fourteenth-Century and Early Fifteenth-Century England," *Comparative Studies in Society and History* 18, no. 3 (1976): 308–309. "Fur-Collar Crime: The Pattern of Crime among the Fourteenth-Century English Nobility," *"Of Good and Ill Repute:" Gender and Social Control in Medieval England* (Oxford: Oxford University Press, 1998), 53–69. *Crime and Conflict in English Communities, 1300–1348* (Cambridge: Harvard University Press, 1979), 99, 100, 123, 153, 181.

[5] Carl I. Hammer, Jr., "Patterns of Homicide in a Medieval University Town: Fourteenth Century Oxford," *Past and Present,* 78 (1978): 3–23.

countryside who fled to the center of Paris. Not only did the Black Death ravage the territory, but multiple crop failures and famines led to large protests in the country areas and urban centers.[6] More specifically, the Hundred Years War created a large number of people (mostly artisans) who had to seek employment or charity in the kingdom's capital. Soon displaced individuals overran the streets, becoming a part of the underground realm of prostitutes and vagrants who lurked in marginal locations such as cemeteries and dark alleys and inns ready to pounce on unsuspecting victims.[7] This situation contributed to a French fear of criminal bandits or beggars, and led to an eventual disregard for the poor.[8] One source base offers the evidence for most examinations of Parisian crime: the only extant criminal register from the royal Châtelet dating from 1389 to 1392.[9] From this register, containing one hundred and seven trials involving one hundred and twenty eight defendants, the majority of offenders were among the poorest inhabitants of Paris who had no permanent residences or possessions in the city, and had committed theft of some sort.[10] As Esther Cohen put it, "first and foremost, crime meant theft, which was an instrument of profit, not an emotional outlet. Secondly, crime was largely petty and nonviolent, also for practical reasons."[11] These particular records do not reveal the professional organized roaming gangs, thieving or otherwise, found elsewhere in France, nor do they contain premeditated violent crimes. But still, fundamentally, the statistical findings from the register of the Châtelet of Paris perpetuate the notion that French criminality can be linked largely to the lower, displaced, migratory class. Jacques Chiffoleau has also proven that most prostitutes, assailants, and

[6] Léon Mirot, *Les insurrections urbaines au début du règne de Charles VI (1380–1383): Leur causes, leurs conséquences* (Paris: Albert Fontemoing, Éditeur, 1906).

[7] Jacqueline Misraki, "Criminalité et pauvreté en France à l'époque de la Guerre de Cent Ans," *Études sur l'histoire de la pauvreté*, vol. 2, ed. Michel Mollat (Paris: Publications de la Sorbonne, 1974), 535–546. Bronislaw Geremek, *The Margins of Society in Late Medieval Paris*, trans. by Jean Birrell (Cambridge: Cambridge University Press, 1987), 6–43.

[8] Claude Gauvard, "Fear of Crime in Late Medieval France," *Medieval Crime and Social Control*, ed. Barbara A. Hanawalt and David Wallace (Minneapolis: University of Minnesota Press, 1999), 1–48.

[9] *Registre criminel du Châtelet de Paris du 6 Septembre 1389 au 18 Mai 1392*, 2 vols., ed. M. Henri Duplès-Agier (Paris: Imprimer par C. Lahure, 1861–1864).

[10] Esther Cohen, "Patterns of Crime in Fourteenth-Century Paris," *French Historical Studies* 11, no. 3 (1980): 307–327. Claude Gauvard, "La criminalité parisienne à la fin du Moyen Âge: une criminalité ordinaire?" *Villes, bonnes villes, cités et capitales: Études d'histoire urbaine (XIIe-XVIIIe siècle) offertes à Bernard Chevalier*, ed. Monique Bourin (Caen: Paradigme, 1993), 361–370.

[11] Cohen, "Patterns of Crime," 327.

thieves came from all over Christendom to commit their crimes in the papal headquarters of fourteenth-century Avignon.[12]

As the political capital of Languedoc, there is little doubt that, like Paris, Toulouse had its share of unemployed transients who had to steal or resort to violence to survive. But if the sergeants or night guards arrested them for some offense, the capitols did not take the time to record the cases or conduct extensive investigation into the matter. Instead, the defendants identified in the capitols' criminal register lived, worked, and (allegedly) committed their crimes in the most thriving districts of the urban space. So whereas other courts, including inquisitorial courts, dealt primarily with outsiders and rural residents, in Toulouse, the municipal court dealt with people explicitly connected to the community. The citizens of Toulouse moved from one region of the city to the next throughout the daily course of their lives, dealing with their neighbors, local merchants, and clergy. This led, not surprisingly to occasional interpersonal conflicts or to violent eruptions. But the city space also became the site of rebellions and protests from the both the urban and the surrounding rural inhabitants alike. People who inhabited the surrounding countryside of Languedoc flocked through the city's gates and flooded the streets when royal policies or new taxation infuriated the masses. Even in times of peace there was always the possibility that a dispute between a citizen and a visitor could turn physical and result in a jurisdictional conflict between the capitols and other authorities. These events transpired in the living and working city space of Toulouse, and whether consciously or subconsciously, these locations then took on connotations of power. The ordering of the social, political, or jurisdictional hierarchy was negotiated in front of the audience of the urban public, and thus confrontations or protests occurred in the most populous districts of the city. This reinforced the notion that the capitols and other civic officials had an obligation, a responsibility, to protect the city space through the enforcement of justice and order.

The purpose of this chapter is to establish the overall social topography of Toulouse to accentuate the experience of living in the city for various social classes, and the public areas available for interaction. It will create a sense of where particular groups of people lived, and where they had to go to buy goods, to seek justice, and to worship. The city was partitioned in such a way that even non-citizens entering the city for the first time would

[12] Jacques Chiffoleau, *Les Justices du Pape*, 256–258.

have little trouble navigating the space in order to achieve a particular goal or function. Like most medieval cities, the population coexisted in fairly close quarters, with privacy a luxury that few could afford. Much of their lives spilled out of their homes or taverns and into streets to unfold in the public squares, courtyards and in front of their neighbors. As such, this chapter will assess the geographical distribution of crime throughout the city, in order to reveal that most of the reported and prosecuted activity transpired in the most densely populated regions of Toulouse. The formalities of the entering the capitols' courtroom, apparently, best served the men and women of Toulouse who could afford the pursuit of justice and who needed a public restitution of their honor.

The Living Space of Medieval Toulouse

The previous chapter explored how several competing realms of jurisdiction divided Toulouse: royal, municipal, and ecclesiastical. As a royal subject, a citizen could appeal to the royal vicar regarding the capitols' criminal verdicts, or, he could be tried as a heretic in the court of the Inquisition, even *in absentia*. In the same respect, economic and social factors partitioned the city space. The tanners lived and worked by the Garonne River, and the glove makers shared a neighborhood close to church of the Carmelites. In other words, people who worked in the same craft congregated in the same area, not only to share equipment and skills, but also for the companionship of their profession, and for mutual aid. The medieval inhabitant would have known where to go in the city to buy the best goods and necessities. On top of that, social and religious groups tended to inhabit the same neighborhoods of Toulouse. Most of the city's Jewish population lived in a district called Joutx-Aigues before Philip IV expelled them from France in 1306.[13] University students resided and studied around the basilica of Saint Sernin. As the administrative capitol of Languedoc, portions of the city space held political importance: the town hall symbolized local sovereignty, while the Château Narbonnais stood for the power of the Raymondine counts, and later the Capetian kings. Thus, each street and city square held several overlapping social, religious, economic, and political connotations for the urban inhabitants, and served as forums for personal and professional interaction.

[13] Gustave Saige, *Les Juifs du Languedoc antérieurement au XIVe siècle* (Paris: Gregg Pub., 1881), 280–283. Gérard Nahon, "Les juifs dans les domains d'Alfonse de Poitiers, 1241–1271," *Revue des Études Juives* 124 (1966): 157–211.

From its earliest origins, Toulouse thrived as the commercial and political center for the surrounding territory. It served as a point of transit between the Atlantic Ocean and the Mediterranean, and between France and Spain. The Garonne River cut through the city, and was a natural thoroughfare for merchants coming to Languedoc. As a result, most of the workers and centers of production were situated around the river and extended north towards the town hall. So, like many medieval towns, economic factors defined and divided Toulouse. The city was a "*fabrica*, an enormous factory whose various branches of activity were widely scattered."[14] The type of work and production served to divide the topography of the city space into various sectors. Individuals and families who worked either in alimentation or in the industries of leather had a tendency to group together in the city. This would include the bread and wine makers, those who worked with meat and fish, and those who prepared leather, such as the tanners, skinners, and shoe and glove makers. The location of their production base would largely be dependent upon the available resources of the city, and so, for example, fishers and millers obviously gathered by the Garonne River, as did the parchment makers, who needed effective drainage into the water. A glance at a map of Toulouse today still reveals that many of the streets bear the names of the artisans who worked there: there is la rue Pargaminières (or parchment makers), and la rue des Blanchers. Beginning in the thirteenth century, workers involved in various strands of cutlery cohabited on la rue des Couteliers.[15]

Although most commercial districts existed in the center of the town, close to the town hall like the Place de St. Georges, or areas in proximity to the Garonne River,[16] other groups of workers in alimentation (most commonly, the merchants of wine and oil and the candle makers) were scattered throughout the city, to provide easy accessibility to each of the individual neighborhoods. Some, particularly the butchers, gathered in clusters at specific designated sites, or *bancus*, where authorities could easily regulate their goods and shoppers could compare wares.[17] A guild statute from 1322 reveals that meat was especially important to the medieval household.[18] The document (an agreement between the capitols and

---

[14] Geremek, *The Margins of Society*, 66.

[15] *DRT*, vol. 1, 329.

[16] Wolff, *Regards sur le midi*, 273.

[17] A *bancus*, was a booth or a table where merchandise for sale was displayed for inspection by the buyer. Apparently in Toulouse, this term only applies to butchers, and meant a grouping of butchers in squares, or the "quarters."

[18] *Early Guild Records of Toulouse*, 69–70.

the butchers), lists around one hundred and seventy seven names of butchers, in addition to the location of their *bancus,* situated in each the twelve *capitoulats* of Toulouse. The majority of the butchers were in the more populated region of the *cité,* including thirty-nine on today's rue Saint-Rome alone. In the *bourg,* which was less populated, there were sixteen names around Saint-Sernin, four names at the place du Bazacle, and there were twenty-one names of butchers holding stalls along the river banks of the suburb, Saint-Cyprien. According to Philippe Wolff's calculations, there was one butcher for every 226 inhabitants (based upon a population of 40,000 inhabitants).[19] In other words, a medieval housewife did not have to travel far to purchase the meat and beef for the household, or to catch up on gossip with her neighbors.

In order to gain some sense of the distribution of wealth in Toulouse, scholars have turned to extant tax registers, known as *estimes,* which date from 1335.[20] The statutes of Toulouse mention tax registers in the early thirteenth century tax registers, especially when the capitols struggled with the local counts for jurisdictional autonomy. Alphonse of Poitiers commanded the capitols to make a register of the moveable and immoveable goods of the heads of each household, and to add up their taxable goods. A statute from 1270 stated that each of the twelve divisions, or *capitoulats,* would have a separate tax register, to be locked in an armoire with five keys; four would be distributed to good men of the neighborhood chosen by the region's capitol, who would guard the fifth. In order to prevent any corruption or mutation to the document, all changes would be enacted at the decision of all five men.[21] The single register which survives from 1335 was a direct result of the royal financial punishment for the city's execution of a squire in 1332 (the "Aimery Berenger Affair" which will be discussed at length in Chapter 5). The capitols needed to tax the population extensively in order to pay their large fines to the king. Unfortunately, the existing records from 1335 only concern the Bourg.[22] Towards the end of the fourteenth century, the more complete tax registers provide a better sense of where people lived and how much wealth they had.

The tax registers divided the population into two categories: the *estimes* and *nichils.* A head of the household who held property that was valued

[19] Philippe Wolff, "Les bouchers de Toulouse du XIIe au XVe siècle," *Regards sur le midi medieval,* 107–124.

[20] AMT, CC 1 and CC1 bis. Published in Wolff, *Les "estimes" toulousaines.*

[21] AMT-AA 3: 128.

[22] None of these documents contain any information about the landholding of the church in Toulouse, which would have been substantial.

over ten *livres tournois* was an *estimes*; if they did not, he was considered *nichils*. In compiling the records, the notary recorded how many houses, land, and inns the citizen owned in the city and the surrounding territory, and then estimated its taxable worth. In 1335, the Bourg was populated by both large landowners (rich nobles and retired business workers) and humble gardeners, and workers (such as artisans who specialized in textiles, metal, and leather). The tax list suggests that many artisans lived by the Garonne River, around the ancient church of Saint-Pierre des Cuisines, and into the area of the Daurade. An examination of the complete tax registers from 1398 indicates that the richest merchants of the city lived in the oldest part of the city, near the shops of de la Pierre, and the poorer sections were isolated to the suburb of Saint Cyprien across the Garonne River. For the most part, however, rich and poor resided and worked side by side, scattered throughout the various neighborhoods of Toulouse.[23]

The inhabitant who earned a modest income, then, just had to walk down the street to see how the wealthy citizens lived: in opulent hôtels. Although it is difficult to gain access to the daily living conditions of the residents, some notarial records do provide important information regarding the material culture of some of the dominant noble families of the city. Several families, such as the Maurand and Roaix, descended from the knights who first came to Toulouse, who established political dominance, and who held the position of capitol in quasi-dynasties. For example, citizens elected the men of the Roaix family to the office sixty-eight times between 1156 and 1482.[24] Other elites gained their wealth later in the fourteenth century, earning large incomes from occupations such as bankers, drapers, and merchants.[25] In addition, the University of Toulouse and the increasingly bureaucratic municipal administration brought in law specialists, notaries and jurists as university masters who also became a part of the city's oligarchy. One of these powerful families, the family of Bertrand Tornier, owned a large home on the rue Temponières (not far from the Church of the Daurade by the Garonne River), that dominated the street from the early fourteenth century. A tax register from a notary's tour of the estate in 1403 gives a sense of this enormous conglomeration of

---

23 Wolff, "Toulouse vers 1400: répartition topographique des fortunes et des professions," *Regards sur le midi*, 269–281.

24 Véronique Lamazou-Duplan, "Les élites Toulousaines et leurs demeures à la fin du moyen âge d'après les registres notaries: entre maison possédée et maison habitée," M.S.A.M.F. (2002), 42.

25 Philippe Wolff, *Commerces et marchands de Toulouse (vers 1350–1450)* (Paris: Plone, 1954).

property in the middle of Toulouse. Smaller buildings to house relatives surrounded a huge familial home creating a complex, which also boasted a tower (a sign of nobility and the classic capitol's status), and a chapel. The house even had its own type of plumbing to send water into the Garonne River.[26] The notary recorded expensive clothes, furs, and precious metals, and also mentioned that the front door to the home was large enough to accommodate the entrance of horses.[27] On a daily basis, servants came in and out of the home, to seek provisions from merchants in the surrounding neighborhoods so that the large home was fully stocked for all of its inhabitants.

Particular areas of the city became identifiable by the status of its residents, and by the social services available to the citizens. A short walk north from the Garonne River led to the centrally located town hall. As we saw in the previous chapter, the town hall served as a sign of the growing strength and sovereignty of the capitols in the thirteenth century. The town hall could also evoke a sense of rebellion, as it was here that the capitols supposedly stored the trebuchet that killed Count Simon de Montfort on June 25, 1218, during the Albigensian Crusade. The anonymous commentator of the *coutumes* of Toulouse mentioned this point in 1296, almost in a casual passing of his narrative.[28] If this was truly the case, we can only imagine that this factor would have influenced royal and local Toulousain relations. The infamous count was one of the key figures in the battle over Languedoc, heralded by northern chroniclers, and condemned by writers from the south. In *The Song of the Cathar Wars*, William of Tudela described his atrocities at length, and included Simon de Montfort's very explicit intention to raze the city to the ground. In one ruthless occupation of Toulouse in 1217, Simon ordered the arrest of about four hundred prominent citizens and commoners to be first imprisoned in the cells of the Château Narbonnais, and to be later condemned to castles scattered throughout Languedoc as hostages. He enacted a huge tax of 30,000 silver marks upon the rest of the population, and confiscated and destroyed the homes of occupants who did not pay. Overall, the demolition of the city was intense, but unfortunately for the northern crusaders, not complete.[29] As Simon de Montfort attended to other campaigns throughout

---

26 Regulation of irrigation had been left for the municipal administration. AA1:19, from November 1180.

27 Lamazou-Duplan, "Les élites toulousaines," 47.

28 Giles, *Les coutumes de Toulouse*, 163, "qui lapis fuit projectus per machinam cum quo dictus comes Montisfortis fuit percussus. Que machine est adhuc in palatio communi."

29 Sumption, *The Albigensian Crusade*, 189.

Languedoc, by 1218, the Toulousains rallied to form a resistance. According to *The Song of the Cathar Wars*, by the time Simon de Montfort returned to lay siege to the city, "there was in the town a mangonel built by a carpenter and dragged with its platform from St. Sernin. This was worked by noblewomen, by little girls and men's wives, and now a stone arrived just where it was needed and struck Count Simon on his steel helmet, shattering his eyes, brains, back teeth, forehead and jaw. Bleeding and black, the count dropped dead on the ground."[30] The text recounts that the whole city rejoiced at this event. They lit candles in all of the churches; they played trumpets, rung bells, cried out in joy, and celebrated throughout the night. Northern author Peter of les Vaux-de-Cernay's *Historia Albigensis*, however, equated the death to that of the martyrdom by stoning of Saint Stephen, the namesake of Toulouse's cathedral.[31] The French crusaders buried Simon de Montfort with great reverence and honors in the cathedral church of Saint-Nazaire in Carcassone, and his death served as a rallying cry for the papacy and Capetian king alike to renew their efforts to take the city of Toulouse. Pope Honorius offered the king, "remission of his sins to bring successful conclusion the Crusade against the heretics of Toulouse, to the honor of God and the glory of his Holy Church."[32] It is striking that the capitols would not only keep, but maybe even prominently store, the deadly siege weapon in the town hall.

Of course, we can only speculate as to whether or not the average man or women living in Toulouse regarded their town hall and officers with pride or reverence based on these historical affiliations. But they certainly acknowledged the town hall's practical importance as an administrative headquarters. Citizens seeking any type of justice or restitution headed to the building to meet with a notary, or to attend a court proceeding. The capitols worked here with their bureaucratic and policing staff on a daily basis, as they dealt with the pressing economic, judicial and political issues of the city. It housed the municipal jail, along with the jailer and his family. On any given day, citizens, lawyers, sergeants, capitols could come and leave the town hall on matters of all things business. The front lawn of the building, then, became a natural site for protests or demonstrations aimed at policies or decisions of the local government.

---

[30] *The Song of the Cathar War:, A History of the Albigensian Crusade*, trans. Janet Shirley (Sydney: Ashgate Publishing Limited, 1996), 172.

[31] Peter of les Vaux-de-Cernay. *The History of the Albigensian Crusade. Peter of les Vaux-de-Cernay's Historia Albigensis*, trans. W.A. Sibly and M.D. Sibly (Woodbridge, Suffolk: The Boydell Press, 1998), 277.

[32] Ibid., 278.

To the west of the town hall, the area surrounding the basilica of Saint Sernin became closely affiliated with the University of Toulouse throughout the thirteenth and fourteenth centuries, as the institution grew along with the proliferation of colleges endowed to house the poor students who come into the city.[33] In the *estimes* of 1335, several Toulousains owned schools in this district of the Bourg, which is hardly surprising considering the area was, and still remains, the university district. Thirteen individuals held multiple schools that valued 1,755 *livres tournois*.[34] In the 1250s, Bishop William of Agen, head of the papal inquisition, donated the College of Saint-Raymond as a gift to the canons-regular of Saint Sernin. The bishop granted a house, located across the street from the Hospital of Saint-Raymond, where poor students could live, under the condition that house would be joined to the hospital by a bridge, its street door blocked up, and turned into a dormitory with rooms for study. Previously, a Bernard de Caux owned the house, and used it as a prison for the inquisition between the years 1245 and 1247.[35] As wealthy patrons and church officials continued to fund colleges for students affiliated with the university, the population of Bourg grew with the influx of foreign scholars. A citizen of Toulouse who walked from the town hall and down the rue du Taur towards the basilica would have been overwhelmed by the large number of young men spilling out of the colleges and into the streets.

As the urban population expanded and diversified, more benefactors established charitable institutions to help the poor or sickly in the city. In 1275, a nobleman named Bernard Bruno bequeathed five *sous* to each hospital of Toulouse, five *sous* to each leper house, and 500 *sous* to provide clothes and supplies for the poor of the city.[36] John Hine Mundy has also demonstrated that despite the proliferation of heresy and the decline of the strength of the church in the thirteenth-century Toulouse, there were still an abundance of hospitals and leper houses. As early as 1080, the hospital of Saint Raymond was located adjacent to Saint Sernin. By the early thirteenth century, leprosaries are mentioned in the documents for the

---

33 Smith, *The University of Toulouse*, 110–120.

34 Wolff, *Les "estimes,"* 60.

35 The eighteenth-century copy of the *vidimus* from the thirteenth century is published in John Hine Mundy, "The College of Saint-Raymond," *Studies in the Ecclesiastical and Social History of Toulouse in the Age of the Cathars*, 215–223.

36 Celestine Douais, "Des fortunes commerciales à Toulouse et de la topographie des églises et maisons religieuses de Toulouse d'après deux testaments (XIIIe-XVe siècle)," *Mémoires de la Société Archéologique du Midi de la France*, vol. XV (Toulouse: Édouard Privat, Libraire- Éditeur, 1894–1896), 27–28.

first time. They were situated at the Narbonnais Gate, the Villeneuve Gate in the Bourg, and the Leprosary of Bruno Baranonus in Saint Cyrprien, was attached to the Daurade.[37] Increasingly, the number of leprosaries grew: one outside of the gate of the Arnaud Bernard is mentioned in a testament of 1246, and another outside of the Pousonville Gate. Mundy has shown that by the mid-thirteenth century there were as many as seven leprosaries and twelve hospitals in Toulouse.[38] Initially, individual sponsors ran the leprosaries, and not the city government. Most inhabitants who could do so felt obligated to donate to these charitable institutions, but they were not regulated or administered by the local officials or bigger church institutions until the late fourteenth century.[39]

In addition to charitable institutions, the city was full of numerous churches and religious orders. These religious buildings forced great changes in the city's topography: monks and friars needed a lot of space to build their cloisters where they meditated. Although it took some time for the number of women's orders to grow in Toulouse, as early as 1217, an old hospital of the Arnaud Bernard Gate was given to the Dominicans for "fallen women."[40] In 1304 and 1309, the sisters of the Augustinian order engaged in a heated dispute with the monastic order of Saint Jean-de-Jerusalem over a small farm and garden located at the gate of Villeneuve.[41] The male patrons insisted that the sisters remain cloistered and respectable, and remember to pay their financial obligations to their sponsors. In fact, because the sisters had been accused of neglecting to make payments, they were asked to pay double their annual rent in gold. In Bernardus Bruno's will, the wealthy merchant left a large amount of money to the churches of Toulouse, which give us some sense of the structures being created at the time and those which were already in existence. He gave money to the cathedral Saint Étienne (located in the northeast portion of the city), Saint Pierre-des-Cuisines, the basilica Saint Sernin,

[37] John Hine Mundy, "Hospitals and Leprosaries in Twelfth and Early Thirteenth Century Toulouse," *Essays in Medieval Life and Thought, Presented in Honor of Austin Patterson Evans*, ed. John H. Mundy, Richard W. Emery, and Benjamin N. Nelson (New York: Columbia University Press, 1955), 185–186. While in the Departmental Archives of the Haute Garonne, I requested to view the documents for the leprosary outside of the Château Narbonnais, (Series H, Grandselve 1). At the time, they were not accessible to the public. I hope to view them in the future.

[38] Mundy, "Hospitals and Leprosaries," 187.

[39] John Hine Mundy, "Hospitals and Leproseries around 1400," *Studies in the Ecclesiastical and Social History of Toulouse in the Age of the Cathars* (Burlington, Vermont: Ashgate Publishing Company, 2006), 225–234.

[40] Mundy, *Men and Women at Toulouse*, 67.

[41] AMT-GG 820 (1304) and GG 821 (1309).

the Church of Taur, and 300 *sous* for the mendicants, who were building a church and a chapel to Christ and Saint-Jacques. One hundred and fifty *sous* were left for Beguines to build a hospital.[42] All over the city of Toulouse, religious orders erected or enlarged churches, to accommodate the growing number of ecclesiastical representatives and the burgeoning population of worshippers.

The influx of royal officials and Dominican inquisitors into Toulouse added new dimensions to the connotations of power and authority in the city space. As early as 1230, a convent, known as the Jacobins, was built specifically to accommodate and serve as the Dominican headquarters for the inquisition. The Jacobins was (and is) situated south of the town hall, close to the Garonne River, and it is here that the inquisitors resided, prayed, and summoned heretical suspects to be questioned. But the heretics could be detained in numerous prisons scattered throughout the city: in the prisons of Saint Sernin and of Saint Étienne, or in the royal prison of the Château Narbonnais. The inquisitors protected and stored their records in the Château Narbonnais as well.[43] Even though the Dominicans carried out their methods and interrogation in secret, they made very public denunciations of specific condemned heretics and heretical behavior most commonly in front of Saint Étienne. For example, in 1308, 1309, 1311, and 1315, an inquisitor mounted the steps of the cathedral and announced the various punishments for heretics, and warned the gathered audience that even the bodies of deceased Cathars could be interred and burned again.[44] The area around the Château Narbonnais became populated with royal sergeants and bureaucrats who had been stationed in the city to protect and to enforce the Capetian king's policies as presented by the vicar. Old and new buildings and sections of Toulouse grew closer in affiliation and function with these 'outside' authorities tasked with the responsibility of fostering the assimilation of the region into a royal and orthodox state.

As Toulouse progressed as the home to an increasingly miscellaneous population of inhabitants, the city experienced a proliferation of taverns. The inns and taverns hosted both the residents of the city seeking food and drink, and the traveling merchants and pilgrims passing through the city on their way to tourist destinations such as Compostela. As the administrative capitol of the region, people came to Toulouse for advice from lawyers, to bring complaints to the capitols, and for the use of a notary in

[42] Douais, "Des fortune commerciales à Toulouse," 25–52.
[43] Given, *Inquisition and Medieval Society*, 27.
[44] *HGL*, vol. 4, 177.

land transactions or inheritance disputes. Inns were scattered throughout the city, and around 1205, the capitols established regulations for the inn-keepers in regard to their clientele, particularly pilgrims. For example, the capitols established standards against seizing pilgrims' clothes or horses; they created standards for the bread, wine and oats that the inn keepers sold to their clients. The capitols instructed the inn keepers to remain open until the night bell, and even then, the proprietor must open the door for the clients who might have missed the last ring.[45] In 1398, tax records show that there were about thirty inns owned by the head of a households. Wolff consulted the tax records from 1440 to situate the inns in the city, and found that most were situated around the bridges, gates, and commercial districts of the city. Few neighborhoods, however, did not have at least one inn or tavern to serve as the public gathering place for social and business interactions.[46]

Although we know where the taverns and inns would have been located in fourteenth-century Toulouse, we can only speculate as to what transpired within these buildings on any given day. A case preserved in the archives of the Parlement (March 8, 1384), does allow us to step inside, and to examine the social and business interactions of the proprietors and their clients. In this scenario, Robinet Tirand, a squire and servant of the king was sent to Toulouse, where he took a room with his men in the inn of Jacomard de Joye, a tailor, and his wife, situated on the rue du Temple.[47] The street was a major thoroughfare towards the Château Narbonnais, where the royal representative would have been conducting his business.[48] The proprietors assigned him a room on the top floor, a choice location away from the scuffle of the street. As he settled into his chambers, his men placed two locked metal boxes that contained both money and jewels, under the third bed in the room. Tirand later testified to the Parlement that he had demanded, in vain, to secure a key to this room: the wife assured him that his luggage would be safe, and promised him the key later on. When he left his room for business, the boxes disappeared. Tirand immediately accused the hostess of the theft. She and her husband defended themselves, and claimed that they did not know that he had the

[45] AMT-AA 1: 52. Published by Limouzin-Lamothe, *La commune de Toulouse,* 358–361. The municipal, and later royal, insistence that food and wine be regulated continued into the mid-fourteenth century. See, AMT-AA 56 (1341).

[46] Wolff, "Les Hôtelleries toulousaines," *Regards sur le midi,* 94.

[47] This case, found in the Archives Nationales, series X 34, n° 92, f° 167, is described in Wolff, "Les hôtelleries toulousaines," 105.

[48] *DRT*, vol 2, 503.

boxes, and they stressed that Tirand had, in fact, received a key. Thus, according to the custom of Toulouse, they were above any responsibility in the crime. The de Joyes did, however, suggest alternative culprits for the theft. One theory blamed a neighborhood pauper, named Jean Denys, who displayed a suspiciously more lavish lifestyle around the time that the boxes were reported missing. However, the Parlement did not buy the defense and ordered the couple to pay Tirand the value of his lost goods, and the court fees.

As we step outside of the de Joyes inn, and back into the streets of Toulouse, we return to the complex urban environment. The city hosted a wide range of inhabitants, including members of the clergy, the administrators, and the men and women who worked in the economic sector, providing the goods which allowed the city to thrive. This was not a city where neighbors were strangers, and after work, people retreated to their home in isolation. Instead, there was a tavern in each neighborhood where the citizens could mingle and meet for business or pleasure. The city had many commercial districts for shopping and production, a university district full of ambitious and rambunctious young men, and administrative regions full of lawyers and bureaucrats around the town hall and Château Narbonnais. The city offered hospitals and leprosaries for the sick and infirm, charitable institutions to take care of the poor, and churches to pray for salvation. In short, the city of Toulouse and its population were active and thriving in the fourteenth century.

The Demographic Composition of Toulouse's Municipal Defendants

Toulouse provided many locations and opportunities for its citizens to gather and interact. Not surprisingly, many of these meetings resulted in crimes and violent conflicts in the city. One extant archival register from 1332 indicated that seventy men and women were named as the primary defendants in criminal charges read in the capitols' court. These citizens were accused of various crimes including physical assault, carrying illegal weapons, and theft. It is difficult to establish the accurate number of people actually involved in the city's criminal activity; the defendants often implicated additional collaborators in their testimony. Some participants were referenced only as either *malefactores,* or "certain bad men" (*mali homines*) during the proceedings.[49] Frequently, the defendant was

49 Ibid., 271, 151.

drinking in a bar with nameless friends before a conflict erupted.[50] In other cases, the notary recorded unnamed participants as *eius consortes* in the charges.[51] But still, overwhelmingly, the primary defendants identified in the capitols' criminal register were men and women directly tied to the community through various occupational and familial links.

The urban administration brought defendants to trial in several manners: the city's municipal officers caught them in the act, or the alleged victim filed a complaint with a criminal notary. In the cases from 1332, occasionally the capitols became aware of other charges against accused criminals through felons already in jail. The convicted criminal, about to be punished by the capitols, found a last opportunity to ensure that all of the collaborators suffer a similar fate. For example, as the capitols convicted a thief called Mon Johan and several others bandits (*latrones*), and sentenced them to run the town and to be exiled, the gang turned in a local citizen, Arnaldus de Santo Martino, for holding and redistributing their stolen goods.[52] The archives do not hold any evidence to suggest that the capitols conducted an extensive trial to convict the roving bandits for their offenses. But they did thoroughly investigate the charges against Arnaldus de Santo Martino: they called in witnesses and issued officers to his home to read the charges brought forth against him. Arnaldus and his lawyer had to attend a hearing in order to attempt to prove his innocence. As I have stressed before, not surprisingly, there *were* transients and vagrants who committed crimes in Toulouse, but they were not afforded the formalities of a trial in the capitols' courtroom.

In Languedoc, most people had a prename, to designate the individual, and an inherited name, to designate the family.[53] The assigned notary recorded when a defendant had a nickname or an alias with multiple spellings. In one example, a co-conspirator in an attack upon a night guard was identified as Rao in the initial proclamation. The notary later referenced him as Radulfus and Rael in the testimony of the case. However, this does not seem to suggest that he was a vagrant of some sorts; he lived in the neighborhood of *Trelhe*, near the *Plateam Affactatores*, located in the center of town.[54] Other times, people were recognized by a different geographical region in or around Toulouse. Men like Peyrotus de Casalis,

50 Ibid., 179. This is the case in the charges against Franciscus Amblayre.
51 Ibid., 139, 141, 203.
52 Ibid., 143.
53 Limouzin-Lamothe, *La commune de Toulouse*, 55–57.
54 AMT-FF 57, 117. *Carreria Trelhe*, is the ancient name of today's la rue and la place de la Trinité. *DRT*, vol. 2, 529.

alias dicitur de Putheo,[55] and Perrotus de Balerno, *alias dicitur Calhan de Colomeriis*,[56] suggest a variable and complex means of social classification. Individuals were not identified by one factor, but wee able to move in a fluid stratum of geographic or familial nomenclature.

For the most part, the notary identified the profession or occupation of the defendants, which ranged from an educated master to shield bearer. Three of the defendants worked for the municipal government: Arnaldus Franciscus, a sergeant for the capitols of Toulouse, who sometimes also served as a messenger,[57] Ramundus Bernardi was a night guard,[58] and Vitalis Nigri was a municipally funded guard of a vineyard outside of the *Porta Matabovis*, north of town.[59] One public notary for Toulouse (*notaire tholosa publice*), Master Guillelmus Petrus de Villa Longa, was involved in a gang attack against a clerk in the city streets.[60] These municipal officials earned their livelihood in service to the community, and city taxes paid their salary to an extent. Two professionals, a medical doctor (*medicus*),[61] and a copyist (*scriptor librorum*),[62] were charged with violent crimes involving illegal weapons. They would have passed certain standards of proficiency to practice in Toulouse. Although the capitols sent most individuals affiliated with the church to ecclesiastical courts, Petrus Guillemus, a priest of the chapel of Saint Salvatoris,[63] faced charges in the municipal court. Aside from two squires listed as defendants in the violent Aimery Berenger affair (both the scandal's namesake and Perrotus de Penna, a bastard from the de Penna family, and a shield bearer),[64] only two other servants were charged with a crime. Talayrannus Guallermi, a squire of Lord Raymundus Arnaldi de Villa Nova,[65] was accused of a physical attack, while municipal sergeants caught Clemenes de Bena, a servant (*famulus*) of Lord Helis de Costello, when he possessed illegal arms.[66]

The remaining defendants had a wide variety of occupations in Toulouse, most of which would have required the individual to be a member

---

55 AMT-FF 57, 139.
56 Ibid., 239
57 Ibid., 155. In a case dated later in the register, Arnaldus Franciscus was called upon to serve as a messenger, reading charges against a defendant, 181.
58 Ibid., 223
59 Ibid., 271.
60 Ibid., 141.
61 Ibid., 147.
62 Ibid., 75.
63 Ibid., 67. Petrus is identified as *clericus*.
64 Ibid.
65 Ibid., 61.
66 Ibid., 253

of one of the local guilds. By the fourteenth century, guilds performed many important functions in the urban environment. In addition to ensuring the quality and fair price of goods and services, the members' dues covered the repairs of the cathedral Saint Sernin and other churches, and the fines collected for failing to comply with the guild regulations went to the upkeep of roads and bridges over the Garonne River and sometimes went to aid the city's poor.[67] In other words, a defendant identified as a money changer (*campsor*),[68] or a tavern keeper (*tabernarius*),[69] was not only economically invested in the city through their employment, but he was also conscious of the guild's social responsibilities to the well-being of the community. In effect, this meant that guild members were accountable to three sectors: the municipal court, the masters of their profession, and the public at large. And if a weaver or brewer, for example, wanted to achieve financial success in Toulouse, he had to have a solid reputation in his community. Neighbors shared their opinions as to which merchant or skilled worker offered the best value and goods. These defendants who worked in Toulouse were intrinsically woven into the social and economic fabric of the community. Much of this notion is further evidenced in the preambles of guild statutes dated between 1270 and 1322, where the masters professed their moral and civic obligation to control the behavior of the members, and to secure a monopoly in the production and sale of goods. Andree DuBourg's study of these documents, in fact, emphasized the importance of both civic pride and Christian sentiment to the formation and aspiration of the guilds.[70] Sister Mary Mulholland contends that the capitols of Toulouse ordered the production and the wording of these early guild records in an effort to bolster the local officials' control over the merchants and artisans. Because at this same time the royal vicar began to infringe upon the capitols' traditional right to appoint regulatory guild officers, to police and safeguard the exercise of the trades, to create new statutes, and to prevent abuses within the guilds.[71] Mulholland's argument that the capitols and the royal vicar competed over control of the guilds ties nicely into the ambition of this book to prove that they struggled over jurisdiction and the right to punish as well.

---

[67] *Early Guild Records of Toulouse*, 27, 56, 65–66.

[68] AMT-FF 57, 141.

[69] Ibid., 79.

[70] Andree DuBourg, "Les corporations ouvrières de la ville de Toulouse du XIIIe au XVe siècle," *Mémoires de la Société archéologique du midi de la France*, XIII (1884–1885), 154–253.

[71] Mulholland, *Early Guild Records of Toulouse*, xvi.

This is certainly not to suggest that these merchants and artisans lived up to the lofty ideal of their communal, religious, economic (and in some cases, political) duty in Toulouse or in other cities. Indeed, some professions gained a reputation for inappropriate behavior, either criminal or professionally unethical. In several locations throughout France, the butchers and the fishermen seemed to be the occupations best represented in disciplinary courts. In Avignon, the butchers nearly topped the list of the most violent professionals of the fourteenth century,[72] whereas in Lyon, butchers more commonly engaged in fraud and theft, although they had their fair share of brutal attacks and revolts against the municipal government.[73] Nicole Gonthier speculated that it was perhaps the very demands and qualifications of the job, such as a willingness to shed blood or to wield cutlery, which attracted the deviant or rebellious sort.[74] Beyond looking for criminal trends along occupational lines, Bronislav Geremek actually challenged the validity of people claiming to be professional in the records of the register of the Châtelet of Paris, and argued that many of the accused criminals simply claimed to be artisans in order to hide the fact that they were career criminals or transients.[75] He alleged only three men could confirm that they were qualified craftsmen.[76] Others simply borrowed the occupation of an acquaintance or family member. Geremek seems to warn scholars that a defendant's declaration of a professional status does not prove that he contributed to and was connected with urban society at large.

But the records of Toulouse contain numerous indications that support my earlier allusion that the city's guild members were, in fact, very much interwoven into the social fabric, and that they were not imposters. First, a defendant might be identified by both his profession and a specific residential neighborhood: there were two lumber dealers (*fusterii*), Arnaldus Mancipii de Tunicci[77] and Bernardus Fusterius Guaynerium de Judey Aquis.[78] Two more were brewers (*brasserius*), Petrus Lequast de carreria

---

72 Chiffoleau, *Les justice du pape*, 157.
73 Gonthier, *Délinquance*, 182–185.
74 Ibid., 185.
75 Geremek, *The Margins of Society*, 243.
76 Ibid., 247.
77 AMT-FF 57, 267.
78 Ibid., 113. In early archival references of Toulouse, the *fusterii* were normally identified as carpenters. However, a guild statute from 1273 pertains to merchants as opposed to artisans. Mulholland therefore concludes that the term could cover carpenters who also sold their wares. *Early Guild Records of Toulouse*, xii, 60–64.

de Cogossato[79] and Bernardi Aymes de Barrio Penitentie.[80] Each listed street is a recognizable and fairly centralized location, which again, firmly allied the defendant with a profession and fixed location in the city space. Second, the accused criminal could be described as the son of a father of the same profession. These included a carpenter, Huguetum de Sanardino (*carpenerius*),[81] an iron worker, Johannes de Manso (*ferratus*),[82] a gardener, Johannem de Castro Novo (*ortolanus*),[83] and a grocer, Bartholmeus Jordani.[84] We also have one example of a third generation weaver, Johannem de Pinolibus,.[85] The hereditary nature of the position validates the occupational claims of the defendant, and family members who shared a common employment probably lived in a common district of Toulouse for generations. This leads us to the third indicator from the documents, which is that many merchants or artisans lived with colleagues, or in the same vicinity. Two defendants, both merchants, Franciscus Bene and Johannem de Moras, lived with Arnaldo de Gualhato, another *mercator*.[86] Six defendants from 1332 all had jobs in the production of textile goods, and lived in the neighborhood of Clotis, close to commercial center of the Place Saint Georges. The criminal notary of Toulouse recorded these identifying traits in the criminal register to keep track of the accused malefactor, but for our purposes, it implies that the professionals would have been legitimate members of their respective civic guild.

If the notary did not record an occupation, the defendant's residency became the identifying factor for the court. It was important for the notary and the court to know where the defendant was staying in the city in case they needed to issue a warrant for an arrest. For example, Vesianus Guarini stayed with Johannes Pascisserio in the neighborhood of *Calida*.[87] Guillelmus Rabant stayed with the *rector* of the neighborhood of *Tauro*.[88] One unusual suspect, Repplanda, was only identified as one who "sleeps in the house of Geralde, wife of Geraldi Fayshoris of Thayo Rotando de Lata."[89] Other references to residential locations could be situated by a

79 AMT-FF 57, 181.
80 Ibid., 203.
81 Ibid., 255.
82 Ibid., 59.
83 Ibid., 167.
84 Ibid, 219
85 Ibid., 203. He is identified as the grandson of Bernardi Ramini.
86 Ibid., 259.
87 Ibid., 93.
88 Ibid., 135.
89 Ibid., 251. "Causa preventionis tradite contra Repplanda qui iacet in domo Geralde uxoris Geraldi Fayshoris de Chayo Rotundo de Lata de vulnere Grize."

gate of the city, such as Johannem Causati of *Porta Ville Nova*,[90] or Johannem de Lapindad, of the area (*lissa*) around the gate of Arnaud Bernard.[91] Specific neighborhoods were listed for Perrotus Guaynerius of Judeys Aquis,[92] Petrus de Tauro Sabaterus of the neighborhood of *Turris deu Guaruguas*,[93] and Jacobus Briconis of near (*prope*) Nazarenium[94] A couple of entries were narrowed to a neighborhood landmark: Franciscus Amblaýre lived in the neighborhood of Hugonis Vitalis, by a closed well.[95] Most of the defendants, in short, lived with friends and family or rented rooms in well-known locations throughout the city.

In addition to the occupational and residential connections, the criminal register reveals that many of the defendants had family members living in Toulouse. Only one defendant was identified as a bastard: Perrotus de Penna, who served as a shield bearer to Raymundus Amelii de Penna.[96] Beyond this exception, the register holds two sets of brothers accused of plotting and wounding other men in the city. For example, Petrus Boerii and Bernardus Boerii, were originally from Sanna, and lived with Bernardus Maiorus de Montis Audranno, the individual they later attacked.[97] The Alsieu brothers, Gualhardus and Raymundus, lived individually with another set of brothers, Bertrando and Raymundus de Samuhato, and attacked a young neighborhood boy.[98] In each case, a man had to take an oath which assured the court officials that he was above the age of twenty-five years old, the legal age to be held responsible for a crime. The fathers of six underage defendants escorted their sons to the capitols' court to serve as legal authority, and to pay the court fines such as bail.[99]

But whereas young men could not be tried for crimes without a parent or guardian present, the capitols did prosecute women without the

[90] Ibid., 81.
[91] Ibid., 99.
[92] Ibid., 121
[93] Ibid., 125
[94] Ibid., 137.
[95] Ibid., 179. "Qui moratur in carreria Hugonis Vitalis prope putheum clausum." Todays la rue Baronie.
[96] Ibid., 1.
[97] Ibid., 71.
[98] Ibid, 73.
[99] Ibid. Johannes de Manso, son of Helio de Manso, 69; Guillelmus de Portello, filius Raymundus de Portello de Montis Gualhardi, 85; Raymundus Donati, macellarius, filius Raymundus Donati Macellarius de Banquis prope Plateam Montis Arsini, 85; Raymundus Vergerii, 117; Franciscus Amblayre, Filius Bertrandi Amblayre, 179; Johannem Sartoris, son of Magister Bartholomey Sartoris de Carreria Bernardi Barriam, 215; Petrus Augerii, son of Petri Augerii of Villata, 263.

involvement of a husband or father. Very frequently, scholars think of women and crime in terms of sexual offenses such as prostitution, concubinage, or adultery. Indeed, the first legal precedent set forth by the capitols of Toulouse in 1176 concerned the adulterous Babilonia, accused of running away with a soldier, and as a consequence, was forced to surrender all of her goods and dowry as compensation to her husband.[100] However, Barbara Hanawalt's investigation of 'female felons,' found that women were just as participatory in theft, burglary, or receiving of stolen goods as they were in violent crimes and murders, although women rarely acted alone in the physical confrontations.[101] In the cases from Toulouse, three married women were listed as defendants, all involved in violent crimes. When the two women were listed as sole defendants, the husband's professions were also identified: Ricarda, was married to Arnaldus de Bolbenas, a merchant of Carreria Nova in Saint Cyprian.[102] Bernarda, was the wife of Arnaldus Durandi, a tavern keeper (*tabernarius*) of barrio Alte Rippe.[103] Gualharda, wife of Arnaldis Aynerii de Petra Lada, was identified and charged as a conspirator with a neighbor, named Guillelmus Calvetti.[104] All three women committed these violent crimes against individuals who were not in their immediate families. The example of these female defendants suggests that wives were not relegated to the private spheres of the homes, tucked away from the social and economic activity of the city. Instead, they actively engaged in the public realm as will be discussed at length in the next chapter: they feuded with neighbors, and stood trial for their misdeeds in the capitols' courtroom.

When the capitols called court into session in the town hall, notaries and lawyers had to be in attendance. Testimony had to be recorded in the official register, and witnesses had to be summoned and interrogated. The citizens who offered their version of the events or paid the court fees for a loved one had to take time from work to report to the building. If the defendant was not being held in the municipal jail, officers had to be

100 AMT-AA 1:33, March, 1176.

101 Barbara A. Hanawalt, "The Female Felon in Fourteenth Century England," *Women in Medieval Society*, ed. Susan Mosher Stuard (Philadelphia, The University of Pennsylvania Press, 1976), 125–140. For a discussion of gender constructs of criminal violence in the early Middle Ages, see Ross Balzaretti, "'These are Things that Men Do, Not Women': The Social Regulation of Female Violence in Langobard Italy," *Violence and Society in Early Medieval West*, ed. Guy Halsall (Woodbridge, Suffolk: The Boydell Press, 1998), 175–192.

102 AMT-FF 57, 129.

103 Ibid., 151.

104 Ibid., 245.

prepared to arrest the malefactor if he failed to appear for a scheduled court appearance. The capitols did not go to such lengths for petty crimes or misdemeanors; instead all of these formalities were reserved for defendants who had extensive economic and social ties to the community of Toulouse. The men and women accused of crimes in the capitols' register had jobs of varying degrees of professionalism, they had their own homes or rented rooms from another citizen, and they had extensive family networks in the city. The people who came into the judicial system needed a good reputation, and an honorable place among their neighbors. They wanted to take the time to make sure that justice had been achieved, or that false accusations had been remedied. There is little doubt that many lesser crimes transpired in Toulouse in the fourteenth century, but the defendants and victims who took advantage of the court system were the citizens invested financially and personally in the social fabric of Toulouse.

The Location of Criminal Activity

It is not surprising that most reported and prosecuted criminal activity happened in the most populous areas as described in the first section of this chapter. Spectators saw the assaults or violent explosions, and then served as witnesses in the capitols' courtroom. Most of these witnesses were the men and women heading through the city streets to conduct business in another district of the city. Other disputes erupted in one of the city's many taverns. Because many of the defendants worked in the city, and lived closely to the site of their employment, again, most fights between business rivals would have transpired in the shared neighborhood.

In the circumstances when a non-resident committed a crime in Toulouse, the capitols and their officers wanted to ensure that they tried the alleged malefactor in their courtroom. The capitols had jurisdiction over the surrounding territory, and because they were under royal authority, they could extradite defendants to stand trial for offenses committed in Toulouse. This again, was a way in which the capitols protected the city space and its inhabitants, and could demonstrate sovereignty to their constituents, especially if the crimes were particularly public or horrific. In September, 1291, the capitols contacted the authorities of Castelnaudry (40 kilometers to the southeast), to capture and to hand over a certain Raymundus Furutrii, so he could be punished for his "excesses and crimes" committed in Toulouse.[105] The most extensive example of the capitols battle over extradition with another jurisdiction transpired in the spring of 1332. In this situation, an inhabitant of the nearby city of Villamuro, named Stephanus Saletas, came into Toulouse and hired men to ambush and to mutilate the face of a municipal business lawyer who he felt had cheated him on a legal transaction. Saletas struck a deal with the thugs, and returned to Villamuro to await news of the vengeful assault. After the attack unfolded in front of a large crowd by the town hall, municipal officers quickly caught the assailants who implicated Saletas in the crime. The capitols mobilized their administration toward preparation for a trial, so that the city's lawyer could receive justice for this public affront and his facial disfigurement. But, the city officials of Villamuro claimed authority over the person of Stephanus Saletas and refused to extradite their citizen to Toulouse. It then took months of legal wrangling between the capitols, the royal seneschal, and the consuls of Villamuro before Saletas came back into the city to stand trial for his conspiracy to commit a crime. In this circumstance royal intervention worked on the behalf of the capitols. Pressured by the authority of the royal seneschal, the consuls of Villamuro handed Saletas into the custody of Toulouse's sergeants, who escorted the prisoner back into the city space that he had violated.[106] Although the records are silent on the outcome of this case, the extant sources establish the importance of utilizing city space to perform various manifestations of justice. Saletas presumably believed he had achieved justice by ordering the mutilation of the lawyer in front of the town hall, and the capitols established justice by holding Saletas legally accountable in the courtroom of the very same building.

The case of Stephanus Saletas demonstrates that the capitols wanted to establish and to perpetuate the city's prominence as the administrative capitol of Languedoc. As a result, this meant that Toulouse became the destination for protestors from the region. In 1304, for example, when famine devastated the surrounding countryside, fifteen thousand beggars

---

105 AMT, layettes II, carton 84. September 21, 1291. "Ex parte domini nostri regis Francie et nostra voca requirimus ac Rogamus quathinus Ramundum Furutrii quem lator seu latores sub fida custodia transmittatis inquirendum et puniendum super quibusdam excessibus et criminibus per eundem Ramundum in Tholosa et sub iurisdictione nostra comissia taliter super his vos habentes ut vos valeatis noci facturos."

106 I have written about this particular case in more detail in "'With Teeth Clenched and an Angry Face:' Vengeance, Visitors and Judicial Power in Fourteenth-Century France," *Urban Space in the Middle Ages and the Early Modern Age*, ed. Albrecht Classen and Marilyn Sandidge (Berlin and New York: de Gruyter, 2009), 353–371.

abandoned their small villages to seek aid in Toulouse. They wandered through the streets and caused such a commotion that the capitols ordered their policing officers to drive them out of the city. This, however, only added to the confusion which led the king to intervene and to name a commission to remedy the situation. The royal commission stipulated that the citizens of Toulouse should be subject to an income tax to provide aid for the needy, but this measure did not prevent the starvation and death of eight thousand peasants.[107] The medieval chronicler Guillaume Bardin described another protest against the Capetian king's high taxes that financed the royal war against Flanders in 1310. The leader of the movement, a knight named Pontius of Boissaco, rode throughout the countryside, and tried to incite a rebellion against the king. After he was captured, he was sentenced to be hanged and to be beheaded in the square in front of Saint Etienne. Before the execution was carried out, three hundred of his masked and armed supporters broke through the nearby Narbonnais gate to his rescue, and then proceeded to ransack the rest of the city, and later trapped the capitols in the town hall.[108] That same year another uprising against the king's taxes resulted in a mob pillaging the house of the head of the royal commission.[109] In each of these circumstances, the participants incorporated the urban space and particular buildings to play a part in their protests, and likewise the administrators sought to control what transpired in their civic realm, through either police forces or public punishments.

An examination of an even more specific and contained set of sources establishes the distribution of individual criminal activity in the space of Toulouse. Many of the violent crimes recorded in the criminal records from 1332 occurred around the capitol square where the town hall was located, and spreading outwards towards the cathedral Saint Étienne, and down to the Garonne River around the church of the Daurade. Four violent scuffles took place directly off of the town square, a bureaucratic and commercial focal point of the city. For example, a capitol named Franciscus de Gaure first encountered a young squire named Aimery Berenger and his gang during a police patrol of the central thoroughfares of the capitol,[110] while a roaming gang accosted a father and son who had a

107 Daniel Borzeix, René Pautal, Jacques Serbat, *Révoltes populaires en Occitain: Moyen âge et ancien régime* (Treignac: Éditions «Les Monédières», 1982), 40.

108 Found in the "Chronique de Guillaume Bardin," *HGL*, vol. 10, cols. 26–29. Lafaille, *Annales de Toulouse*, 40–43.

109 Borzeix, *Révoltes populaires*, 41.

110 AMT-FF 57, 1.

home in the neighborhood Pascalis, a small street just off of today's rue Saint Rome to the east of the town hall.[111] Many of the defendants lived in the thriving commercial district a stone's throw away from the town hall, today known as Place de Saint Georges (*planum montis Aygonis*), and four of the crimes were specifically attributed to the locale. Guillelmus de Portello robbed an inhabitant of the area,[112] Raymundus Donati attacked a grocer,[113] Franciscus Bene and Johannes de Moras stalked and assaulted a lantern bearer who was walking through the neighborhood,[114] and Vitalis Nigri, who lived by the city gate of Matabovis, was reported to have threatened and wounded Guillelmus de Bordis, in a small alley just off of the square.[115] As many citizens lived and worked in this area, or deliberately came to the district to make purchases for their home, it is little surprise that conflicts would arise and come to violent blows.

Just beyond the place de Saint George, extending towards the cathedral, the notary recorded that five additional violent crimes took place. This area was populated by some of the richest inhabitants of the city, and also clerks affiliated with the bishop. Johannes de Manso was accused of rape and kidnapping a young woman from the neighborhood of Borbona, and stashing her away in his home in the area of Saint Salvatore.[116] As lawyer Bernadus de Bosto walked towards the capitol square to conduct business at the town hall, several armed men jumped him, and severely disfigured his face in the same neighborhood.[117] The three additional recorded attacks erupted around the cathedral Saint Étienne, including one altercation provoked by a priest.[118] Moving from the cathedral towards the Garonne River at today's Place Esquirol, four more incidents occurred, all

---

111 Ibid., 203. The two other attacks near the capitol were committed by Johannes de Castro Novo (around *Villenovo*), and Bartholmeus Jordani, who attacked Bernardus Raynes on today's rue Saint-Rome (*carreria bancorum majorum*), 167 and 219 respectively.

112 AMT-FF 57, 69.

113 Ibid., 85.

114 Ibid., 259.

115 Ibid., 271.

116 Ibid., 59. *Borbona*, today known as la rue Boulbonne, is one of the oldest nomenclatures of Toulouse's city streets. The name *Borbona*, derives from a religious group of Cistercians from the abbey of Boulbonne, who built a home in the locale. The street finishes in the Place Saint-George. *DRT*, vol. 1, 173–174.

117 AMT-FF 57, 31

118 Ibid., Petrus Guillelmus (*clericus* from the parish church of Saint Salvatores), attacked a man outside of the church, 67; Raymundus de Lugio and Johannem de Causidis attacked Bernardus de Carcassona as he was passing through neighborhood of *Portam Novam* (today's rue de Penitents Blancs), 63; The Boerii brothers ganged up against a man just outside of Saint Étienne, 71.

of them involving physical assaults.[119] The capitols heard two separate charges against residents in the neighborhood of Judey Aquis, who apparently decided to resolve a feud between them with violence. Bernardus Guaynerius and Perrotus Guaynerius each assaulted the other on separate occasions in the same neighborhood.[120]

A few crimes were scattered in the neighborhoods in front of the Château Narbonnais, although the scarcity of incidents could be attributed to the presence of royal officials, who would have perhaps discouraged criminal activity, or would have been tried for their indiscretions before the vicar. Regardless, an altercation between a group of men and the night guards took place by the gate *Montis Olini*, today's Montgaillard.[121] Officers arrested two individuals, Guillelmus Rabant and Jacobus Briconis, for carrying illegal arms by Nazarenum, a street off of the lawn in front of the Château.[122] Along the southern banks of the Garonne River, one tavern keeper was assaulted off of the *barrio Alte Rippe*,[123] while the inhabitants of the small bank of Tonitus took in upon themselves to arrest Arnaldus Mancipii for multiple thefts in the specific neighborhood of Puta.[124]

Nine crimes transpired on both of the populous, centralized banks of the Garonne River, where much of the city's industry and commercial production was located. Three occurred in the small region of Saint Cyprian, the suburb of Toulouse, where the majority of the poor population lived. Magister Geraldus Seretas, a copyist, attacked a man in the neighborhood of Turris of Saint Cyprian.[125] A female defendant Ricarda attacked a woman in carreria Nova of Saint Cyprian.[126] Guillemus Calveti and Gualhardam, lived in the neighborhood of Petra Leda of Saint Cyprian.[127] One individual was arrested while carrying illegal arms leaving Saint Cyprian and heading back to his home by the ancient bridge, Pontis Veteris.[128] Six other offenses occurred on the right bank of the Garonne,

---

119 Ibid. Vesianus Guarini attacked a guy by Petrum Santi Geraldi (Place Esquirol), 93. Franciscus Amblayre attacked Johannem de Bosto in Hugonis Vitals, 179. *Carreria Hugonis Vitalis*, is today known as rue du Baronie. It was named after Huc Vitalis, a fourteenth century notary from the district of Saint-Pierre-Saint-Géraud. *DRT*, vol. 1, 115.

120 Ibid., 113, and 121 respectively.

121 Ibid., 117.

122 Ibid., 135, 137

123 Ibid., 151.

124 Ibid., 267.

125 Ibid., 75.

126 Ibid., 129.

127 Ibid., 245. The neighborhood of *Petra Lada* was located between today's la rue des Teintures and la rue Chairedon, in Saint Cyprian.

128 Ibid., 253.

particularly surrounding the church of the Daurade, where it should be remembered, many of the artisans lived and worked. All of the attacks were violent in nature, and one included the assault of a young girl who was innocently walking to the river to fill a water pitcher.[129]

Only four crimes from the 1332 register took place in the Bourg, where most of the university students and clerks lived. A night sergeant arrested Petrus Augerii carrying illegal arms as he was walking through a neighborhood located by the gate of Arnaud Bernard.[130] Defendant Petrus Laquast allegedly wounded his neighbor in the street *Pracheri Pelherioris*, north of Saint Sernin.[131] A second attack with illegal arms occurred near the small parish church of Saint Julian.[132] From the charges brought forth against Arnaldus Franciscus, a municipal sergeant, witnesses placed his illegal activities around the gate of Badacley (today's Bazacle), where there was a brothel as well as a bar in which he claimed to have first met the women who later accused him of selling her into prostitution.[133] The reason for the scarcity of crimes committed in the Bourg could be attributable to a number of reasons. Perhaps the area's less dense population managed to avoid the sparks of conflict. Or, more likely, the large number of clerks who lived in the area, residing in one of the plentiful colleges, would have been held accountable for their offenses in an ecclesiastical court, not the capitols' tribunal.

On a daily basis, the citizens of Toulouse had many opportunities to come into contact with friends, and perhaps, rivals in the various districts of the city. A trip to the Place Saint Georges to purchase goods for the household could lead to an encounter with an adversary in the street, and after an exchange of words, the interaction could result in physical blows. Each of these locations had many spectators, who could then come forth and offer testimony to the capitols. The defendants, who had personal

---

129 Ibid., 215. Johannes Sartoris, attacked the young girl. The other attacks are as follows: Stephanus Furneres de Plathea Piscatorus, attacked a night guard by Capelle Rotundes, by the Garonne, 89; a group attacked a canon by the church of Saint Pierre des Cuisines, 141; Raymundus Martini attacked a man by the Daurade, 165; Natus de Barbenthis de carreria Bernardus Barravi (today rue Jean-Suau, by the Daurade) attacked Heliam Stephanus de Capella Rotunda, 211; Gualhardum Boneti attacked Guillelmus de Bassolas around *ecclesiam Santi Petrus Martini*, 183. The *ecclesia Sanctorum Petri et Martini*, was the name of an ancient capitoulat. It was a little church dependant upon the Daurade, and was completely destroyed in a fire in 1463. Today it is known as *rue de Prieuré*. *DRT*, vol. 2, 437–438.

130 AMT-FF 57, 263.

131 Ibid., 181. Today's rue des Trois-Piliers. *DRT*, vol. 2, 265.

132 AMT-FF 57, 125. The church of Saint Julien was destroyed after the Revolution. *DRT*, vol. 2, 425–246.

133 AMT-FF 57, 155.

interests in the city financially and socially, came into the courtroom to stand before the capitols to seek justice and restitution for the offenses that transpired in the neighborhood where they lived and worked. There is little doubt that at the geographical margins of the city, including cemeteries or in the streets the city gates, transients and bandits committed transgressions. Within private homes, domestic violence certainly occurred between husbands and wives, and parents and children. But the cases that came to the capitols' court were committed in the most populous and commercially relevant areas of the city.

Conclusion

The register that has been discussed in this chapter is certainly not indicative of the many crises and injuries that occurred on a daily basis. But I have argued that charges of corruption, theft, and violence were represented by a wide demographic in fourteenth-century Toulouse. Even the lesser charge of carrying illegal arms was an equal opportunity offense. The individuals charged with crimes in front of the capitols were not just from the lower class, or vagrants. It appears that the majority of the defendants had clear vocational ties and social networks in the city. The location of the crimes (when recorded), were not relegated to the geographical margins of the city, where one might expect drifters or foreigners congregating. There is a paucity of offenses which took place by the gates of the city, where one would expect roaming gangs to gather, to take advantage of tourists or travelers resting in the inns and taverns of the city. Instead, most of the crimes were committed in the most populous and central portions of the city, where rich and poor, professional and artisan would mingle and work. The tension and friction that resulted in violent crimes existed between neighbors, coworkers, and family members, in the common areas they inhabited. In the next chapter, the public nature of these crimes and the capitols' role in the pursuit of justice will be explored further.

CHAPTER THREE

"WITH AN ANGRY FACE AND TEETH CLENCHED:" PERSONAL CONFLICT AND PUBLIC RESOLUTION

To the modern imagination, a fringe underworld of transients, thieves and murderers plagued medieval cities, as they lurked around every dark street corner and in the smoky taverns. One would assume that these offenders packed the municipal courts and jails as they waited to be judged and to be held accountable for their alleged abuses. But in the early fourteenth century, the capitols conducted criminal trials for individuals who inhabited the commercial and populous areas of the city. Most of the defendants were well established in the community, and had extensive social and occupational contacts that provided financial and emotional support in court. In Toulouse, therefore, the function of the judicial process was not to prosecute the dangerous criminal element that existed on the margins of society, even though there is no doubt it was a real threat. Instead, the capitols and their officers used the criminal proceedings to investigate conflicts between neighbors, and to demonstrate their authority by passing judgment upon their constituents caught, or suspected of, breaking municipal laws. The trial transcripts of accusations and defense testimony also reveal the open and public nature of life in the medieval urban environment. The alleged crime, the trial and the proclamation of the sentence all transpired so that the greater population of the city was aware that an injustice had occurred, and that the capitols and the municipal officers had fulfilled the duty of their office by restoring law and order to the city. By examining the characteristics of the offenses recorded by the capitols' notary, we gain the sense that because the crimes were performative in many respects, the trial and punishment had to involve the public so that the capitols could establish their legitimate power over the citizens of Toulouse.

Rather than provide examples of random, impersonal acts of bloodshed, the criminal records from Toulouse reveal a nuanced escalation of exchanges between neighbors before their conflict turned violent, and they ended in the capitols' court for resolution. The majority of the crimes occurred in public locations, which allowed bystanders to intervene, or at least to create witnesses to verify guilt or innocence in the courtroom. On the occasions when the dispute did turn physical, the trial became an opportunity for the municipal officers and the public to perform the ritual function of determining the standards of socially acceptable or deviant behavior. This argument will be developed by first establishing the public nature of the crimes reported in the city. From slanderous insults to the conspicuous locations of attacks, all assured that an audience would be present at the time the offense transpired. Although most of the violent attacks occurred between two individuals, the people of Toulouse did not always stand by and simply watch events unfold. There were circumstances in which the public participated in efforts to prevent the crime, and the other occasions where people protected the criminals from the municipal officers' detection. The criminal process of apprehension and the subsequent trial set into motion a ritual series of oaths, testimony, and proclamations of power which gave shape and structure to notion of law and order for the community. The trials became a judicial spectacle in which the Toulousains and their officials could acknowledge, and then reject the individual who brought chaos and violence to their city.

The Public Nature of Crimes

As individuals moved from the countryside to the medieval city, they discovered that the conditions provided little opportunity for privacy from their neighbors. People lived in close proximity to each other in residential buildings that grew higher to house families, lodgers, and lower class servants. Most of the economic activity took place in the open to comply with guild regulations. Urban shoppers moved from one display of goods to the next to purchase the household necessities, haggling over prices and the merchandise's quality. The streets of Toulouse, like most medieval cities, became the venue for social interaction, as men and women left their crowded accommodations and ventured into the courtyards or squares to meet friends or business contacts. Each foray into the public, then, became a performance of status and identity, and posed new opportunities for conflicts between neighbors who competed for dominance within their communities. The court records reveal that even if there was a private dispute between individuals, it still played out in the city streets, so that spectators could recognize the adjustment or reaffirmation of the social hierarchy. In his study of fourteenth-century Avignon, Jacques Chiffoleau found similar results: most attacks transpired in the city streets and squares with few exceptions.[1] Although the nature of the sources

[1] Jacques Chiffoleau, "La violence au quotidian," 350–352.

limit, to some extent, what we may say about domestic violence within the household and other petty crimes, we may analyze the augmenting levels of other conflicts as they moved from verbal threats to physical confrontations, allowing plenty of time for alternative and peaceful resolution.

The most common performative aspect of crime found in the records is the use of words against an enemy, either as a slanderous attack, or as a declaration of planned violence against an individual.[2] Chiffoleau argues that individuals intended verbal injuries both to precede and to justify the subsequent physical actions, and were also meant to challenge the moral, physical and sexual integrity of the enemy in extremely crude terms.[3] This seems to be the case as well in the small Languedoc town of Moissac, which reveals that public insults were a very serious affair. Between the years 1301 to 1308, the city's consuls heard and recorded eleven cases, of which eight concerned accusations of slander in some form.[4] In one trial, a woman named Oliva demanded 20 *livres* of redress because her neighbor, Guillelma, proclaimed that their shared street had "four whores and one is Oliva."[5] Another woman pressed charges against a man who grabbed her by the dress and struck her, calling her an "evil, foul hearted, whore."[6] A citizen named Johannes Cardaillac complained to the consuls that he suffered insults from a man Aymericus de la Lande and his mistress. Johannes testified that Aymericus hit his face and told him that he deserved to live with the lepers. Aymericus's mistress cursed all of Johannes' children and loved ones.[7] What we find is that in both large cities like Avignon, and in small towns such as Moissac, verbal attacks were intended to challenge the good name and sexual reputation of the individual and his or her family, and to discredit the person's standing in the community. Authorities in Ghent took this notion so seriously that they punished a defendant found guilty of false slander or 'scandalmongering' by having him return to the neighborhood of the person defamed, and in

---

[2] Ronald Gosselin, "Honneur et Violence à Manosque (1240–1260)," *Vie priveé et ordre public à la fin du moyen- âge: Études sur Manosque, la Provence et le Piémont (1250–1450)*, ed. by Michel Hébert (Aix-en-Provence: Université de Provence Service des Publications, 1987), 45–63.

[3] Jacques Chiffoleau, "La violence au quotidien," 352–353.

[4] All of the cases are recorded in AMM-FF1, the city's only extant medieval criminal register.

[5] AMM-FF1, fol. 1r: "i avia quatre putas, de que la una era la dicha Oliva."

[6] Ibid., fol. 9r: "puta, malvada, corredissa."

[7] Ibid., fol. 20r. and fol. 22r.

front of all of neighborhood residents, admit that he lied when he uttered the verbal attack.[8]

Toulouse's criminal register from 1332 does not contain examples of trials that concentrated extensively upon charges of defamation. Fortunately, the municipal archives do have one example of a slander case from 1287 that reveals how the courtroom became the setting for neighborhood dynamics and grievances to be played out in the arena of criminal justice. In November of that year, the capitols began the proceeding and recorded the complaint of Guillelma, the wife of a merchant. She argued that a young neighborhood man (under the legal age of twenty-five years old), Bernardus de Martel, insulted her in a "public street," and called her a "false, mean, stinking piece of nothing," and expressed regret that he had not rolled her in the mud.[9] Numerous women from the neighborhood came forward to the capitols and supported Guillelma's accusation. But, more importantly, the female witnesses also took advantage of the officials' audience to express their grievances about Bernardus de Martel, whom most of the women considered a rude chauvinist. One wife argued that Bernardus was a "hostile and quarrelsome man who is not good with his neighbors, as he never speaks to them."[10] Another woman "heard it said in the neighborhood" that Bernardus de Martel had a troublesome home life and a tumultuous relationship with his wife. She testified that he had thrown his wife out of their conjugal home after only one year of marriage, because he thought she was poisoning him. Bernardus de Martel delayed his day in court as long as possible, and tried various legal maneuvers through his attorneys to avoid the charges. But after he had exhausted all of his appeals, he told the capitols that his neighbors could not have seen any incriminating interaction between himself and Guillelma, as they were all in their homes on the day in question. Besides, he continued, they were "liars, gamblers and drunks, who will say anything for a small bit

---

[8] Nicholas, "Crime and Punishment in Fourteenth-Century Ghent," 1161.

[9] The case is written upon a large roll of eighteen smaller sheets of parchment, sewn poorly together, and both numbered and lettered by an unidentified archivist. The overlapping numbers and letters make it difficult to designate accurate folio citations. The dates for the case are November 19, 1287 to March 1, 1288. AMT, layette series II, 92/4: "carreria publica...vocando ispam actricem, mendigam malvadam, pudentam, venguda de nore." Henri Gilles examines this case and offers some transcriptions in "Une cause d'injures à Toulouse à la fin du XIIIe siècle." *Annales de la faculté de droit et des sciences économiques de Toulouse* 17 (1969): 121–144. His focus is the legal ability of women to file complaints in the city's judicial system.

[10] Ibid., "Idem Bernardus est homo iniquus et rixosus et non est bene cum vicinis suis ut aparet in tantum quod non loquitur eis." Cited in Gilles, "Une cause," 122.

of wine."[11] The capitols' verdict is missing from the archives, but the real significance of this trial resides in the fact that many of the neighborhood's residents (especially the women who rallied behind Guillelma) eagerly became involved in the case in order to establish certain standards of social conduct within their community.

The importance of verbal exchanges in the streets of medieval Toulouse goes beyond that of publicly defaming the character of a person's adversary to their neighbors. The criminal notary also recorded whether or not the violent attacks being tried in the capitols' court were preceded by threats of harm: words which conceivably announced the intentions of the perpetrator to the surrounding bystanders.[12] Even if the attack was instigated seemingly without provocation, the involved parties usually had an implied history of disagreements. In one example, a clerk of the Church of Saint Savior named Petrus Guillelmus expressed previous "injurious words" to an inhabitant of a neighborhood close to the cathedral Saint Étienne.[13] But on the day in question, the victim claimed that Petrus struck him with his fist "without any cause," and after he had been knocked off guard, Petrus drew his sword and finished the altercation with a second blow, causing a wound by his eye.[14] In this instance, the tension which had existed between the clerk and a citizen turned physical only after some perceived insult transpired between the two men crossing paths in the city streets. It is more common in the criminal records to find that multiple "injurious words" and "threats were made night and day" on "many different days and hours" before an assault erupted.[15] It was only after the defendant wanted his or her "threats to come into effect" that events set into motion which left the parties before the capitols' court facing criminal charges.[16]

This menacing behavior intensified when the individual venting plans of attack also carried prohibited arms throughout the streets of the

[11] Ibid., "Guillelmus Maurelli testis est et erat tabernarius tempore lati testimonii, vilis persona, lusor qui ludit ad talos, potator qui sepe inebriat se et homo qui pro una denariata vini diceret omne malum." Printed in Gilles, "Une cause," 144.

[12] Valérie Toureille, "Cri de peur et cri de haine: haro sur le voleur. Cri et crime en France à la fin du Moyen Âge," *Haro! Noël! Oyé! Pratiques du cri au Moyen Âge*, eds. Didier Lett and Nicolas Offenstadt (Paris: Publications de la Sorbonne, 2003), 169–178.

[13] AMT-FF 57, 67: "injuriam verbo." The defendant is listed as "Petrus Guillelmus, clericus de Capellis Santi Salvatoris Tholose." This church was situated close to the cathedral Saint Étienne. *DRT*, 2, 441.

[14] Ibid., 67: "Sive aliqua insta causa cum pugno percussit Raymundus Imberti…et gladium cum quo invasit percussit et vulnerit dictum Raymundum uno vulnere in cilio."

[15] Ibid., 167: "pluries minatus fuisset de nocte et de die."

[16] Ibid.: "dictas minas ducere ad effectum."

city.[17] In most medieval cities, only certain officers of the government, soldiers, and established nobles had the privilege to carry weapons. Lawmakers hoped that by limiting the availability of dangerous weapons, injuries from fights would be less severe.[18] But the women and men of the urban realm were fairly resourceful not only in securing a wide range of illegal weapons, but also in incorporating everyday objects into their attacks. The most commonly used weapons were different types of swords, knives and daggers made of iron (*gladius, ensis, ferrum, cultellus*), considered all the more dangerous when the defendant carried them without a sheath. The more primitive weapons included staffs (*baculus*), swords made of stone (*ensis lapidibus*), or simply large rocks. In one brawl outside of a tavern of Toulouse, the offender grabbed either a stone or a roof tile (*lapide seu tegula*) to wound his opponent in the head.[19] It is no wonder, that the municipal officers made concerted efforts to arrest people whom they saw carrying any arms at night. Towards the end of June, 1332, the night guards arrested three young men within a few days of each other, all found lurking suspiciously in front of the Château Narbonnais. Guillelmus de Comera, of Burgneto Novo was stopped, and taken to the town hall by a night guards Johannes Probihominis and two other officers, for carrying a large staff or javelin of some sort.[20] Officers caught Guillelmus Rabant with a sword and they took him to jail in the town hall.[21] On the same night, and in the same neighborhood, the officers seized Jacobus Briconis for carrying a sword as well.[22] Apparently, the night guards for this *capitolat* were either trying to reach a quota, or were extremely intent on finding malefactors. But this indicates that the individuals making verbal threats to their enemies added the extra element of recklessness to their tactics of performative intimidation by carrying illegal weapons: they were willing to risk arrest by the night guards and sergeants in order to see their threats carried out in the public streets.

Some defendants, however, did insist that they had a legitimate and non-threatening reason for carrying illegal weapons at night, which no doubt added to the municipal officer's confusion and danger when on duty. For example, the night guards stopped Guillelmus de Comera because he carried a staff that he insisted he used for work, and not a

---

17 Ibid.: "parasset cum armis prohibitis."
18 Hanawalt, "Violent Death," 310–311.
19 AMT-FF 57, 81.
20 Ibid., 133: "unam magnam barram." It is also spelled "bariam" in the document.
21 Ibid., 135: "unum gladium extra pagelam."
22 Ibid., 137.

weapon.[23] Another defendant, Jaconis Briconis, testified that he intended to sell the sword he was carrying to Johannes de Castro Novo, a client waiting for him in a vineyard, when the night guards arrested him.[24] Perhaps the most intriguing defense comes from Petrus Augere de Villata, arrested by a sergeant who saw him threatening a monk with a sword.[25] Petrus' father immediately responded to the charges after the sergeant imprisoned his son. He explained that his son carried the weapon because he had just returned home from a journey to Villata, and he had intended to spend the night in the house of Nicolaý Hostalere, by the gate of Arnaud Bernard. Petrus Augere was in Toulouse to resolve a dispute between his father and several citizens regarding some property and windmills held close to Villata.[26] The sergeant came upon him just as he had entered through the city gates, and as he was waiting outside an inn for the other men. This location happened to be situated by the monastery of the Augustines. In other words, the municipal officers found it difficult to discern the motivations and intentions of armed men in the middle of the night, and thus arrested individuals based upon their perception of threats to pubic safety. Because the court records do not reveal the resolution for many of these accusations, we do not know if the capitols believed these claims of innocence. But the sergeants and night guards had the discretion of their office to determine which citizen should be held accountable for suspected crimes in the civic court. The officers in many respects served as a bridge between the capitols and the citizens because they walked the streets of Toulouse and interacted with the public, as they tried to enforce law and order.

If we return to our discussion of grudges, the following example traces how one man ensured that his ill-feelings towards a neighbor resulted in a very public and dramatic incident. According to the notary's transcript of the trial, defendant, Perrotus de Balerno, despised an artisan named Petrus Bernadus. Throughout the course of eight days, Perrotus extended "many threats" against Petrus Bernardus, and even informed acquaintances that his nemesis would come into "bad fortune within two days."[27] Clearly, Perrotus was both determined and patient enough to wait for the perfect opportunity to unleash his resentment upon Petrus. The occasion

---

23 Ibid., 133.
24 Ibid., 137.
25 Ibid., 263.
26 Ibid., 264.
27 Ibid., 239: "ipsum pluries minatus fuisset…videlicet ab octo diebus…et asserendo pro *infra* duos dies eidem Petro Bernardo veniret malum infortunium."

presented itself when Perrotus saw his intended victim riding a horse to a business meeting on the other side of the city. Perrotus, armed with a rod (*baculus*), "openly and quickly followed him through the public journey." When he caught up, Perrotus struck him from behind so hard that Petrus fell from the animal to the ground. While Petrus Bernardus lay helpless, Perrotus gave him a second blow to the head, which left him in "mortal danger." The case establishes the premise that tensions between the two individuals were not always private affairs. This inter-personal hostility was announced, and criminal intentions proclaimed, to all who would listen and who could potentially intervene to aid in the resolution. When these ill-feelings turned violent, the instigator struck when the victim's vulnerability presented itself in the public arena.

In the situation described above, Perrotus attacked Petrus Bernadus when he dropped his guard on his way to conduct business in a different district of Toulouse. The passages of the city, always described by the notary as "public streets" (*carreria publica*), were not necessarily rife with random violence, but were instead the most convenient and common place to gain access to an irksome neighbor or business competitor. As David Nicholas puts it, "increased contact provided increased opportunities for friction."[28] For example, Johannes de Lapinada lived near the gate of Arnaud Bernard, and held a certain "hatred" for his neighbor Bernardus Mancipii.[29] One day, Bernardus passed before Johannes' home. Johannes seized this moment for his attack, and grabbed a large staff covered in iron. He then struck and wounded Bernardus in the head. As Bernardus ran to seek refuge in his own home, Johannes chased after him, brandishing the staff in a threatening manner. After a little while, Johannes somehow gained access to Bernardus' home, and gave him a second near-fatal blow to the head. With a spectacle such as this in the populous streets of the Arnaud Bernard Gate, there would have been an extensive audience to Johannes efforts to harm Bernardus for the undisclosed tension between them.

David Lord Smail studied this notion of "hatred" as a motivation for physical assaults, and he has shown how many personal grudges between citizens evolved into acts of violence in medieval Marseilles.[30] Through an examination of numerous law suits, he argues that the emotions invested

---

28 Nicholas, "Crime and Punishment in fourteenth-century Ghent," 1176.

29 FF 57, 99: "haberet hodio."

30 Daniel Lord Smail, "Hatred as a Social Institution in Late-Medieval Society," *Speculum* 76, no. 1 (January 2001): 90–126. *The Consumption of Justice: Emotions, Publicity, and the Legal Culture in Marseilles, 1264–1423* (Ithaca: Cornell University Press, 2003).

in these feuds, primarily "hatred," was a form of "cultural capital and therefore a necessary and more or less permanent feature of the landscape of social relationships."[31] It reaffirmed rank in the community, and solidified alliances between neighbors. But he reveals that Marseilles' criminal officials did very little to unpack the history behind the feud of the antagonists in an effort to rhetorically present the case in the records as another example of "common and petty" violence.[32] Barbara Hanawalt found a lack of interest in the motives behind violent deaths in the coroners' rolls of fourteenth- and fifteenth-century England. She believes that this comes from the basic function of the records themselves, which were intended to assess the value of the suspect's goods rather than find a reason behind the attack; but it also suggests that the king and his officials were more interested in the immediate cause of the murder rather than any malice aforethought.[33] Similarly, Toulouse's documents rarely reveal the origins of these long standing feuds or "hatreds." We may still deduce that most of the long standing bitterness which translated into violence existed between Toulousains who lived in close proximity, or had economic relations with one another. Raymundus Donati, a grocer, injured Petrus Hodini, another grocer who lived and worked in the same commercial district of today's Place Saint Georges. Raymundus Donati's father was also a grocer, so perhaps this rivalry went back for generations.[34] Women engaged in feuds with their neighbors for a variety or reasons, including malicious gossip or competition for male attention. For example, a woman named Ricarda publicly threatened her next door neighbor, named Vitalia, and eventually struck her with a large rock (*magnum lapidem*). With one blow, Vitalia collapsed to the ground and had to be confined to bed for a long time, believed by her husband to be in "mortal danger."[35] But again, very little context to the attack is preserved in the court records or witness testimony. When feuds dissolved into violence, however, the capitols' and their court became a broader venue for these fights, beyond the immediate vicinity of the city streets. The litigants brought cases to trial to seek some public retribution and acknowledgement of the tensions that could sprout during the daily frustrations of urban living.

---

31 Smail, "Hatred as a Social Institution," 110.

32 Daniel Lord Smail, "Common Violence: Vengeance and Inquisition in Fourteenth-Century Marseilles," *Past and Present* 151 (May, 1996): 57.

33 Hanawalt, "Violent Death," 311.

34 AMT-FF 57, 85. The medieval name of the location is Montis Arsini.

35 Ibid., 129.

On a few occasions, the perpetrators in the trial transcripts used theft as a means of disgracing one's opponent after an attack. As a night guard named Guillelmus Sartoris performed the "duties of his office," he came upon a gang of four young men carrying a variety of illegal weapons, including swords and lead rods. When the night guard tried to exert his authority and disband the group, they attacked him, wounding his left shoulder and hand. As he was lying helpless on the ground, the ruffians robbed him of his twenty *sols tols*, and took his official weapons, leaving him completely vulnerable and defenseless.[36] The night guard perhaps got off lightly in this case, because a sergeant from Lyon had to fight off a group of malefactors trying to steal his wife![37] In another circumstance, a citizen of Toulouse named Franciscus Amblaýre plotted with fellow accomplices in an assault against a despised tavern keeper, Johannes de Bosto. After they located Johannes de Bosto in their shared neighborhood, the group threatened him, and then drew their weapons and struck him several times in the head and left hand. As he lay writhing on the ground, calling for help, the men scattered in different directions. One of the unnamed friends of Franciscus, however, returned to steal his hat.[38] These thefts seem senseless, almost an afterthought to the violent crime that proceeded. But the items that were stolen added insult to the injury that the victims suffered. After all, one of the privileges of being a night guard was the right to carry arms while on patrol. A perpetrator who stole them from an officer, bleeding in the street, directly challenged his status and position in the social and political hierarchy of the city.

The criminal cases suggest that the perpetrators in premeditated attacks, who secretly planned among collaborators, wanted the citizens of Toulouse to be witnesses. None of the calculated assaults were meant to be clandestine events. Spectators needed to be present in order for the physical violence to convey the meaning that the perpetrators intended. Take, for instance, the case of Stephanus Saletas, an inhabitant of Villemuro, who came to Toulouse for the services of a business lawyer (*advocatus negotiaris*), named Master Bernardus de Bosto. At one fateful meeting, Bernardus informed Stephan that he needed to pay twenty six *sol tols* for the lawyer's seal upon a document. Stephan Saletas responded to the price with an "angry expression and said he did not owe Master

---

36 Ibid., 117.

37 Gonthier, *Délinquance, justice et société*, 262.

38 Ibid., 179.

Bernardus money or love."[39] Apparently, Bernardus and Stephan had previously agreed upon a specific payment, and had sworn an oath confirming the deal. Stephan complained bitterly to friends that Bernardus had broken this promise, and changed the price at the last minute. After several verbal exchanges and grudging negotiations between the two, the men agreed to involve an outside mediator to resolve the dispute. Unfortunately for Stephan, this too proved unsatisfactory, as he now owed six *denarius tol* to the notary for his mediating services. Either way, the financial transaction left Stephanus increasingly upset, and visibly so. He became so infuriated that witnesses remarked that he bore an "angry expression and clenched teeth."[40] From that day and to the next he continued to carry the grudge, and started throwing threats that very soon he would get his revenge. As he spewed his threats to witnesses he maintained a "raging and angry face."[41] In his plot for payback, he decided to leave the lawyer perpetually deformed. Anger, in this example, does not appear to be a sudden outpouring of impulsive, irrational behavior. Instead, Stephanus Saletas found a specific way to rectify what he perceived as an injustice to his honor, and to find an outlet for his emotional ire through calculated revenge.

Next, Stephanus Saletas hired some men he knew through his social networks in the city to stalk and to attack the attorney, and to enact his vengeance. When he initially met with two men who were willing to accept money for the assault, he informed them that, "a certain lawyer called Master Bernardus de Bosto has done me wrong; I want vindication, and so I am asking you to wound him so badly in the face that he will be deformed for the rest of his life."[42] By focusing upon the mutilation the lawyer's face, Saletas attacked the very honor of de Bosto, and designed to render him impotent as a respected professional and member of the community.[43] After they agreed upon the payment, Saletas left the city to await

---

39 Ibid., 44: "tunc respondit irato animo et dixit pro sibi magistro bernardo non debebat pecuniam nec amorem."

40 Ibid., 45: "cum vultu irato existens et dentibus fremens."

41 Ibid., 45: "vultu furibando et irato."

42 Ibid., 45: "bacallaris in legibus vocatus Magister Bernardus de Bosto fecit michi aliquas injurias ita pro modis omnibus volo ipsos vendicari et ipsos rogano instanter ut dictum Magistrum Bernardum taliter in facie vulnerarent pro totaliter vita sua esset defformatus."

43 Valentine Groebner concentrates upon the significance of facial mutilation in medieval Germany in, "Losing Face, Saving Face: Noses and Honour in the Late Medieval Town," trans. Pamela Selwyn, *History Workshop Journal* 40 (1995): 1–15, and elaborates upon the meaning of disfigurement in, *Defaced: The Visual Culture of Violence in the Late Middle Ages*, trans. by Pamela Selwyn (New York: Zone Books, 2004), 67–86.

word that his revenge had been carried out by his mercenaries. When no notice arrived, Saletas came back to Toulouse on numerous occasions to speed things along with promises of additional money, meeting with the hired thugs in taverns and in the houses of his social connections.[44] The fact that the men dragged their heels suggests that they did not trust that Stephanus Saletas would follow through in his agreement of payment, a fear that in the end was completely warranted.[45] When the men finally coordinated their attack, they met with one of Stephanus Saletas' trusted accomplices, named Petrus Cortesii. They headed towards the town hall on a tip that lawyer Bernardus de Bosto was there for work. After Petrus Cortessii identified the lawyer for the assailants, they attacked him with their swords "without any warning" in the most frequented square of the city, and wounded him so badly that he was left in mortal danger and permanently deformed in the face.[46] Stephanus Saletas, thus, conspired to satisfy his desire for revenge by leaving his mark upon Bernardus de Bostos's face. Saletas' coordinated attack and end result required an audience to defame and to disgrace the lawyer.

The archival evidence makes it difficult to discern whether or not the household provided any means of protection from the violence and scuffles unfolding in the public streets and courtyards of the city. According to customary law, the Toulousains had the right to kill anyone who "secretly broke into their home at night, or invaded."[47] This statute did not discourage assaults against individuals seeking refuge in their households. The perpetrators simply concentrated their efforts towards driving their targets out to the streets so the confrontation could be settled in the open. The trial records reveal several means to this end. A carpenter named Hugnetus de Sanardino first assaulted and wounded his adversaries, Petrus de Montis Gualhardo and son, with a sword as they were walking through the city. After the attack, the father and son retreated into their home. Hugnetus decided to continue the affront against the family members by gathering and throwing large stones against the house, hoping to force them outside. In another instance, the victim of an alleged attack revealed that he and his family were "gathered together in their house that night, sleeping and resting in their beds peacefully and quietly, believing

44 AMT-FF 57, 46, 47.

45 Municipal officers found the conspirators hiding in a church after the attack. The men complained that Stephanus Saletas did not pay them, and he fled the city without letting them know he was leaving. AMT-FF 57, 50.

46 AMT-FF 57, 31.

47 AMT-AA 1:4, fols. 5r-5v. Printed in Limouzin-Lamothe, *La Commune de Toulouse*, 268.

to be in a protected place," when their defendants passed by the home several times.[48] Several women inside noticed this threat, either looking through the windows or hearing taunts, and began to "scream for their lives."[49] The menace lurking outdoors provoked the large brawl which ensued, as the men of the household gathered arms and charged outside to defend their women and maintain a sense of manhood among their neighbors. Instead of breaking into someone's home in the middle of the night, and risk being killed in the process, the determined perpetrator of violence was better served by drawing his or her intended victim into the public forum, which also insured an audience for the dispute.

Neighbors and business competitors did not only fight for dominance in the city streets. Taverns served as a public environment where social and professional activities could transpire, as the owner provided food and comfortable shelter to residents and travelers at a reasonable price. The tavern owner had the responsibility to regulate the behavior of his clients, otherwise he could be held accountable legally for injuries or disorderly conduct.[50] Although statistically, it seems as though alcohol and drunkenness played a small role in most violent attacks,[51] still the efforts of tavern owners to control their patrons could result in disastrous conflict. In fourteenth-century London, a taverner and his brewer tried to eject eighteen young men who were armed with weapons such as stones and knives, and who tried to abduct a young woman from the place. After a scuffle erupted between the owner and the rowdy patrons, the brewer ended up killing one of the young men with a staff.[52] On one occasion back in Toulouse, a tavern owner who lived and worked a neighborhood by the Garonne River experienced the repercussions of

48 AMT-FF 57, 203: "Petrus Mercerii et Bernardus eius filius existentes tunc una cum eos famula et quibusdam amicis et perentibus quos in dicto hospitio dicta nocte recolligerent et etiam dormientis et requiestentis in eos lectis pacifice et quiete credentis esse in loco tutissimo."

49 Ibid., 205: "Quedam mulieres qui intus erant…inceperunt clamare ad mortem."

50 B. Ann Tlusty, *Bacchus and Civil Order: The Culture of Drink in Early Modern Germany* (Charlottesville: University Press of Virgina, 2001), 158–182. Barbara A. Hanawalt, "The Host, the Law and the Ambiguous Space of Medieval London Taverns," *'Of Good and Ill Repute:' Gender and Social Control in Medieval England* (Oxford: Oxford University Press, 1998), 104–123. Nicole Gonthier, *Cris de haines et rites d'unité: la violence dans les villes, XIIIe-XVIe siècle* (Turnhout: Brepols, 1992), 111–149.

51 In England, Hanawalt found in her record base that the drunken brawl occurred only in 4.3 percent of the rural homicides and in 6 percent of urban homicides, "Violent Death," 312. Chiffoleau only found one case of a drunken attack in the records of Avignon from 1336. "La violence au quotidian," 350.

52 Hanawalt, "Violent Death," 312.

enforcing his authority over his establishment. As Guillelmus Amusse sold wine and other goods to his many clients, Bernarda, the wife of a fellow tavern owner from the same neighborhood, entered his business. Bernarda wanted to return a dish (*scutella*) she had purchased from Guillelmus' wife, but the proprietor refused to issue a refund. As the transaction occurred in front of several witnesses, Bernarda perceived this as an insult, and she became furious and started screaming at the wife that "bad things would come to her body."[53] Bernarda stormed out of the tavern, only to return a short while later with a dagger concealed beneath her clothes. After confronting Guillelmus, she withdrew the dagger and stabbed him in the chest until he fell back to the floor. This, however, did not satisfy the *ira* of Bernarda. The next day she recruited several "corrupt" men to assist her plan. She instructed the men to go to Guillelmus' house in the middle of the night and bang on the door, shouting that they wanted to buy some wine. When Guillelmus opened the door to greet his customers, the armed men attacked him, wounding him in the head. Bernarda was an angry woman, but not irrational. She took the time to secure male accomplices to complete her vengeance, and fulfill her desire to see Guillelmus suffer. She realized that Guillelmus would not allow her back into his tavern, and so she had to find a sneaky way to gain access to him at his most vulnerable. Bernarda believed that Guillelmus and his wife humiliated her by dismissing her business transaction. She converted her anger into revenge, striving to reestablish her pride by fooling and injuring her foil.

Although it is difficult by our standards to consider the medieval home a 'private space,' the criminal records rarely reveal any cases of domestic violence. Chiffoleau suggests that this absence in Avignon's records can be attributed to a certain jurisdictional power of the *pater familias* over his household.[54] If the records describe a crime within a home, the incident rarely transpired between family members. Instead, external perpetrators found their way into the home in order to commit their particular offense. Gonthier found in Lyon that many of the accused criminals employed trickery to gain entrance into the home. In 1410, Pierre Fucheron presented himself at the home of an acquaintance under the guise of sampling his wine, but then, with the help of two accomplices, proceeded to rape the host's young wife. Two other men in 1504 succeeded in convincing a couple to open their door after ten o'clock at night by claiming to be night

53 AMT-FF 57, 151: "Ex hus mota ira incepit rixari…et dicendo pro malium infortunium eveniret eis."

54 Chiffoleau, "La violence au quotidien," 350.

guards investigating a murder. Once inside the house they seized and kidnapped the couple's two young daughters.[55] In Toulouse, the external threat to the household came in the form of an invited guest, not in deception. The one accusation of theft presented to the capitols provides an example. In early June of 1332, Johannes Arnaldus, of the neighborhood of Montis Aygonis, complained that he had received his young neighbor, Guillemus de Portello, into his home for a drink which he served in a silver cup. After Guillelmus left, Johannes Arnaldus realized that his guest had taken the silver cup with him.[56] Evidently the host knew Guillelmus well enough to bring him into his house for a social visit, and to entertain him with refreshments. The theft, then, was an affront to Johannes' hospitality, especially because the stolen item was valuable. In a second case concerning an assault, the defendant was a professional brought into the home, presumably on business. Magister Bernard Geraldus, a doctor (*medicus*), attacked and injured Sclarmonda, the wife of Guillelmus of Totenthis, in her house with a sword and "other arms."[57] The listing of weapons clearly indicates that the wounds Sclarmonda suffered were not related to any types of treatments. The doctor was in fact a resident of Toulouse, with social and familial roots, and so we may assume he was not a mobile practitioner, as found in other cities of France.[58] The court records identify him as living in the neighborhood of Badacley, a region by the Garonne River. In addition, his father and another resident of Toulouse came forward to pay the trial's expenses.[59] As there is no indication that this was a forced entry, we may only speculate as to what went wrong within the home that would result in the doctor physically assaulting a woman.

The court records reveal many individuals sought revenge against an adversary by taking matters into their own hands, rather than to involve municipal officers in their conflicts. One citizen of Toulouse, named Hugnetus de Sanardino attacked a father and son he encountered in the street. He testified in his defense that he only injured the men in an

55 Gonthier, *Délinquance, justice et société*, 110.
56 Ibid., 69.
57 Ibid., 147: "Magistrus Bernardus Geraldi medicus."
58 For a discussion concerning the differences between doctors and licensed medical surgeons, see Noël Coulet, "Quelques aspects du milieu médical en Provence au bas Moyen-Âge," *Vie priveé et ordre public à la fin du moyen- âge: Études sur Manosque, la Provence et le Piémont (1250–1450)*, ed. by Michel Hébert (Aix-en-Provence: Université de Provence Service des Publications, 1987), 122–125.
59 AMT-FF 57, 148.

attempt to ward off their blows.[60] They threatened him and cornered him to instigate the fight, Hugnetus continued; he could not escape their attack. In other words, he had no choice but to protect himself with violence. Johannes Causati, from the city gate of Villeneuve, tried a similar excuse in his trial to justify his altercation with Hugnetus de Masto Faýsherius. As the two men drank in the Durandi bar, Hugnetus began a fight and hit him in the forehead with a roof tile. Later that day, still stewing over the confrontation, Johannes saw Hugnetus as he passed through a neighborhood. This was his opportunity for revenge. He grabbed a rock and pummeled Hugnetus in the head; later they met up in the town hall, Hugnetus' head wrapped, as he pressed charges against Johannes.[61] This would suggest that Johannes did not realize the severity of the attack when he hit him. In both of these instances, the accused culprits decided to take matters of revenge and perceived self-defense into their own hands through physical retaliation, instead of asking an officer to become involved in the matter.

In many respects, the streets and taverns of medieval cities served as the arena for shouting matches, exchanges of insults and violent altercations during the process of everyday life. But this disruption of the civic peace was not limited to marginal individuals fueled with alcohol and easy access to weapons who erupted into random attacks for no substantial reason. Instead, the criminal records from Toulouse suggest that perpetrators of violence pronounced their intentions and aired their grievances with friends and neighbors, brandished weapons to reinforce their seriousness, and bided their time until they had an opportunity to confront their adversaries. The social and economic relationships between the citizens of Toulouse were established within the daily interaction of the smaller realms of neighborhoods. These verbal and physical jousts served as one way in which the hierarchy of status and dominance was defined and negotiated, until the exchange resulted in bloodshed. Because the nature of medieval criminal activity was open and public, a wide range of the community served as resources in both the prevention and propagation of deviation from the law and order of Toulouse.

[60] Ibid., 257.

[61] Ibid., 81: "Dictus Hugnetus esset in taberna Durando dictus Hugnetus incepit rixari cum ipso [Johannes] et cum quadam tegula percussit et vulneranit [Johannes] in frontis...dicta die decero cum dictus Hugnetus esset in carreriam idem [Johannes] volens se vendicare progessit quendam lapidem contra dictum Hugnetum cum quo percussit *supra* capud...et post modum vidit eum in domo communi in caput cum panus involuto."

Public Involvement in Crimes

But the people of Toulouse did not stand idly by as criminal transgressions occurred before them. The public helped the municipal officers regulate the behavior of their fellow citizens: they seized malefactors, or they intervened to protect those who could not help themselves. In this respect, many individuals felt an obligation to maintain the sense of prosperity and prestige of the city and their own immediate environment by refusing to allow misdeeds to go unpunished. Not all of the public involvement (as described in the court documents) was motivated by good intentions to uphold the law. The testimony of the trials also indicates that many of the defendants had extensive social networks that helped to conceal the crimes, or to participate tangentially in the overall offense. Even though the role of the people varied between those trying to suppress crime and those sustaining its existence, people were actively involved in the lives of their neighbors and in the events of the streets, including the occasions when they needed to protect the liberties they valued as citizens.

The capitols realized that in addition to the numerous policing forces that patrolled the streets of Toulouse, they had to appeal to the broader population's sense of civic obligation to help enforce municipal criminal laws. An individual who witnessed a crime should come to the aid of the city officials and uphold the standards of law and order. In Italian city-states like Siena, the commune paid secret informers to identify citizens who had broken laws.[62] The French customary law of Phillippe de Beaumanoir granted the theoretical right of 'citizen arrests:' "It is to the common profit that each man should be sejeant and have the power to seize and arrest malefactors."[63] In practice, however, it seems as though citizens rarely took advantage of this privilege. In the northern French city of Arras, Carola Small found that of 968 criminals held in the municipal prison in the fourteenth century, only 38 were not arrested by municipal sergeants.[64] Nevertheless, in Toulouse, the capitols worked in collaboration with the royal vicar, and offered citizens the right of seizure. In 1304, two of the town criers traveled to the most populous quarters of the city,

---

62 William M. Bowsky, "The Medieval Commune and Internal Violence: Police Power and Public Safety in Siena, 1287–1355," *The American Historical Review*, vol. 23 (October, 1967): 7.

63 Phillip de Beaumanoir, *Coutumes du Beauvaisis*, ed. T. Salmon, I, p. 482.

64 Carola M. Small, "Prisoners in the Castellany of Artois in the Early Fourteenth Century," *Histoire sociale – Social History*, vol. XXVI (November 1993): p. 352.

accompanied by the municipal trumpeter, and read a proclamation regarding the carrying of illegal arms.[65] The statement reinforced the prohibition of certain weapons, and clarified that if authorities caught an individual in possession of arms, either night or day, the offender had to pay sixty *sols tols*, and the city government would confiscate the weapons. The town criers insisted that the citizens had an obligation to denounce the offense to the vicar or to the capitols. If anyone witnessed an attack that involved illegal arms, the citizen had to defend the victim by capturing the perpetrator, violently if necessary. The citizens were exempt from any fines or punishment if the assailant was harmed in the process. A very similar obligation can be found centuries later in early modern Augsburg, as male citizens had the right and duty to interfere in fights, to disarm disorderly people, and authorities sanctioned the use of physical force in apprehending the malefactor.[66] These proclamations display a certain amount of trust that the citizens would not abuse this power due to a sense of obligation to the greater good of the city and to their own safety. On the continent, there seems to be little legal concern about the abuses this privilege might incite in the hands of indiscriminate citizens, but this seems to have been the case in England, where malicious arrests were prevalent.[67]

The municipal government encouraged the inhabitants of Toulouse to take a direct hand in the control of prostitutes as well. An early statute of the city from 1201 limited prostitutes to practice only outside of Toulouse's walls.[68] By the end of the thirteenth century, prostitution had become more pervasive and audacious in the adjoined suburb of Saint Cyprian. In other cities of Languedoc, prostitutes did not share the same legal protection as 'honest' people, and could be especially vulnerable to spontaneous physical attacks when their actions were perceived as insulting to citizens.[69] If an 'honest' woman of Arles, for example, saw a prostitute wearing a veil (a sign of chastity), she had the right to rip it off. Toulouse's municipal government granted the people of Saint Cyprian the right not only to arrest a woman they saw soliciting customers for sex, but also to undress them, and to drag them, nude or clothed, to the vicar's or capitols'

65 AMT-AA 4:19. August 5, 1304. Copied in *HGL*, X, doc. 134, cc. 446–447.

66 Tlusty, "Civic Defense and the Right to Bear Arms in the Early Modern German City," 495.

67 Small, "Prisoners," 352.

68 AMT-AA 1:27. August 31, 1201. Printed in Limouzin-Lamothe, *La commune*, 316–317.

69 Leah Lydia Otis, *Prostitution in Medieval Society: The History of an Urban Institution in Languedoc* (Chicago: The University of Chicago Press, 1985), 66–67.

court where she would be tried and charged a fine.[70] This is reminiscent of King Louis IX's campaign against prostitutes in the realm at large. In 1254, the monarch issued a decree that ordered not only an expulsion of all 'common women' from towns and villages, but also the confiscation of all of their property, including their clothing.[71] Studies have shown that these efforts to eradicate prostitution ultimately failed, and resulted instead in the marginalization of the profession to designated sectors in the city space.[72] But still, conceivably, the statute of Toulouse gave citizens the right to seize someone they thought was breaking the law, and to humiliate the sexual perpetrator by parading her through the city streets to jail.

Other individuals employed these municipally sanctioned powers of regulation and policing to humiliate a neighbor they hoped to drive out of the city. One instance of this situation occurred in a small district of the suburb of Saint Cyprian on the left bank of the Garonne River. A merchant named Guillelmus Calveti and a woman named Gualharda, the wife of Arnaldus Aýnorii, conspired against their neighbor Alamanda, wife of Petrus Bergonhonis.[73] What we know of the case is that Alamanda complained to the capitols in court that the two defendants publicly defamed her character, and threatened her safety on numerous occasions. She said that they told their neighbors that they would not break bread with her, and would in fact "break bread in her bed," and leave a mark on her face so she would "always be recognized," and "deformed in her face."[74] These disparaging remarks, taken as a whole, seemed to accuse Alamanda of illicit sexual conduct, and to allude to outright prostitution. Prostitutes were not allowed to socialize or to be welcomed into respectable homes, and the threat of "breaking bread" in her bed could serve as a symbolic accusation that she had hosted many men in that location. And aspiring to scar her face not only would create social isolation, but some cultures believed that a woman who had a permanent mark on her face did not have sexual integrity. Valentin Groebner argues more specifically that the severing of a nose signified an assault against the sexual honor of an individual, both in

---

70 AMT, layette series II, 77. April 1271, copied in February 1299. Printed in Georges Boyer, "Remarques sur l'administration de Toulouse au temps d'Alphonse de Poiters," *Mélanges I: Mélanges d'histoire du droit occidentale* (Paris: Sirey, 1962), 200.

71 *Ordonnanaces des rois de France*, vol. 1, p. 65, art.34.

72 Geremek, *The Margins of Society*, 215–222.

73 AMT-FF 57, 245.

74 Ibid.: "panem suum comedent in lecto"..."taliter esset signata in eius facie pro semper cognosceretur et esset defformata dicte eius facieý."

criminal punishments sanctioned by the municipal governments, and through duels fought between rivals. A husband in late medieval Germany, for example, could punish his wife for infidelity by cutting off her nose.[75] But the accused defendants Guillelmus Calveti and Gualharda were not content to slander Alamanda's reputation and social standing in their neighborhood. They also coordinated a ritual humiliation that drove her from their neighborhood. The couple forced Alamanda to cross over a bridge from the suburb and into the city of Toulouse, and "denounced" her way of life as they made her walk like a "poor woman." The procession ended in a vineyard outside of the gate of the Château Narbonnais.[76] The two conspirators then directed some malefactors to the location where they had left Alamanda. The men beat her so badly that she was later discovered half-dead. When the capitols summoned Guillelmus Calveti and Gualharda to stand trial for these accusations, both proclaimed their innocence of any misdeed, and brought in Lord Geraldus Capellanus from their neighborhood church to discredit Alamanda's reputation.[77] The sources do not reveal the outcome of this case, but it is clear that the men and women of this neighborhood tried to enforce their idea of civic order and dignity.

There were some citizens of Toulouse who upheld their civic obligation to intervene and to protect helpless victims, like women. The urban environment was always a precarious place for the 'weaker' sex, especially for those who walked alone night or day in the city streets. In most accounts from medieval France, violent attacks against women transpired in the shadows of dark alleys or in the cover of taverns.[78] But in an example from Toulouse from 1332, a man assaulted a young girl named Finas as she headed home after she filled a pitcher with water from the Garonne River. Johannes Sartore, the son of a Master Bartholomeý Sartore, approached her and apparently made sexual advances against Finas, and when she ignored his flirtation, he became angry and violent. Johannes "struck her with his fists and mistreated her with many blows," until bystanders became involved in efforts to protect the girl. He then pulled out a knife and continued to "strike Finas, and others who tried to intervene, resulting

[75] Groebner, *Defaced*, 81–82.

[76] AMT-FF 57, 245.

[77] Ibid., 246.

[78] See, for example, Walter Prevenier, "Violence against Women in a Medieval Metropolis: Paris around 1400." *Law, Custom and the Social Fabric in Medieval Europe: Essays in Honor of Bryce Lyon*, eds. Bernard S. Bachrach and Davis Nicholas (Kalamazoo, Michigan: Medieval Institute Publications, 1990), 263–284.

in many wounds among them."[79] In this scenario, then, we see that citizens could and would get involved to prevent an assault. Johannes' rage must have been so intense that it inspired other bystanders to risk their own well-being to protect Finas from his fists and weapons. Perhaps the people who got involved in the assault were determined to preserve the general sense of community and civic order, and to exert protection to those in need.

Even though the capitols appealed to the public to monitor crime in their neighborhoods, the archival documents suggest that there were just as many social networks available to the defendants to either aid in, or to help conceal, deviant activity. Spouses became common allies in violent attacks, especially in instances against a third party who had insulted the honor and status of the couple.[80] On September 3, 1261, Petrus de Monthel, a miller, brought charges in front of the capitols against Raymundus Salevat, another miller, and his wife Geralda, seeking financial compensation of 200 *solidos tolosanos* for a physical attack he suffered.[81] Petrus argued that as he walked down a street, he passed in front of the couple's house, where the two sat with some other people who looked to Petrus like "criminals." Suddenly, the husband and wife charged him, and began hitting and kicking him with their fists and feet. After this assault had gone on for awhile, they dragged him by his clothing and hair into their house where they continued to strike him in the face, and to trample him under foot, until a neighbor who heard the screams came to his aid. Because the two men worked in the same profession, it is likely that the rivalry started because of business competitions. The husband and his wife resolved to make a spectacle of their ill feelings towards Petrus, and to exert their united dominance over him by beating him into submission.

When the citizen of Villamuro, Stephanus Saletas, began his tumultuous relationship with Toulouse's lawyer Bernardus de Bosto, he called upon his familial and social ties to aid in his revenge. For instance, after the financial transaction between the two proved unsatisfactory, Stephanus asked his first cousin (*consobrinus*) to confront the lawyer in the streets before the Château Narbonnais.[82] When this verbal mediation failed to

---

79 AMT-FF 57, 215: "cum pugnis percussit et maletractabit pluribus ictibus et cum intreparetur peraliquos de predictus perventus evagniant quodam cutella cum quia invasit dictas Finas et illos qui ipsim interpaverant faciendo posse suum percussiendi et vulnerandi eosdem cum eadem."

80 Gonthier, *Delinquance, justice et société*, 130.

81 AMT, layettes series II, 60/1.

82 AMT-FF 57, 44.

satisfy Stephanus, he began to conspire with some men he hired through a friend, Petrus Cortesii, to attack Bernardus de Bosto. The organization of the assault does not appear to have been the most sophisticated, because suspicious neighbors kept questioning the intentions of the men when they congregated to plot. In one scenario, all of the men exited the home they used as a headquarters for their operation, armed with illegal swords. When a couple who lived close by interrogated the home owner (a friend of Stephanus Saletas), he explained that the men were about to take a long journey, and they were not a threat to the security of the area.[83] The conspirators all hid in the same home with their wives and prostitutes, gathering weapons and courage for months. The wife of the homeowner assured the men that Stephanus was her cousin, and that he would keep his promise to pay them after the assault on Bernardus de Bosto.[84] And so the attack of one of Toulouse's business lawyers which transpired in front of the town hall, took place in large part due to the loyalty and connections that Stephanus had secured through his family and friends who lived in the city. The case also reveals that people questioned their neighbors if they observed untrustworthy behavior by unknown men lurking around Toulouse.

Most of the criminal activity the capitols and the lawyers prosecuted did not unfold under the cover of darkness, or in marginal areas of Toulouse. Instead, the citizens witnessed violent confrontations erupt before their homes, or passed a person carrying illegal arms while they headed to a different neighborhood in the course of a day. Either deliberately or inadvertently, disputes between two people frequently evolved to incorporate a wide range of public involvement. Some spectators could not stand idly by and allow vulnerable people suffer an attack, and so they stepped forward to intervene. Others participated by seizing men who carried illegal arms, or women who engaged in illicit prostitution. But the court records also reveal that many defendants relied upon friends and family to help them in their criminal activity, either as perpetrators in the assaults, or they provided shelter for the conspirators. Because the crimes were so public in their nature, and involved a broader audience of the people of Toulouse, the capitols and their judicial system needed to incorporate designated portions of the city space and its population, in order to conduct an open ritual of inclusion and exclusion within the community.

[83] Ibid., 46.
[84] Ibid., 46–47.

The Public and the Pursuit of Justice

The capitols' courtroom hosted the formalities of the criminal process, and it became a forum for establishing the cycles of inclusion and exclusion within the community at large. For instance, if the capitols discovered that someone falsely accused another citizen of a crime, honor had to be restored in the public opinion through a ritual cleansing of the defamation by bringing the accuser to court. In this respect, the judicial trial become a "trial of transformation" for an accused or slandered individual to be reinstated among the respectable people of the society.[85] Similarly, if the capitols found a person guilty of their crime, they had to conduct the trial and the punishment in a public and prescribed manner, so that the citizens could witness that justice was served. This final section will explore the various steps of the capitols' judicial procedure in order to elucidate the ways in which the officials employed the public, and the city space, in the determination of guilt or innocence.

The capitols received criminal cases in three ways: a complainant could bring a grievance to the court in the town hall where a notary would record the testimony, the municipal officers caught the suspect in the act of committing a crime or they could solely rely upon the unanimous clamor of unnamed informants.[86] In all circumstances, the notary would then pass a copy of the charges to the civic messenger who would go to the home of the accused, and announce the indictment and cite the specific day and time that the accused must come to the court for trial.[87] According to municipal regulations from 1273, the complainant was obligated to pay both the notary and the messenger two *sous tournois* for this function. Frequently, these messengers, or more commonly town criers, wore a particular outfit that symbolized the office, such as a vest in the municipal colors. In Marseilles, the town crier wore a vest of blue and white, so perhaps in Toulouse, he would wear the city colors of black and red.[88] The capitols employed men who best represented the authority and prestige of the municipal government, and chose candidates with clear and loud voices, able to attract the attention of a crowd.

85 Courtemanche, "Medical Expertise," 123.

86 Gilles, "Une cause d'injures," 121–124. Trevor Dean, *Crime and Justice in late Medieval Italy* (Cambridge: Cambridge University Press, 2007), 18.

87 AMT-BB 204, fol. 9.

88 Michel Hébert, "*Voce preconia*: note sur les criées publiques en Provence," *Milieux naturels, espaces sociaux: études offertes à Robert Delort*, ed. by Élisabeth Mornet and Franco Morenzoni (Paris: Publications de la Sorbonne, 1997), 689–701.

In return, the public crier received a lot of benefits from the office. For example, in 1293, the capitols guaranteed that Raimond Arnaud, son of the late Raimond Arnaud of Fanjeaux, would hold his office of town crier *in perpetuum*, and would be financially protected by the capitols even after he retired.[89] In the early fourteenth century, Guillelmus Johannes, who lived in a neighborhood close to the town hall, held the official position of town crier and trumpeter, and again, made a good living serving the capitols in a variety of functions.[90] He was paid 20 *sol tols* during the year 1322–1323 for pledges he announced between merchants in the market place.[91] From a legal perspective, the municipal archives hold one example of a complete proclamation made by the same Guillelmus Johannes that concerned the criminal accusations made between the years 1292 to 1293. Here he summoned a thief accused of stealing a blanket worth 300 *sol tols* (which he resold for 15 *sol tols*) who had failed to appear in court three times. He announced that seven other defendants who faced charges of physical violence needed to appear before the capitols' court.[92] Even more significantly, he made the announcements in the neighborhoods where the crimes took place, so that the men and women who had perhaps witnessed the event knew that someone would either stand accountable for the deed, or prove his innocence in the courtroom.

After the town crier read the citation, the accused could postpone the hearing at least three times. Once all legal delays had expired, the defendant either reported before the capitols willingly, or the municipal sergeants set out and made the arrest. Lawyers joined their clients in the courtroom, and the royal procurer gathered with the capitols as well. If the defendant or a witness wanted to offer testimony, he or she had to swear a variety of oaths so that the statement could be included in the trial transcripts. First, they had to pledge to the capitols and the court that they were over the legal limit of twenty-five years old. If the defendant was under age, a father or guardian had to be present in the courtroom as the capitols interrogated him or her. Next, the suspect or witness raised the right hand to God and "swore to tell the truth."[93] When released on bail, the accused promised to return to the courtroom wearing lay clothing.

[89] AMT, layette series II, 70/4. April 13, 1293. A second example of the same privileges to a different crier is found in AMT-layettes series II, 70/5, dated August 22, 1299.

[90] AMT-FF 59, fol. 12v. *DRT*, I, 27.

[91] *CR*, 70, no. 1064.

[92] AMT, layettes II, 84/6. January, 1292 to January, 1293.

[93] AMT-FF 57, 147: "jurem de veritatem dicenda."

This oath guaranteed that the defendant would not appear in clerical garb and in turn, demand clerical privilege, which would complicate the capitols' criminal jurisdiction and prolong the trial. In these ritual exchanges of oaths, the defendant placed his honor and reputation on the line, he agreed to be a part of the larger judicial process and he recognized the legitimate authority of the capitols and their court.

Medical specialists (*surgicus iuratus et expertus huius ville tholose*) joined the lawyers and capitols in the trial's ceremony as they fought to determine guilt or innocence in the courtroom. The capitols summoned doctors to investigate a victim's wounds, and to report whether or not he would recover from the injury. As cities grew in importance and in population throughout the thirteenth century, municipal administrations began to associate the regulation of medicine with the policing of crime.[94] For example, a statute from Venice in 1281 required that all medical practitioners report to the police any occasions when they treated patients with wounds from a physical assault.[95] In Marseilles, Jewish surgeons were frequently called upon by the judicial court to offer their testimony concerning alleged acts of violent crime.[96] The city of Ghent actually employed its own surgeon who treated injured municipal officials, and assessed the severity of wounds for victims who sought financial amends from the city council. In extreme cases, the municipal surgeon was aided by other local doctors, because, David Nicholas argues, the "testimony of the doctor was perhaps the most important part of the trial proceedings, since a penal assessment would be measured according to the extent of the injury."[97] In these examples, the judicial officials did not rely on the doctors to serve just as witnesses. They made the medical experts part of the judicial system determining admissible proof. Each doctor in the capitols' criminal trials of Toulouse swore that he "saw for himself and diligently inspected"

---

94 Courtemanche, "The Judge, the Doctor, and the Poisoner," 114–115. Joseph Shatzmiller, "Médecins et expertise médicale dans la ville médiévale: Manosque, 1280–1348." *Vie priveé et ordre public à la fin du moyen- âge: Études sur Manosque, la Provence et le Piémont (1250–1450)*, ed. by Michel Hébert (Aix-en-Provence: Université de Provence Service des Publications, 1987), 105–117. Catherine Crawford, "Medicine and the Law," *Companion Encyclopedia of the History of Medicine*, ed. W.F. Bynum and Roy Porter (London: Routledge, 1993), 1622–1624.

95 Guido Ruggiero, "The Cooperation of Physicians and the State in the Control of Violence in Renaissance Venice," *Journal of the History of Medicine and Allied Science* 33 (1978): 155–166.

96 See, Smail, *The Consumption of Justice*, 78–79. Joseph Shatzmiller, *Médicine et justice en Provence médiévale: documents de Manosque, 1262–1348* (Aix-en-Provence: Publications de l' Université de Provence, 1989), 30–44.

97 Nicholas, "Crime and Punishment in Fourteenth-Century Ghent," 1142–1143.

the wounded defendant.[98] The capitols called upon medical inspector Master Guillelmus Nicholaý most frequently during their criminal trials, but in the more controversial cases, six additional medical experts could offer their opinions as well.[99] By the early fourteenth century, the University of Toulouse had an established medical faculty, which provided these men with the necessary training and expertise to aid the capitols in their administration of justice.[100]

It should be stressed that the medical experts did not conduct their examination of the victim in the town hall or in the isolation of a doctor's office. Instead, on a designated day, they walked to the home where the injured person was recuperating, many times escorted by a civic notary who would record the doctor's comments. Again, the inhabitants of the neighborhood and the family of the victims could witness the local authorities come into their district of the city, and could see that all paths were pursued towards the determination of the assault's severity. The medical experts most often visited victims of head wounds. For example, one man received a blow to the head that he believed left him in "mortal danger." Master Guillelmus Nicholaý's examination concurred, and municipal officers promptly arrested the perpetrator.[101] In other circumstances, as in Ghent, the doctors cared for municipal officers injured while performing their professional duties. Guillelmus Sartoris, a night guard of Toulouse, was attacked while he patrolled the city; he suffered a wound in his left hand and arm, which left the appendage impotent, although the doctor speculated it might heal in the future.[102] The doctors returned to the court after they made these examinations, and offered their findings in order to help the capitols' shape their punishment so that it appropriately fit the severity of the crime.

The capitols and their officers proved their authority and the legitimacy of the city's judicial system through both the extensive trials and by sending their experts and town criers into the neighborhoods of Toulouse. The courtroom also became an environment for the defendants to call upon

---

[98] AMT-FF 57, 64: "dicta die se vidisse et diligenter inspexisse Bernardum de Carcassone."

[99] Ibid., 120. Additional medical experts included: Master Micahelis de Castris, Aymericus de Locis, and Petrus Simonis, Raymondus Bernardus, Bertrandus de la Greze, Petrus Aurier.

[100] Philippe Wolff offers a brief examination of the licensing of doctors and barbers in "Recherches sur les médecins de Toulouse aux XIVe et XVe siècles," *Regards sur le midi*, 125–142. Smith, *A History of the University of Toulouse*, 210.

[101] AMT-FF 57, 100.

[102] Ibid., 117.

their social networks for a public showing of support. Most often, friends and family members demonstrated their loyalty to the person on trial by posting bail and paying court costs. One tavern owner, accused of attacking a candle maker by the Garonne River, had a burgher pay his fines, although the documents do not reveal their connection.[103] It was more common for the accused men and women to have their relatives pledge their goods in order to post their bail. A grocer named Raymundus Donati, who was emancipated from his father, relied upon a relative named Petrus Donati, to pay the appropriate fines so that municipal authorities released Raymundus from jail, where he was being detained an alleged assault.[104] A woman named Ricarda needed her husband and two of his acquaintances to post her bail when the capitols held her in custody for harassing a neighbor.[105] And Bartholmeus Jordani, a merchant, called upon the assistance of both his father and son- in-law after he was charged for striking a rival merchant in the face with a staff.[106] These men came forward and gave their money to the capitols in order to demonstrate publicly that they stood behind the defendant and they had faith in the judicial process.

Even though there is no record of a woman who offered property or money to cover the various court costs, a wide demographic range of people did come into the courtroom to testify before the capitols. According to the customary law, women could offer testimony in crimes of injury, and even attend the trials unescorted by their husbands.[107] In the trial of Stephanus Saletas (the man who coordinated the assault of lawyer Bernardus de Bosto), dozens of professional attorneys and notaries were recorded as witnesses, which is not surprising considering the attack took place close to the busy and bureaucratic town hall. But among the over one hundred and thirty-four names, the notary listed the testimony of a fisherman, a tavern owner, a silversmith, a barber, a tailor, several wives (unattended by their husbands), a female servant (*ancilla*) and a notary accompanied by his trainee.[108] In a separate case, the servant girl of a lord offered supporting testimony for a fellow servant, named Clemens

---

103 Ibid., 79 "Raymundus Catalam Burgenis de Capella Hugolezii."

104 Ibid., 85.

105 Ibid., 129.

106 Ibid., 219.

107 Gilles, *Les Coutumes*, 217. For a discussion of women in the legal structure and protection under the law, see Mundy, *Men and Women in Toulouse*, 22–27.

108 AMT-FF 57, 104: "Magister Petrus de Hertia notaire et eius discipulus."

de Bena, who had been arrested for carrying illegal arms.[109] Conversely, victims' family members and friends came forward to speak to the capitols and to plead for justice in these cases. When the capitols tried Perrotus de Balerno for attacking a man, the notary recorded the victim's mother and sister among the other people waiting to give testimony.[110]

Whereas the Dominican friars perfected a system of inquest that relied upon secrecy, and they conducted their interrogations behind closed doors, the capitols and their municipal judicial structure was an open forum for grievances, resolution and support. After the notary registered the offense, the town crier pronounced the complaint to spectators within the neighborhood where the crime allegedly occurred. These officers provided a legitimate voice of authority for the municipal administration, and demonstrated to the people that city officials did pursue justice. Similarly, the medical experts of the city added an element of professionalism to the ritual criminal proceedings. But the trials were also an opportunity for the defendants' families and social networks to come exhibit their support if they felt as though they were falsely accused. Likewise, the victims in these crimes could rely upon witnesses to provide evidence to the capitols. The courtroom became an environment which served dual purposes: in one respect, it allowed the capitols and their officers to further advance the legitimacy of their power and authority in the municipal judicial system, while it also allowed men and women of varying social status to receive an audience with the capitols to help shape the outcome and verdict in the trial.

Conclusion

The criminal sources available from medieval Toulouse do not allow much discussion concerning any clandestine or dark underworld of bandits and thieves. Undoubtedly, these unlawful elements of society existed in the urban environment, but they were not brought into the capitols' courtroom in the town hall. Instead, the records reveal a city in which disputes and grievances between adversaries were aired to their neighbors for extended periods of time. Violence erupted in the city streets only after tensions had mounted too high and other means of interpersonal resolution had failed. The majority of the attacks and disputes occurred in the

109 Ibid., 254: "Aladaý suam Ancillam."
110 Ibid., 244.

most public arenas of Toulouse: streets, taverns, close to city landmarks, and commercial squares. Witnesses to these events could intervene at any moment, and fulfill a civic duty to the capitols and each other to preserve the peace of the community. But the cases also reveal that networks of support for defendants determined to see their crimes and grudges take a violent turn. The process of uncovering the guilt or innocence of these individuals, then, also had to be a very public and involved process, in which the lines of inclusion and exclusion were established somewhere in the middle of the negotiations between the municipal officers, and the people living in Toulouse.

CHAPTER FOUR

FORCES OF ORDER, FORCES OF DISORDER: CORRUPT OFFICERS AND THE CONFUSION OF AUTHORITY

In 1268, a fight over jurisdiction between the capitols and the vicar resulted in a gruesome death. One afternoon, the vicar's messenger, named Michael, stood before the capitols and their officers in the town hall's court and proclaimed he was taking a young citizen of Toulouse into custody. When the citizen resisted arrest in front of everyone in attendance, Michael struck him several times with a club. The capitols sprung into action, and ordered their officers to take the messenger to the municipal jail, where he would be incarcerated until they could resolve the matter with the vicar. According to the tenuous jurisdictional agreements of the city, the vicar's messenger had no authority to seize a citizen of Toulouse without the consent of the capitols, and especially not in the court which symbolized the local administration's power and autonomy. Word of the messenger's attack spread quickly from the municipal officers to the citizens of Toulouse, and before much time had passed, seven thousand protesters gathered before the town hall. Suddenly, some members of the crowd broke through the doors of the building with either a tree trunk or a wooden beam and raced towards the jail, where they discovered the messenger held in shackles.[1] Several citizens removed the restraints, and carried Michael to the protesters who were waiting outside armed with rods and staffs. After the crowd beat the messenger to death, they carried his body throughout the city streets in celebration.

During the vicar's inquest into death of his messenger, a local banker, named Garnerius, found himself standing in the courtroom charged with the murder. On March 5, Garnerius' year-long trial began as dozens of citizens and municipal officers came forth to offer testimony against him. According to witnesses present that fateful afternoon, he gave a rousing speech to the mob that denounced the messenger's disregard for their civic liberties and for the honor of the capitols. Moved by his words, the

---

[1] Élie Berger, ed. *Layettes du trésor des chartes,* vol. IV (Paris: Plon-Nourrit, 1902), 321–326, no. 5487. Witnesses described the instrument used to break through the door as a "pertica magna vel trabe."

audience charged into the town hall to retrieve the messenger. Garnerius' defense testimony, not surprisingly, offered a very different description of events, which implicated both the capitols and their officers in the orchestration of the murder and subsequent attempt to cover up the crime. He claimed that two of the capitols' messengers ordered him to go to the town hall, and when he arrived, a capitol recounted to the crowd what had happened in the courtroom earlier that day. Garnerius insisted that the capitol, not he, instructed the crowd to seek revenge against the vicar's messenger. After the mob paraded the messenger's body outside of the town hall, he continued, three of the capitols and their sergeants tried to conceal the evidence by hiding the corpse in the Church of Saint Rome, forbidding anyone to enter.[2] Because the extant records do not reveal the outcome of this case, nor do they suggest that the vicar tried any other citizen or municipal official for the offense, it is impossible to determine who was held accountable for the death of the messenger.

But why did Garnerius accuse the capitols and their officers of wrongdoing in the horrific death of the vicar's messenger? Was it merely a legal ploy to establish his innocence? Or does his testimony ring true? Did the capitols and their officers take advantage of the citizens' frustration and public demonstration to oppose external authority without being directly accountable? In the defenses employed by accused criminals in the capitols' court in the fourteenth century, municipal officers did emerge as active participants in the violent conflicts which erupted in the city streets of Toulouse. In fact, the disruptive behavior of civic sergeants and night guards often instigated the confrontations. The officers stirred up trouble in order to enhance their status within the community and to subvert the power and judicial privilege of royal representatives. Not unlike today, the men and women accused of crime in the capitols' court expressed a variety of defenses, such as self-protection or vengeance for an insult. But the testimony of individuals such as Garnerius, who incriminated the capitols and their officers in criminal activity, reveals that the lines of legitimate authority were often ambiguous and difficult for the citizens of Toulouse to discern. What we find is that many officers (including the capitols) took advantage of their positions of authority to manipulate and intimidate the people they had vowed to protect, in order to advance their own political or personal agendas. In other words, the

[2] The Church of Saint Rome was a small chapter dependant upon the Cathedral Saint Étienne, situated off of the central town hall. It was demolished shortly after the French Revolution. *DRT,* vol. 2, 441.

forces of order could also be the forces of disorder in fourteenth-century Toulouse.

As the judicial structure became a better organized and central fixture in the lives of the city's inhabitants, administrators hired physically strong men to serve as their policing officers: they had to be large enough to enforce the city's laws, and to secure criminals resistant to seizure. As Bernard Guenée put it, "fear and blows [were] the daily bread of the sergeant."[3] In Lyon, the public called their officers by nicknames such as "Well Built" and "All Heavy," obviously suggesting their menacing physique.[4] These sergeants and night guards represented the most immediate form of authority in the urban milieu as they patrolled the streets of the city and interacted with the public. But they not only had to be prepared to fight, they also had to loyal and supportive of their local politicians.[5] Although Susan L'Engle argued that, "they rarely wield their arms to wound or kill…since their function is primarily for the preservation of order rather than retribution," this was far from the case.[6] No doubt many believed in the integrity of their office, and sought to maintain the peace of the city. Others, however, were more susceptible to bribery, violence, and overall disruption of the city's order. Due to the prevalence of suspected corruption, these municipal guards frequently became convenient scapegoats for both the capitols and the populous who tried to shift blame from themselves towards the supposed wayward sergeant. The sergeants and night guards, then, played an integral, but liminal, role in the relationship between the municipal government who made the laws, and the citizens expected to obey.

To elucidate the dynamics of the relationship between the municipal officers, the public and the capitols, we have to add into our consideration the role of royal and ecclesiastical officers in the city of Toulouse, who battled for primacy in the streets. Beyond this competition between policing officers, the defendants in criminal trials from the fourteenth

[3] Bernard Guenée, *Tribunaux et gens de justice dans le bailliage de Senlis à la fin du Moyen Âge (vers 1380-vers 1550)* (Paris: La Société d'éditions Les Belles Lettres, 1963), 213.

[4] René Fédou, "Les sergents à Lyon aux XIVe et XVe siècles: une institution, un type social," *Bulletin Philologique et Historique (jusqu' à 1610)* (Paris, Bibliothèque Nationale, 1967), 287–289.

[5] William M. Bowsky, "The Medieval Commune and Internal Violence: Police Power and Public Safety in Siena, 1287–1355," *The American Historical Review* 73 no. 1 (October, 1967): 11.

[6] Susan L'Engle, "Justice in the Margins: Punishment in Medieval Toulouse." *Viator: Medieval and Renaissance Studies* 33 (2002): 139.

century do depict the city's sergeants and night guards creating disorder for the people of Toulouse by readily abusing their position of authority. One example comes from a town and gown row from 1336, in which several municipal night guards arrested a university student for controversial reasons, apparently with the sanction of a capitol. This conflict returns to one of the major issues addressed in Garnerius' trial which opened this chapter: namely, how jurisdictional overlap between municipal and royal representatives concerning the arrest and seizure of an individual led to spectacles which erupted in the city streets. I should emphasize here, though, that the sources I am dealing with accentuate the negative aspects of these men, and much like today, we cannot definitively claim that the actions of a few should tarnish the policing force as a whole.

The Agents of Law and Order: The Right to Arrest

The three competing administrations of Toulouse did not simply combat for legal dominance in the courtroom through proclamations and correspondence. They aspired to secure particular privileges for their policing officers, who represented their authority and legitimacy by interacting with the Toulousains. The power to arrest and to hold people in custody was a powerful aspect of delimiting the spheres of jurisdiction in the town. But in addition to the demonstrations of authority provided by seizing and intimidating the citizens with their weapons, an examination of these policing forces suggests that the officers of these three courts approached the general public in very different ways. The capitols and their officers were much more woven into the social fabric of the city, and aspired to protect the people in general (even though they frequently failed in this endeavor). Ecclesiastical officials and royal sergeants sought to restrain the public in a more detached fashion, one that lacked the intimacy or local traditions that the capitols and their agents employed. Some royal officers were more inclined to make a profit by accepting bribes from the citizens they seized, rather than enforce the regulations of the city.

As early as 1222, the counts granted the capitols of Toulouse the right to have an armed guard to survey the inhabitants, public places, roads and buildings of the city. The statute proclaimed: "From now and forever the capitols may defend the city and suburb of Toulouse and may defend and protect religious and lay homes, and all of the men and women who visit and live here from all of the spiteful men, robbers, and bandits."[7] The capitols had a large network of men working for them, whose responsibility it was to persuade and to coerce the people of the city to comply with the law, and maintain some semblance of order. In a statute from 1264, made in a general council at the town hall (called in this rare instance the "communal palace"), the capitols vowed that if any of notaries, messengers, guards of the day or night, sergeants and officers were accused of any criminal offense while performing their duty to the city, the commune of the *cité* and of the *bourg* would serve as their council, and would guarantee to pay the fines of the hearings, and to continue to pay their salary.[8] Even if they had to use undue force, the guards had to maintain the peace. The capitols also controlled several sub-organizations of the police division. For example, they had a rural patrol, an organization of men who monitored the gaming practices of Toulouse and a group who regulated funerals. With these various groups of men on surveillance, granted authority by the capitols, the municipal administration could regulate both the moral, personal, leisure, and criminal activities of the inhabitants of the city.

The sergeants (*servientes*) were the primary policing force of Toulouse, authorized by the capitols to carry weapons and to arrest anyone suspected of breaking the laws. On April 25, 1310, King Philip IV sent word to Toulouse supporting the seneschal's ban upon carry illegal arms during the day. The king's one exception permitted the capitols' sergeants to keep their weapons, because they bore the responsibility of "stopping malefactors."[9] In a declaration from Parlement, the king prohibited the vicar from seizing the arms of the capitols' sergeants, with the injunction to give restitution of any arms they had previously seized.[10] In this respect, the king acknowledged the importance of allowing these officers to be armed; it was a recognizable instrument of their right to represent authority. When any of the king's men tried to claim these weapons or seize them, it was a direct insult to the officer and his power to fulfill his civic duty. The official documents from medieval Toulouse never establish the specific "official weapons" that the sergeants were allowed to carry, although in

---

[7] AMT-AA 1:79. September 23, 1222. Cited in Limouzin-Lamothe, *La commune de Toulouse*, 415–416. "Quod nunc et semper consules civitatis Tolose et suburbii deffendant et possint deffendere et custodire a malignis hominibus, raptoribus et latronibus domos videlicet ordinum et religionum et omnes homines et feminas ibi manentes et habitantes."

[8] AMT-AA 5:139. September 6, 1264.

[9] AMT-AA 3:136, 5.

[10] AMT, AA 4:7, no date.

sixteenth-century Germany, civic ordinances required their guards to report to duty with a breastplate, helmet, and pike.[11] Illustrations from a manuscript from Toulouse, now situated in the Bibliothèque Nationale in Paris, depicts sergeants wearing heavy chain mail and helmets, carrying swords, shields and other weapons; certainly a figure who would intimidate the average citizen he encountered in the streets of the city.[12] The image shows the sergeants in coordinating uniforms of cloaks in the city colors of red and black to further reinforce a sense of uniformity in their appearance, making them even more recognizable figures of authority.

Unfortunately, the records are fairly silent as to the demographic origin of the class of municipal sergeants. In some Italian communes, like Siena, the government hired many foreign policemen to work in the city. By William Bowsky's estimation, by the "mid-1330s there was a foreign policemen to each 145 inhabitants of Siena, men, women, and children, lay and cleric."[13] There is no indication in the archival documents of Toulouse that there was a division of the sergeants into mounted or foot groups, as was the case in Paris.[14] In general, the mounted sergeants surveyed the surrounding county of the Île-de-France, while the foot sergeants worked within the royal city walls with the same powers to arrest, to issue official decrees, and to carry out the civil decisions of the Châtelet. Despite these policing and administrative responsibilities, however, the Parisian sergeants did not work in this capacity full time, and had a supplementary employment in the crafts.[15] In Toulouse, it seems that the men hired to serve as sergeants were local: in general they hailed from Languedoc. And the records suggest that the capitols employed a singular troop of sergeants to survey both the city and country, and entrusted them with so many duties that this was the officer's only occupation. This arrangement is certainly due to the fact that Toulouse had a much smaller population than cosmopolitan Italy or Paris, and the capitols could employ a permanent group of policing officers to work on their behalf both preventing crime and enforcing municipal statutes in and out of the city. In all scenarios, we should keep in mind that the governments never had a sufficient amount of sergeants to regulate the vast and unruly urban

---

[11] B. Ann Tlusty, "Civic Defense and the Right to Bear Arms in the Early Modern German City," *Acta Histriae* 10 (2002): 496.
[12] BN, MS lat. 9187, fol. 33r.
[13] Bowsky, "The Medieval Commune," 7.
[14] Geremek, *The Margins of Society*, 23.
[15] Ibid., 25.

population. What they lacked in numbers, the police force had to compensate for through sheer determination and intimidation.

Traditionally, authorities also coordinated a night patrol, or *guet*, when the city faced some sort of immediate crisis. Heads of families would volunteer one or two members of their household to patrol buildings, gates, bridges, and the urban streets as an obligation to their community and people.[16] For the most part, municipal authorities called upon fathers and oldest sons to serve in times of war to prevent any night time surprise attacks at the city gates. In Ghent, these men were known as *scerewetters*, and they served as night watchmen only when the city was in danger, rather than as a permanent nocturnal policing force. David Nicholas does not believe that there were ever a lot *scerewetters*, nor did they seem to have the power to arrest local malefactors, but still they were helpful supplements to the formal municipal policing officials in an emergency.[17] During periods of outright war, however, everyone ostensibly participated in protecting the city, day or night. Chronicles from the Albigensian Crusade provide some evidence of these night time patrols in Toulouse, as the armies of the dreaded northern crusader Simon de Montfort laid siege to the city. In a lull in the fighting from 1217, William of Tudela recalled how the Toulousains united to protect the city against the attacks and the invasion of the French. William marveled that, "never in any town have I seen such magnificent labourers, for the counts were hard at work there, with all the knights, the citizens and their wives and valiant merchants, men, women and courteous money-changers, small children, boys and girls, servants, running messengers, every one had a pick, a shovel or a garden fork, everyone of them joined eagerly in the work. And at night they all kept watch together, lights and candlesticks were placed along the streets, drums and tabors sounded and bugles played."[18] In other accounts, after nightfall the townspeople positioned themselves at city gates or towers and scoured the city walls for any breach of security; this civilian guard was armed with impromptu weapons and noisemakers to fulfill their civic duty of protection. This tradition continued into the Hundred Years War,

---

16 Nicole Gonthier, *Le châtiment du crime au Moyen Âge, XIIe-XVIe siècles* (Rennes, Cedex: Presses Universitaires de Rennes, 1998), 59–62. In Florence, a night time police force and judiciary magistracy was created to prosecute homosexual behavior in the fifteenth century. Michael Rocke, *Forbidden Friendships: Homosexuality and Male Culture in Renaissance Florence* (Oxford: Oxford University Press, 1996).

17 Nicholas, "Crime and Punishment in Fourteenth-Century Ghent," 308.

18 Guillaume de Tudela, *The Song of the Cathar Wars*, 124. "E la noit a la gaita son guit cominaler/Estan per las carreiras li lum el candeler."

especially in regions that became occupied by the English army, such as Poitou.[19] Even well into the early modern period, many urban governments expected their residents to participate in the defense of their city, rather than to rely upon professional soldiers. In Augsburg, Germany, the oath of citizenship required men to possess proper weapons and arms, and to be willing and able to fight to protect the city when needed. Any failure to comply with this expectation resulted in a serious punishment fitting a breach of oath.[20]

The *guet* maintained this core of civilian participants in its other manifestations, as is evidence by what emerged in Paris throughout the course of the fourteenth century. Night time crime became an increasing concern to the city magistrates, and after the bells signaled the beginning of curfew and marked the closing of all of the city taverns and homes, greater numbers of officers needed to patrol the city after dark. The magistrates' solution in Paris was to place the burden upon the city guilds: each guild had to supply representatives to serve as the night time patrol, to the number of about sixty burgesses each night. According to a royal ordinance of 1364, the night guard was to be distributed throughout particular sectors of the city, in order to secure the city walls, to guard the prisoners of the Châtelet, and to prevent such dangers such as rape, fire, and attacks and murders. But this night guard was known as a *guet assis*, which meant that they were not supposed to abandon their designated post. Instead, mounted royal sergeants and a company of foot soldiers walked the city streets and arrested malefactors out after curfew.[21] The sedentary component of the job made it a highly undesirable obligation for many of the guildsmen, who put forth concerted effort to be exempt from the post. Some offered bribes to the officers responsible for checking attendance, others claimed illness when summoned, and one guild set forth a petition to the crown arguing that the expectation of the service of the night guard put the honor of their wives at risk. Needless to say, the Parisian *guet* was not the most regular or effective means of protecting the urban population or of preventing crime.

In the same era, the night patrol became a permanent fixture in the municipal authority of Toulouse. Although archival information about the organization of the night patrol is rather scarce for the thirteenth and

---

19 Géraud Jarousseau, "Le guet, l'arrière-guet et la garde en Poitou pendant la Guerre de Cent Ans," *Bulletin de la Société des Antiquaires de l'Ouest* 8 (1965): 159–202.

20 Tlusty, "Civic Defense," 495.

21 This paragraph's discussion draws heavily from Geremek, *The Margins of Society*, 26–27.

fourteenth centuries, many references to the night guards (*custos nocturnus*) can be found in a criminal register of 1332. Each capitol who lived in one of the twelve districts of the city selected a group of night guards: in one of the criminal proceedings from 1332, Raymundus, also known as Almusseres, was identified as a night guard from the "part of the Daurade, fulfilling the duties of his office."[22] The capitol granted privileges to his night guards, such as the right to arrest people, and the right to bear arms as they patrolled the *capitoliat*. The night guards supplied their own weapons, however, unlike the uniformed sergeants. In one example in 1336, the criminal documents described the officers as having to gather their weapons from their homes before they could commence their evening rounds.[23] Like the *guet* of Paris, each night guard seemed fairly regional, in that they patrolled their neighborhoods of Toulouse in a predetermined route, and many times they paused to practice impromptu militia drills. The documents indicate that there would have been four or five men serving each *capitolat* as night guards, which would mean that as many as sixty night guards were roaming the different portions of Toulouse (which had a population of around 40,000 inhabitants in the fourteenth century) each night on the behalf of the capitols. As a means of comparison outside of France, about 120 men patrolled the streets of medieval Siena (with a population around 50,000) in a similar capacity as night guards, although the men primarily seemed to be retired members of the military.[24]

After seizing a suspect caught in the act, the sergeants and night guards could take the prisoner to jail. Apparently this included domestic crimes as well, because the city's *coutumes* lists a nameless *custos nocturnus* who arrested a youth while in the arms of a married woman, and the officer immediately escorted him to the town hall's jail.[25] On other more pressing occasions, the night guards and sergeants could escort the arrested perpetrator to the home of their sector's elected capitol for instruction, although this circuitous route did provide an opportunity for the prisoner to escape. A sergeant named Raymundus Vitalis arrested a fisherman for a violent

---

22 AMT-FF 57, 89: "Raymundus alias dictus Almusseres custos nocturnos pertite de Aurate faceret ex tubiam suam excercendo suum officium." In the sixteenth century, the night guards of Toulouse became more organized, and the records are much more extensive. It also appears that they became more centralized as a unit, like a modern police force. In the municipal archives of Toulouse, series FF 616 to FF 634, hold the nightly reports of the guet for the dates June 16, 1539 to September 4, 1639.

23 AMT-FF 59, 1336.

24 Bowsky, "Medieval Commune," 11.

25 Giles, *Les Coutumes*, 187.

attack, and brought him to the house of capitol Vitalis Durandi, but the perpetrator "fled the house and hands of the sergeant."[26] In each of these scenarios, however, sergeants and night guards needed to be careful when arresting citizens, even when acting on official orders. Because in most French cities, they were alone "responsible for wrongful arrests, and if these involved encroaching on somebody else's jurisdiction, they could be in trouble."[27] For instance, Carola Small uncovered a case from 1270 which concerned two sergeants who seized a suspect later deemed to be under the jurisdiction of the Bishop of Arras. Even though the sergeants acted on the municipal government's commands, the bishop punished them for the arrest with a public penance of humbly participating in his Christmas procession. They wore little more than a shirt and trousers and carried rods. In many respects, this example from Arras really elucidates the notion that policing officers were placed in a very precarious, and sometimes confusing, position. They could be reprimanded for either following, or not following, orders of arrest. It also reveals that the lines of jurisdiction were not always clear in the immediacy of the urban environment.

This last factor became even more pronounced because the municipal administration of the capitols and their guards had to compete for territorial prowess with the ecclesiastical and royal officers who walked the streets of Toulouse. The Dominican inquisitors – most of whom were not natives of Languedoc – were highly skilled in the pursuit of heretics, but their bureaucratic structure was not entirely sophisticated. The leaders of these tribunals had to rely upon servants and assistants who sought out the heretics, but who were not as well trained (or as righteous) as the inquisitors themselves. Many of their officers, especially notaries, cruelly took money from the people they encountered, and, worse, they captured and tortured men and women until they secured confessions. The most notorious figure of the era was Menet de Robécourt, a notary who exploited and violently persecuted the inhabitants of Languedoc.[28] His career was marked by the wrongful imprisonment and torture of unlikely heretical suspects in Carcassone, and of the financial extortion of the residents of Albi. In addition to notaries, the inquisitors also relied upon armed sergeants, often supplied by the king, to serve as the strong arms to bring

---

26 AMT-FF 57, 93: "de dicta domo aufugit et manus dicti servientis evasit."

27 Small, "Prisoners in the Castellany," 352–353.

28 See, Jean-Marie Vidal, "Menet de Robécourt, commissaire de l'inquisition de Carcassone," *Moyen Âge* 16 (1903): 425–449. Given, *Inquisition and Medieval Society*, 145–146.

resistant defendants before the court, and to confiscate goods forfeited by convicted heretics. These sergeants were prone to corruption, as they could use the power of the inquisition for their own agenda. James Given provides one situation where two royal sergeants (who delivered citations to appear before the inquisitor in the region of Carcassone) conspired with a notary, Bernard de Saint-Martin, and some residents of Montaillou, in order to frame their enemies with heresy. Apparently, the group plotted to draw up accusations of Cathar tendencies against two particular men who had previously physically attacked the sergeants. The sergeants asked the notary to write a forged letter of citation, based on the evidence provided by the men of Montaillou, to which they would attach an authentic inquisitor's seal.[29] It appears that the Dominican friars, stationed in Toulouse, had a difficult time regulating the behavior of these men once they were released upon the population of Languedoc.

The bishop and religious orders had aspirations to demonstrate their authority in the space they controlled in Toulouse, and employed sergeants whose power they aspired to equal their royal and municipal counterparts. We know that the bishop of Toulouse had access to patrols to oversee the land under his jurisdiction, because a witness in a manuscript from 1155, was identified as, "Petrus guard of the close of Saint Étienne."[30] Although the archives do not reveal the number of officers at the bishop's disposal in Toulouse, the archbishop of Lyon had at least a dozen sergeants working on his behalf in the fifteenth and sixteenth century.[31] The pope commanded about forty sergeants in Avignon around 1325, and these numbers continued to grow to beyond eighty sergeants after the reforms of Pope Benedict XII. Jacques Chiffoleau argues that these figures are more impressive then those of Paris in the same era, where the capital city had no more then 220 foot sergeants patrolling a population six to seven times larger than that of Avignon.[32] The pope's sergeants had the responsibilities to survey the city, to visit taverns, to regulate commerce and prostitution, and had to vow to follow certain standards of ethical conduct (for example, to not arrest innocent people for profit, or to keep confiscated illegal weapons). The bishop of Toulouse, however, had to negotiate with the king, not the pope, in order to secure powers for his officers.

---

29 Given, *Inquisition and Medieval Society*, 146–147.

30 BN, MS lat. 9189, fol. 221v, July 1155. Cited in Mundy's *Liberty and Political Power in Toulouse*, 346, no. 6.

31 Gonthier, *Délinquance, justice et société*, 40.

32 Chiffoleau, *Les Justices du Pape*, 66. Geremek, *Margins of Society*, 25.

As the population of clerks increased within Toulouse (or at least individuals claiming the privileges of clericature), the Episcopal office became preoccupied with the regulation of criminal clerks' behavior. Geremek remarks that many men in the underworld of Paris simply shaved their head or had a conspiring barber complete the deed in order to assume clerical status and the privileges that went along with it, and hide from secular law courts. Many of these false clergy betrayed their true identities when it became evident to investigators that the men could not supply their appropriate *letters de tonsure* or even read or chant – clear signs they were imposters.[33] But Nicole Gonthier has found just as many confirmed clerks committing a wide variety of crimes, such as adultery, rape, and homicide in medieval Lyon.[34] In Toulouse, though, if clergy were committing crimes, the bishop wanted to ensure that men representing his office arrested him, and brought him directly to his court.

As a result, the bishop quite eagerly sent sergeants out into the fray. In 1294, a royal ordinance commanded the bishop to stop circulating armed men throughout the city and surrounding diocese looking for these "criminal clerks."[35] In fact, the king suggested that the bishop make his inquiries into suspects and their locations without arms, and to call upon royal sergeants to make the arrests that could be dangerous. The proclamation stipulated that the bishop's men should avoid arresting clerks in "honorable houses" or lay homes. Instead, the seizure of the clerk must occur in a public place like the streets, city squares, or taverns.[36] The bishop, then, was continuously balancing the protection and privileges of the ecclesiastical office with his desire to exert his authority into the political realm of Toulouse. He asserted his right to be the sole authority to conduct trials for clerks. In a proclamation from 1283, the king granted the bishop permission to try clerks, especially those who have sinned and committed crimes in the city of Toulouse. But King Philip made a very clear statement that the church must announce, *in public*, the decisions and punishments rendered.[37] It seems as though the people needed to know that these criminal clerks were being held accountable for the chaos they brought to their city.

A final group of men walking through the streets of Toulouse, seizing suspicious citizens, or simply strutting their stuff in the local taverns, were

---

33 Geremek, *Margins of Society*, 135–147.

34 Gonthier, *Délinquance, justice et société*, 159–169.

35 AMT-AA 4:31, January 13, 1294.

36 This issue concerning where bishop's men could arrest criminal clerks is also addressed in the arrêts from the Parlement of Paris in 1277. AMT-AA 4:29.

37 ADHG-1 G 345.

the royal officers sent as professionally trained and commissioned sergeants, assigned to uphold and to enforce the interests of the king. In the fifteenth century, smaller towns like Lyon had anywhere between nineteen to twenty-eight royal sergeants, Dijon had about fifteen, and sixteen royal sergeants surveyed the *bailliage* of Arras, while twelve regulated the town's *bourg*.[38] By 1500, the royal provost of the Châtelet of Paris commanded a troop of 440 sergeants necessary to bring order to the streets of the royal capital, and it is reported that one hundred and fifty royal sergeants occupied Toulouse at the same date.[39] The royal administration hired many men from their respective communities to serve in this position, realizing the benefits of having officers with local knowledge, local relations and a grasp of the local language. But we have evidence that some of these officers were more concerned with finding opportunities for financial gain, rather than protecting the well-being of the people of any given region. This is perhaps best evidenced from King Louis IX's *enquête* into the behavior of his sergeants in the upland region of Ardennes in 1247.[40] Villagers complained bitterly to the *enquêters* about the sergeants' arbitrary seizure of property, and their imprisonment of men for their own profit. Part of the confusion in Ardennes was the sergeants' claim to two privileges: the "right of prise," which granted them the authority to acquire goods (like horses) needed for royal service, and the "right of distraint," which allowed them to take property from people who owed a debt to the crown. It is not surprising that the ambiguous nature of these rights could easily lead to corruption of the sergeants and the financial exploitation of the villagers. In Toulouse, royal officers found an opportunity for revenue through the arrest of citizens. If an individual was brought to a prison to await trial, the arresting officer received a commission from the fines acquired by the jail. Royal sergeants abused this system to such an extent that King Philip VI had to send a mandate in 1331 prohibiting the vicar's men from arresting defendants out on bail from the capitols' prison.[41] In addition, the royal officers could only be tried under the jurisdiction of the king's court, presided over by the vicar. The capitols, their own sergeants and night guards, had no means of holding these men accountable to any of the local laws or stipulations. The streets of Toulouse, then, were very

---

38 Gonthier, *Délinquance, justice et société*, 40.

39 Jean-Pierre Leguay, *La rue au Moyen âge* (Rennes: Ouest-France, 1984), 187. A. Vialia, *Le Parlement de Toulouse et l'administration royale laique (1420–1525)*, vol. 1, 175.

40 Robert Bartlett, "The Impact of Royal Government in the French Ardennes: the Evidence of the 1247 *enquête*," *Journal of Medieval History* 7 (1981), 83–96.

41 AMT-AA 35:10.

crowded with a variety of patrolling officers advancing different agendas and interests in their interaction with the urban inhabitants.

We should take note that none of these officers were immune to the resentment, and in some cases, retaliation of the public. They may have represented the various manifestations of municipal, ecclesiastical, and royal authority, but this did not mean that they earned the outright respect of the people they interacted with on a daily basis. In fact, most studies suggest that the public held policing officers in relatively low regard and outright disdain. Throughout France, most of the urban population loathed the night guards and sergeants because the officers used brutality and intimidation to secure order, and to attack the weak and innocent indiscriminately. There were several instances in Lyon when the people hurled insults and stones at the guards without provocation. A mob came after one unfortunate officer, Jean de Vienne, on two separate occasions in 1406. In the first instance, an angry crowd beat him brutally as he attempted to arrest a malefactor under orders from the municipal government; one perpetrator claimed he did not know that Jean de Vienne was a sergeant, but others conceded that the attack was a deliberate act of personal vengeance. A few months later, a group greeted the same Jean de Vienne with a chorus of barks as he left a tavern, clarifying that he was no better (to put it delicately) than "dog excrement."[42] Even in Paris, royal officers were vulnerable to the temperament of crowds, especially when delivering unpopular new policies.[43] In 1388, a group of valets came together to beat an officer who was trying to impose a royal tax on the sale of wine. The vast unpopularity of some of these royal officers drove the French monarchy to punish a chosen few through dramatic public executions in order to appease, what Claude Gauvard identifies as, public opinion. Beyond the actions of mobs, even singular women were not afraid to thwart sergeants' efforts to seize their husbands by refusing to open doors to their commands, or by shouting insults at the arresting officer in defiance.[44] From a literary perspective, famed criminal and poet François Villon mentions some of the most notorious sergeants of his time in his *Le Testament*, including officer Michault du Four who he bequeathed to the "Prince of

---

[42] Gonthier, *Delinquance, justice et société dans le lyonnais médiéval*, 262.

[43] Claude Gauvard, "Les officiers royaux et l'opinion politique en France à la fin de Moyen Âge," *Histoire comparée de l'Administration (IVe-XVIIIe siècles)* (Munich: Artemis, 1980), 583–593.

[44] Gonthier, *Delinquance, justice et société dans le lyonnais medieval*, 125.

Fools."[45] These policing officers secured privileges and safeguard by the nature of their profession and their affiliation with a particular administration, but it certainly did not make them immune to the ire of the public.

The Municipal Officers and Their Criminal Transgressions

Witnesses who testified in the trial that opened this chapter speculated that between three to seven thousand Toulousains gathered in front of the town hall the afternoon the mob murdered Michael, the vicar's messenger.[46] Sergeants, armed with weapons, stood outside of the building prepared to regulate the crowd's behavior, but in this instance, they did little to protect the messenger from his imminent death. The banker, Garnerius, testified in his defense that he played no role in the crowd's behavior that led to the death of the messenger. He explained that on the day in question, two of the capitols' messengers approached him in his neighborhood by the Garonne River, and ordered him to proceed to the town hall.[47] They proclaimed that a gross injustice had occurred against the city, and threatened that if he did not go immediately, he would be forced to pay a fine and betray his oath of loyalty to the capitols and the city of Toulouse. His presence at the town hall, thus, was not to cause trouble, but to avoid the repercussions of ignoring the capitols' order. In the end, however, only Garnerius stood accountable for the messenger's murder in the vicar's court. What we find in the criminal records of Toulouse is that the municipal officers greatly contributed to the criminal element and confusion of the city. Even though the capitols held these men accountable for the crimes they committed against the citizens of Toulouse, the elected officials also found opportunity to advance their own political agendas using their sergeants' physically authoritative presence in the districts they regulated.

One of the most common ways in which many officers exploited their position's power was by soliciting bribes from the people they

---

45 François Villon, *The Legacy and The Testament*, trans. Louis Simpson (Ashland, Oregon: Story Line Press, 2000), 91.

46 Berger, *Trésor des chartes*, 322.

47 Berger, *Trésor des chartes*, 321, The document lists the neighborhood as *Badaculo*, which is a location by today's Place Saint Pierre. *DRT*, vol. 1, 124–127. This street is quite a distance from the centrally located town hall.

encountered. This corruption only added to the public's confusion surrounding legitimate authority, and led to the people's general mistrust of the motives and actions of the officers. One of the most extensive criminal cases from Toulouse involved a municipal sergeant Arnaldus Franciscus. The length of his trial, the number of witnesses, and amount of testimony rivals that of any case from city in the fourteenth century. In June of 1332, a woman being tried for prostitution made explicit charges against Arnaldus Franciscus. She claimed that she first met him in the nearby city of Moissac. As a municipal officer, he knew that the capitols had banned her from Toulouse for various thefts, but he also knew that she was very wealthy. He approached her, and assured her that through the power of his office, he would be able to have the punishment of exile eradicated.[48] She believed his promises, and agreed to move into his home in Toulouse within a few days. Johaneta soon discovered that Arnaldus had no intention of using his political connections with the capitols to exonerate her, even though he comforted her, saying, "I promise you and assure you; do not doubt that I am doing everything to ensure you will be free from this banishment."[49] Instead, Arnaldus assumed the role of the stereotypical medieval pimp.[50] Her possessions began to disappear after she came to Toulouse, at times redistributed to Arnaldus' wife and daughter. When he had swindled all her money and goods, he arranged for "many clerks and men" to "know her carnally" in his home and other locations of the city.[51] After Arnaldus grew tired of this arrangement, he sold Johaneta to a pimp (*leno*) for four *sol tol*, where she stayed for three or four weeks before being arrested by some other municipal sergeants for prostitution. From a chronological perspective, Johaneta's crime may have come from the fact that she was working in an unauthorized brothel, because the city had houses of prostitution operating openly by the end of the thirteenth century.[52] However, the municipal brothel and designated red-light district of Toulouse only seems to become manifest by the later part of the fourteenth century, so Johaneta may have been caught in the middle of the community's efforts to deliberate and to define where prostitution best fit into the city space.

---

48 AMT-FF 57, 161.

49 Ibid., 161–162. "Ego promitari tibi et asseturo te pro non oportet te dubitare quia ego faciam tantum pro tu eris inmunis et evades ab illa relegationem."

50 Geremek, *The Margins of Society*, 229–230.

51 AMT-FF 57, 156.

52 Otis, *Prostitution in Medieval Society*, 28. The first mention of a brothel comes from the commentary of the city's *coutumes* in 1296.

During the capitols' inquest into Johaneta de Santlo's complaints, ten other Toulousains stepped forward to assert that Arnaldus Franciscus released several violent criminals from his custody in exchange for money. In the words of the notary, he "completely trampled down and cheated the law," and prohibited other officials from seeking and achieving justice in Toulouse.[53] His case reinforces the notion that the officers had a lot of autonomy and discretion when interacting with the people of Toulouse, and could use their rank and position with the capitols to satisfy a desire to make more money than he earned from the city. In general, medieval sergeants did not receive a large salary, if any salary at all. Most officers only earned an income from the fees they could extract from their various policing duties. But in Lyon the sergeant received the equivalent of one *sou* (or a penny) each day.[54] The first to offer testimony against Arnaldus was Johannes Datier who had been accused of killing a lord, Petrus de Lauro, who served as a rector from the Church of Nativity. In this particular case, the capitols sent Arnaldus Franciscus to a church where the defendant was hiding, and theoretically protected from municipal authority through the rights of asylum. Johannes Datier testified that after Arnaldus entered the church, violated this ecclesiastical privilege, and the sergeant proposed he would let him go if he was paid a large sum of money.[55] In another instance, Arnaldus Mitanerii, of the neighborhood of Comitali, struck his neighbor, Guillelmus Portelli, while he was waving around illegal arms. Arnaldus Franciscus witnessed the incident, and allowed Arnaldus Mitanerii to go unpunished in exchange for a bribe.[56] He extorted money from another unnamed criminal, advising him that he would not be denounced to the capitols, even though the man attacked a fellow sergeant named Ranýarc.[57] He arrested Jacobus Boerii and his brother of Bastita, Johannes Senherii, both accused of several night time thefts, but told them he would not take them to the town hall if they gave him money.[58] A final allegation concerned Guillemus Macellarii and Guillerinus de Valle, both fugitives wanted for various crimes. Not only did Arnaldus Franciscus take money from them, but he also welcomed them

---

53 AMT-FF 57, 157. "totaliter occulcando et defraudando."

54 Gonthier, *Cris de Haine*, 156.

55 AMT-FF 57, 156–157.

56 Ibid., 176.

57 Ibid.: "[Arnaldus Franciscus] recepit pecuniam a quodam homine vocato [BLANK] ad hoc ut non revelaret nec denunciaret ad domino de capitolo."

58 Ibid., 176–177.

into his home frequently, "allowing them freedom and comfort."[59] This is reminiscent of the sergeant at Sucy-en-Brie, as mentioned in the records of the Parlement of Paris, who would not reveal local thieves to the authorities because they were his drinking companions.[60] From these numerous accounts, Arnaldus Franciscus abused his position of authority in a variety of ways, and betrayed the confidence of the capitols that retained him, and the citizens he was meant to protect. He utilized the liberties of his office (the power of seizure) in order to intimidate offenders for money, and expressed nothing but disregard for the sanctity of asylum or the capitols. In his corruption, he left the public vulnerable to the violent criminals still at large.

Beyond financial exploitation of the public, other municipal officers resorted to brute force and intimidation in order to satisfy their desire for power or enhanced masculine status among their neighbors. As was previously mentioned, the night guards and sergeants wore weapons and could do just about anything in the name of the capitols, and the documents betray a sense that the officers directed much of this hostility towards women and the weak. In Avignon, the papal sergeants exerted this kind of violence in the fourteenth century: in 1367, a sergeant beat a pregnant woman so rigorously that she lost her child, and in 1363, a group of sergeants struck a peaceful notary as he simply headed home one winter night.[61] Although the papacy tried to regulate their behavior both in the city and in the surrounding countryside, these acts of menace suggest one of the solutions that the sergeants offered to the fact that they were outnumbered by the rest of the population, namely to establish order through violent intimidation. But this assessment seems dissatisfying when discussing the policing officers' cruel behavior towards women. In many medieval cities, women were perceived as an extension of their male protectors: namely, fathers or husbands. If a man committed violence against a woman, it showed his prowess and dominance over other men, and only further demonstrated the vulnerability of women in the city.[62] The physical affront against a female, then, was another way in which the sergeant could perform his power and authority over the urban public. Raymundus Bernardus, a night guard from Toulouse's *capitolat* of Saint-Pierre, hit and

---

59 Ibid., 177.
60 Dean, *Crime in Medieval Europe*, 37–38.
61 Chiffoleau, *Les Justices du Pape*, 66.
62 See Jacques Rossiaud, *Medieval Prostitution*, trans. by Lydia G. Cochrane (New York: Blackwell, 1988), 1–30. Prevenier, "Violence against Women in a Medieval Metropolis," 263–284.

wounded Vincetii de Alta Fulha with his sword. He then turned his attention to Vincetii's concubine. The night guard wielded a large staff (*magna barra*) and struck the concubine, named Mondina, in the head so savagely that the notary recorded there was an "outpouring of blood."[63] He continued to hit her with the staff in various other parts of the body. In other words, she received most of the abuse. When municipal sergeant Arnaldus Franciscus faced charges for selling Johaneta into prostitution, his defense provides interesting details which further illuminate the interaction between the night guards and women. Arndaldus Franciscus claimed that he frequented a tavern near the gate of Badacley, and on several occasions he witnessed Johaneta de Santolo (the woman he allegedly sold to a pimp) drinking and socializing in the same establishment, sometimes with a female friend called Doneta.[64] One evening, a night guard named Petrus Aýmerici, from the *capitolat* of Saint Pierre, punched Johaneta in the face, and forced her out of the bar and into the street. When Arnaldus Franciscus came upon her, she was greatly shaken up and blinded by the blood flowing in her eyes. At that moment, Arnaldus testified, he noticed two night guards lurking around the corner of the tavern with apparently bad intentions. Arnaldus decided to "protect" Johaneta de Santolo by taking her home with him. In both of these instances, it becomes clear that women outside of the traditional family structure were particularly vulnerable to assault by the night guards who, perhaps, viewed them as easy targets to assert their masculine prowess.

Of course, beyond theorizing about officer's violent actions against women, we could just accept the explanation that some cases are based on sheer lust and brutality. A former officer of Bourges, Jean Brunet, confessed to several atrocious crimes of corruption in 1334, including the rape of a servant girl, the abduction of another man's wife, the torture of a pregnant woman that resulted in the death of the fetus and a stillbirth, the beating of another pregnant woman that led to a miscarriage, and the seduction of a young wife with promises that he would release her husband from custody.[65] The archives of Toulouse contain one additional example of how the municipal officers abused the power of their office in order to satisfy their own criminal desires against women. In 1392, a young

63 AMT-FF 57, 223. "et vulneranit Mondinam concubinam dicti Vincetii in capite usque ad sanguinis effusionem."

64 Ibid., 158. Badacley is the ancient name for the territory of today's Bazacle, situated by the Garonne River.

65 Douët-D'Arq, "Lettres de remission pour Jean Brunet, prévot de Bourges, 1334," *Bibliothèque de l'Ecole des chartes* (1856), tome 17, 54–75.

girl named Guiraude approached the house of Petrus Johannes, a carpenter who lived in the neighborhood of Roaix.[66] After Petrus opened the door to her knocks, she begged Petrus, "for the love of God receive me for this night and day," because she was being pursued by officers and fearing for her own safety. The carpenter, who was in the middle of dinner with his wife, Bonne, and eighteen-year-old son, Arnaud Jean, allowed the girl to enter the house. When the family was getting ready to go to bed, several noisy municipal officers, carrying an excessive number of weapons, stood outside the house and demanded that the young girl come out. Petrus Johannes, suspicious of their motives and menacing weapons, refused to let them take the young girl away without proper documentation of their authority. The documents do not reveal how the officers knew that Guiraude was hiding in the carpenter's home, or why they were pursuing her in the first place. But it is clear that a citizen such as Petrus Johannes had reason to question the intention behind their demands, and require some validation from the administration which supported their claims for seizure.

The officers sent some of their servants to seek jurisdictional support or a letter which proved that they had the authority to arrest Guiraude. But the remaining officers grew impatient, and broke through the door of the home and grabbed the young girl, dragging her outside as she screamed, "Death! Death! Rape! Rape!" They then took turns raping her against the outside wall of the home, causing a commotion which left Petrus Johannes and his family cowering indoors. This whole case survives in the municipal archives today because the men were charged with possessing illegal weapons during this patrol. In other words, royal and municipal authorities vied for jurisdiction to convict the officers, but ignored the accusations of the assault and the rape of this young woman. This case effectively demonstrates that in the fourteenth century, the citizens of Toulouse had reason to be frequently suspicious of a congregation of armed men, even if they claimed to be officers of the law. Petrus demanded some form of legitimate documentation before he surrendered the young girl. The officers could not offer any real explanation as to why she had to be taken into custody, such as the offense she had committed. Instead, it appears their only intentions were to mistreat Guiraude.

There was certainly a potential criminal element to this class of policing officers, as they had weapons and authority to advance their personal agendas and to supplement their humble income. By the 1430s, former

---

66 AMT-FF 61, 1394. It is also found AMT-AA 6:193.

and current sergeants were members of an organized crime gang in Provence.[67] But Toulouse also possesses peculiar instances in which the municipal guards commanded and recruited citizens, through the power of their office as sanctioned by the capitols, to engage in activities which could be perceived as illicit. Again, we return to the case of Garnerius, who claimed to be only guilty of responding to an order of the capitols as transmitted to him by messengers. In the following example, which at first glance appears to be simple neighborhood dispute in a district north of the town hall, a much more complicated interaction between the citizens and night guards emerges. In September of 1332, the criminal notary recorded the accusations against several weavers who lived in a small region off of today's Place Saint Georges, a thriving commercial district in the fourteenth century with a market dating back to the city's origins. The weavers, named Guillemus Bertrandus, Raymundus Aýmes, Jacobus Calveti, Johannes Ranini, and other "accomplices," were charged with conspiring against and attacking a father and son, Petrus and Bernardus Mercares.[68] The father and son lived in the neighborhood of Penitentie, or more specifically, a small side road call Pascalis.[69] This street is directly north of the town hall and main square of the city. It is a short distance, probably a five minute walk from the Place Saint George where the defendants lived. On the night in question, the named defendants gathered with four night guards from the *capitolat* of Saint Rome, identified as Petrus Rimis, Johannes Malquestre, Jordanus Barreris, and Stephanus Roderii. Everyone, including the night guards, was armed with prohibited swords and some sort of metal rods. After a bit of discussion, the group headed towards the house of Petrus and Bernardus Mercare, recruiting other unnamed "enemies and ill-wishers" as they headed down the street.[70] The father and son, in their house with friends and family "sleeping and resting in their beds, in peace and quiet, believing they were in a completely safe place," awoke to their door broken open by the accused,

---

67 Dean, *Crime in Medieval Europe*, 37.

68 It is possible that Petrus and his son were merchants of some sort, considering their last name has a close resemblance to the root "mercator." Petrus is also listed as "Petrus Mercares alias dictus Bequas," which could suggest that he was identified by both his profession and place of origin.

69 AMT-FF 57, 203: The victims are said to, "morantur in barrio penitentie videlicet in carreria Pascalis." Pascalis has also been identified as d'Agulherès, which is a part of today's La rue Lafayette. *DRT*, vol. 1, 27.

70 Ibid., 203. The other unnamed members of the gang were identified as "inimicos et malivolos."

and were soon driven out into the street.[71] The men then attacked the father and son with their weapons, administering blows to various parts of their bodies, leaving wounds to their heads, arms and legs. In this accusation, the night guards played a small role in the overall chaos, whereas the named weavers were held accountable in the capitols' court for the crime because of their initial threats and conspiracy against the father and son.

The night guards did not offer any testimony nor were they formally indicted for this attack before the capitols and their court. But the weavers recounted a defense very similar to that of our banker Garnerius. Guillelmus Bertrandus, the first to appear in court, argued that in the preceding weeks, several unidentified armed men had threatened one of his friends on three or four occasions. On a chance encounter, he reported this to a night guard, Petrus Rimis. On the night of the attack, Guillelmus Bertrandus swore, Petrus Rimis, Jordanus Barreris and other night guards sought him out in his neighborhood and said they were prepared to find the men, and get revenge.[72] A short while later the guards were joined by several other men, including Jacobus Calveti and Raymundus Aýmes. One carried an illuminated lantern as they headed off for the neighborhood of Penitentie, passing through the neighborhood of Pascalis. When they did not discover anyone, they group went to the house of Franciscus de Gaure, capitol of the district of Saint Rome.[73] This detail is important because it points to a hierarchy of authority, stemming from the capitol to the guard, and then transmitted to the citizens, who were for all intents and purposes, minding their own business when they were recruited into action. According to Guillelmus Bertrandus' testimony, one of the night guards knocked on the capitol's door and spoke for several minutes in the doorway of the house with two of the servants of the house.

When the guard returned to the group, they set off a second time to the top of the street, Pascalis. At first, some of the men advanced a short distance into the neighborhood, until two or three of them passed before the house of Petrus Mercere. Inside the house, several women sensed the imminent danger and began to scream. At that moment, Guillelmus recounted, four or six men poured out of the house brandishing swords and spears, running towards the defendant, the night guards, and other men waiting at the top of the neighborhood. The night guards captured a

[71] Ibid.: "dicta nocte recolligerant et etiam dormientes et requiestentes in eorum lectis pacifice et quiete credentes esse in loco tutissimo."

[72] Ibid., 205.

[73] Lafaille, *Annales de Toulouse*, 69.

chaplain who had run out of the home, confiscating his sword, while some other guards fled. For a while, the fighting and shouts of "to the death, to the death" resounded through the night air.[74] Guillelmus Bertrandus' perspective provides us with several important components of this case. It suggests that the guards were eager to get involved in the fight without any proof of a crime, and were willing to fight anyone, although they tried to present it as though they were attacked by surprise by the father and son. But it also reveals the role of the capitol, namely Franciscus de Gaure, who seemingly sanctioned the night guards' activity in the area. The capitols played some part in the actions of their officers, even though they may claim not to be accountable when these events turn criminal.

Apparently, Guillelmus Bertrandus willingly participated in the street fight with the night guards. In the testimony of two other defendants, Raymundus Aýmes and Jacobus Calveti, both argued that they happened upon the fight by accident, and only joined in the brawl because the night guards commanded it. Raymundus Aýmes said that it was just one night, as he passed through the town towards the area of Pascalis, that he heard a big commotion and saw men hitting Petrus de Rimis, Malquestre and other night guards who he did not know. As soon as the night guards became aware of his presence, they turned to him and "ordered him on behalf of the capitols of Toulouse to help them willingly."[75] The attackers, he recalled, were Petrus Mercere and his son Bernardus. He also testified that it was only the night guards who were carrying weapons, not the other defendants, such as Guillelmus Bertrandus, Jacobus Calveti and Johannes de Pinolibus.[76] Jacobus Calveti testified to a very similar story, namely, that the night guards compelled him to assist on behalf of the capitols.[77]

This case leads us back to one of the opening questions of this chapter: what were the responsibilities of the citizens to their municipal authority in the maintenance of civic order? How did they know whether or not their government would protect them? Or prosecute them for their involvement in these disputes, even if the night guard ordered them to comply? As elected officials, the capitols had an obligation to maintain law and order through their creation of municipal statutes, and through the criminal process of trials. A portion of their authority was certainly the

---

74 AMT-FF 57, 206: "Moriantur moriantur amlor amlor."

75 Ibid., 207: "Quidem custodes mandaverunt sibi ex parte dominorum de capitolo tholose pro iuvaret ipsos qui dixit pro libenter."

76 Ibid., 207.

77 Ibid., 233.

privilege, as granted by the king, to employ their own sergeants and officers to regulate the behavior of the citizens of Toulouse through their weapons, and ability to arrest suspected offenders. The men who held this office possessed a great deal of responsibility, as they received their authority from the capitols, and walked the streets as representatives of the city's political system. The relative autonomy of their office, however, provided the opportunity for corruption and their unnecessary involvement in the criminal activity and neighborly grudges which unfolded in the streets of Toulouse. The capitols found it increasingly difficult to monitor the behavior of their officers, especially the night guards who found many prospects to add to the chaos of the city. But the capitols could also find opportunity in these officers and their willingness to use their force and established position as intimidator in their neighborhoods to advance the broader agendas of the municipal government, especially in their competition with the royal sergeants who tried to advance the power of the king in Toulouse. As shall become evident in the next section, the capitols needed these officers to assist them when they directly challenged and disputed the royal vicar and the royal representatives in the city.

A Town and Gown Conflict, 1336

Again, the citizens of Toulouse killed the ill-fated messenger, Michael, who was under jurisdictional protection of the throne. Even though he had struck a citizen of Toulouse while in the presence of the capitols and their officers, he could only be tried for this offense in the vicar's court. This legal privilege no doubt infuriated the people and officials of Toulouse, who aspired to see the messenger pay for his crime. Similarly, university scholars shared this somewhat tenuous existence in their host city of Toulouse. On the one hand, the king's mandate of clerical privilege exempted them from municipal jurisdiction, and forbade the local inhabitants to harm them in any way. On the other hand, the students and masters became easy targets for the aggression of the Toulousains who resented royal authority and its representatives, and many inhabitants challenged this protected status. This final section will examine such a situation from August of 1336, in which the royal seneschal heard a case concerning several municipal night guards and high ranking officers, including a capitol.[78] The accuser was a university student, named Michael

[78] AMT-FF 60. This manuscript is in Latin, with 55 pages of parchment, numbered in a modern hand, and is in rather worn condition. The first several pages are particularly

Lemosini, who claimed the men formed an illicit congregation, carried illegal arms (identified in the testimony as various types of swords and rods), and deliberately "broke and violated the royal safe guard" by physically attacking him.[79] Why were multiple high ranking citizens of Toulouse willing to face the dire consequences of assaulting a royally protected individual, in this case, a university student? Either they did not care about the royal repercussions, or identities within the social hierarchy were still so blurred that status (protected or otherwise) was indistinguishable.

Before we turn to the events of 1336, it might be helpful to consider some of the common characteristics of town and gown rows in the same era, in order to gain a greater perspective of the environment simmering in Toulouse. Although each conflict had its own particular impetus, there are some overlapping factors at play. Alcohol, for example, seemed to be a bigger instigator in the violence between scholars and townsmen, then in the fights between just citizens. And when drunken brawls erupted in town and gown rows, the ramifications were felt for days. We have already discussed the events in Paris in 1228–1229, which led to the flight of scholars to places like Toulouse. In Oxford in 1354, during an event known now as the "Fray on Saint Scholastica's Day," students and townsmen argued in a tavern, over a cause that none of the sources reveal. Regardless, the townsmen were angered to such an extent that they returned with full ammunition the next day, destroyed university property and buildings, and killed several students and masters.[80] Not surprisingly, women were frequently the cause of a fight, and help elucidate the masculine competition between scholar and townsmen. In the patriarchal urban hierarchy, local women were meant to be under municipal male control, and theoretically, students were meant to respect the celibacy of their position as clerks. As such, university administrators frequently warned students to avoid contact with the townswomen at all costs, citing not only martial entrapment,

---

tattered, missing the right hand corner of the first three sheets. This case has largely been ignored by historians. It is mentioned in René Gadave, *Les documents sur l'histoire de l'université de Toulouse et spécialement de sa faculté de droit civil et canonique (1229–1789)* (Toulouse: Imprimerie et Librarie Édouard Privat, 1910), 92, no. 83. Gadave, and subsequently Cyril Smith's *A History of the University of Toulouse* (1958), both situate the register in Toulouse's municipal archives, but designated as document FF 102. Smith did not offer any details or analysis of the case in his book. Apparently, when the archives updated their catalogues, the archivist mistook the register as part of the Aimery Berenger affair of 1332. Today it is listed simply as "la même affaire" of the preceding FF 57, FF 58, and FF 59, which is probably why no one has bothered to examine it in any detail over the years.

79 AMT-FF 60, 1: "et frangendo et violando salvam gardiam regiam."

80 J. E. Thorold Rogers, ed. *Oxford City Documents, 1268–1665* (Oxford: Clarendon Press, 1891), 248–268.

but the hostility of the urban man.[81] But in Orléans, 1387, a law student named Guillaume Entrant felt the impact of overstepping these sexual boundaries when he was attacked brutally by two thugs, who had been hired by the husband of the student's mistress.[82] When Jean Rion, the husband, was charged with the crime of commissioning the beating, and he had to apologize publicly to the students and the university, the entire town revolted. Citizens looted student housing, shouting "*moriantur scholares*," and drove the student population to a mass exodus out of the city of Orléans. Presumably, the townspeople could understand the reaction of the Jean Rion, who needed to restore his public honor by seeking vengeance against the foreign man who had penetrated not only his community, but his wife as well. Still other town and gown rows were prompted over property disputes, the most renown being the Parisian university's dispute with the monastery of Saint Germain. By 1278, most of the students lived in the *quartier latin*, which was surrounded by several monasteries. On the outskirts of the city walls was an open meadow that the monks of Saint Germain believed to be theirs through ancient property right. When the university formed as a corporation, its faculty claimed the land as its own, compelling the monks to launch organized attacks against the scholars who played games on the property, driving the students back to the protected walls of the university.[83] At the end of these disputes, when immediate physical reactions had calmed down, royal jurisdiction traditionally favored the university student and reaffirmed the scholar's privileges and legal protection. The public atonement of Jean Rion, mentioned above, is not an uncommon resolution for these town and gown cases. In Paris in 1304, a provost who had wrongfully hanged a student was ordered by the king to cut down the corpse, which had been hanging for some months, and kiss it, while all of the clergy of Paris marched to the provost's house to throw stones at the building, and to utter a solemn exorcism.[84] All of these examples reveal a sense of spontaneous violence, stemming from the difficult assimilation of foreign scholars into the urban realm.

---

[81] See, for example, the many anecdotes of *The Manuale Scholarium: An Original Account of Life in the Mediaeval University*, trans. Robert Francis Seybolt (Cambridge: Harvard University Press, 1921), 88–97. This anonymous student handbook includes mock dialogues between students warning each other against the foul intentions of the urban female.

[82] Fournier, *Les Statuts*, vol. I, nos. 211–212, 155–158.

[83] *Chartularium universitas Parisiensis*, vol. I, no. 480, 564, no. 482, 567–568, no. 484, 569–570, no. 524, 635–636..

[84] *Chartularium universitatis parisiensis*, vol. II, no. 650, 116.

What happened in Toulouse between townsmen, municipal officers and a university student falls a bit outside of these generalizations, and has a few more layers of nuances that we may unpack. Several significant events took place in Toulouse during the year 1336. Perhaps most significantly, the king reduced the number of capitols elected in the *Bourg* from six to four men, realigning the division of *capitolats* as punishment for the death sentence of a university students' squire (which will be discussed extensively in Chapter 5). But political changes were not the only memorable occurrences that year. According to chronicler Guillelmus Bardinus, in April, a comet unlike any other seen in Toulouse's memory crossed the sky.[85] Witnesses described it as full as a moon, but red as blood, and on that first night it appeared, a great wind and rain blew through the city streets. An earthquake accompanied the storm, a seismic disaster which opened the earth and engulfed fourteen houses, including the home of the capitol Petrus de Gamevilla.[86] The citizens of Toulouse viewed this natural calamity as a sign of the coming of Judgment Day. Many abandoned all civic responsibilities for refuge in their churches, praying for salvation during the thirty-six nights the comet frequented their sky. To make matters worse, in autumn, a great plague infiltrated the town, killing more than a thousand members of the population, regardless of sex and age. The symptoms started with a light fever, escalating to continuous hemorrhaging and vomiting, killing its victim within three days. That same year an outbreak of fighting commenced between the French and English in the Hundred Years War around Toulouse, threatening the city as the conflict drew closer.[87] As disease and the weather disrupted the daily lives and faith of the people, from a larger perspective, war marked the implications that accompanied being royal subjects: Toulouse was now an opportune, and vulnerable, military target for the English who occupied nearby Guyenne. The treaty agreements from the Albigensian Crusade stipulated that Toulouse tear down its defensive walls. It was only as late as 1350 that the king allowed the capitols to rebuild the walls, due to the increasing threat of the English position.

The combination of the king's weakening the traditional political structure of the city and the natural disasters perhaps left several municipal

[85] *HGL*, X, no. 1, col. 36–37. Lafaille, *Annales de Toulouse*, 80–81. Bardin attributes the date to 1329, but Lafaille dates it 1336.

[86] Bardin, "terra concuss tremuit, et quatuordecim hospitia hiatus terrae absumpta sunt et absorta, inter quae corruit medietas domus a parte carreriae Petris de Gamevilla, domicelli et capitolis Tholosae hujus anni."

[87] Wolff, *Histoire de Toulouse*, 183–191.

officers with a feeling of resentment and helplessness. In order to reclaim their power and status, they redirected their aggression towards university scholars, a symbol of royal authority who lived in their midst. Like Garnerius' trial which opened this chapter, the initial accusation and the defendants' explanations of the case are contradictory. So in an effort to simplify the details, I will begin with the basic allegations brought by the scholar Michael Lemosini to the seneschal, and then unpack the witness testimony, in order to present, what I contend is the real motivation for the attack. Throughout the extensive trial transcripts, interrogation of the defendants, and wrangling of lawyers, the whole case pulls together the first two sections of this chapter. In one respect, we see that there are many levels of complicated relationships and interactions played out in the city streets which led to violence and conflict, intensified by mistaken identities and misunderstood intentions of the defendants established in the trial records. Secondly, the municipal officers only added to this mayhem when they plotted to advance their own self-serving agendas and blurring the lines of authority, rather than simply fulfilling the duties of their office and upholding the law. In this town and gown row from 1336, the municipal officers had a premeditated desire to seek revenge against the royally protected clerical population of Toulouse, and the capitol of their district actively participated in the plot.

The official notary recorded the charges as follows: on July 25, as the town bells rang in the night sky, the defendants gathered at a field situated in front of the city's basilica, Saint Sernin.[88] The men were identified in the document as capitol Petrus Maurandi of the district of Saint Sernin, Master Bernardus Bretz, a notary, Master Guillelmus Serra, Johannes de Turre, Stephanus de Castro Novo, Johannes Belengarii, Vitalis de Castaneto, Ramundus Benedicti, Arnaldus Costa, and Hugo Fortis, a local grocer. All lived in the neighborhoods surrounding the basilica. On the night in question, the ten men brought various weapons from their respective homes to the meeting, and decided to form an impromptu surveillance of the surrounding neighborhoods. Since the thirteenth century, the majority of university students lived in this area of the *Bourg*, which the king had also just rezoned so that two fewer men would serve as capitols. After a while, the armed patrol approached a house and forced themselves into the

[88] AMT-FF 60, 20. For a discussion of concepts of time in a medieval city, see Jacques Le Goff, "La ville médiévale et le temps," *Villes, bonnes villes, cités et capitales: Études d'histoire urbaine (XIIe-XVIIIe siècle) offertes à Bernard Chevalier*, ed. Monique Bourin (Caen Paradigme, 1993), 325–332.

premises where a party of some sort was taking place. The men seized Michael Lemosini, a student at the university, and as they were leaving the house, they wounded the host in a scuffle. The group then paraded the scholar around the city. First, they marched him towards the town hall, and then eventually made it to the home of capitol Petrus Berenger, who lived in and represented the nearby *capitolat* of Saint Julian.[89] The patrol called through the door to the capitol seeking either advice or adulation (the sources are unclear), but they were greeted by a servant who instructed them to release the scholar and disband their revelry. According to the opening statement, then, the night patrol deliberately ignored the royal mandate which prohibited municipal officers from arresting scholars, from entering the private premises of a clerk, and certainly added insult to injury by creating a spectacle of his seizure in the city streets. Only capitol Petrus Berenger managed to retain a distance from the indiscretion of the officers of Saint Sernin by refusing to sanction the arrest.

Initially, the defendants employed a variety of means to evade all summons to appear before the royal seneschal's court. The capitol, Petrus Maurandi, sent in his brother, Mancipius Maurandi, a soldier, to offer his excuses, saying he would be out of town on the designated day of his hearing. Johannes de Turre pleaded illness for his absence, and Bernarda, wife of Ramundus Benedicti, informed the court that her husband would also be out of town and not able to appear when the court required them to be present.[90] During these delays, the accused men of Toulouse certainly made an effort to secure a proper defense, to recruit a competent lawyer, or even to search for an alibi. The possibility also exists that the men took this time to coordinate their testimony, creating a unified front against the royal representative overseeing the inquest. Regardless, the royal official in charge of the proceedings, named Guillermo Barte, did not interrogate a witness until three months later, in mid-October. Capitol Petrus Maurandi and Johannes Belengarii were the first to appear on the same day with counsel, and as the men slowly trickled into the court, offering their memories of that night, striking similarities emerged. In fact, this case provides rare insight to the patrol paths taken by night guards, the varying perceptions of the roles and civic responsibilities of municipal officials, and the liminal position the guards held between chaos and order.

---

89 Lafaille, *Annales*, 80.

90 AMT-FF 60, 8.

According to the corroborated defense testimony, after the men procured various arms from their own houses, they met in front of capitol Petrus Maurandi's home. Hugo Fortis, a grocer who had joined the patrol that evening, claimed he was carrying his sword under his clothes. The defendants left the home of the capitol in order to fulfill the night patrol of the *capitolat* of Saint Sernin, as led that night by the elected official of the neighborhood. By the very virtue of their cooperation with the capitol, they too were now officials of the city. The testimony is very explicit in outlining the route taken by the men that night, and it is one of the few occasions that the archival documents walk the reader through the city space and its neighborhoods in such detail. The armed men circled around the immediate vicinity of Saint Sernin and its back neighborhoods, passing in front of the house of Ramundus de Aurinalle, which must have been a recognizable landmark, then stood around for a pause listening and trying to hear if anyone approached. They went back to Saint Sernin next to the church of Saint Raymond, and decided to march in a different portion of the city, this time moving beyond the jurisdiction of their *capitolat*, and into that of Saint Julian's.

This diversion into another district of the city is significant in that it points to the spontaneous nature of these patrols. At any given moment municipal officers could decide to abandon their posts and obligations to their neighbors and pursue their own interests. They began by passing through the neighborhood of Lansinorium (today's rue des Peyrou), and then made a brief descent towards the Garonne River. After a short distance, they turned right and marched through the neighborhood of Fulhanium (today's Puit Creuses), where they ended up at the parish church of Saint Julian. The armed men cut through a field to the gate of Arnaud Bernard, where they made an abrupt turn to cut through the street of Putheum Pelherioii (today's rue des Trois Pillers), returning towards Saint Sernin. It was in this neighborhood that the men claimed to have heard a ruckus emanating from a house.

In order to fulfill their duty as the regulators of civic peace (as they claimed in their defense testimony), the men decided to investigate the commotion. At that moment, a man ran out of the house with a large staff (*barria*), and headed towards them. Even though the officers were fully armed, they feared for their safety and that more malefactors were going to join this man. This is the reason Hugo Fortis grabbed the suspicious figure, and placed him under arrest. All of the night guards and their accomplices argued that they did not enter the house and that the man they took into custody, later identified as Michael Lemosini, did not identify himself as a clerk at the time, nor was he wearing recognizable academic dress.[91] When asked if they hit him on the head with the staff before arresting him, they said no.[92] Time and again the defendants stated that Michael Lemosini was carrying illegal arms and that they had every right to arrest him.[93] They also claimed that they escorted their prisoner to the house of Petrus Berenger, capitol of Saint Julian, at Lemosini's request to speak to another capitol, and not as a means to punish him by parading him throughout the streets of the city.

Most of the municipal officers charged with this crime were well versed in the rhetoric of defense strategies. They had structured their testimony to reveal that they were threatened by Michael Lemosini, who had been brandishing a weapon. His clerical status had been an unfortunate oversight while they were fulfilling the duties of their office and removing a danger from the streets. They vowed to keep the population of Toulouse safe, and anyone bearing illegal arms should be arrested and taken off of the streets. But testimony from one of the defendants, named Master Guillelmus Serras, provided a different angle to this story, and a very significant motivation for this particular night time patrol. And this needs to be emphasized. Earlier that month, Serras gathered with his fellow defendants (including capitol Petrus Berenger and three of the night guards who had been patrolling the area) in front of the home of capitol Petrus Maurandi.[94] In the course of the conversation, one of the guards revealed that two or three of their associates had been killed. When capitol Petrus Berenger asked them who did it, they responded that although they did not know names, they knew the murderer was a clerk. Guillelmus Serras then testified in the courtroom that the capitol Petrus Berenger encouraged them to patrol well, and if they caught someone, to put him in the

91 At this time in Toulouse the student would have been wearing a long, black robe as a distinctive clerical dress. Hilde de Ridder-Symoens, "Rich Men, Poor Men: Social Stratification and Social Representation at the University (13th-16th Centuries)," *Showing Status: Representations of Social Positions in the Late Middle Ages*, ed. by Wim Blockmans and Antheun Janse (Turnhout, Belgium: Brepols, 1999), 169.

92 AMT-FF 60, 16.

93 Ibid., 44–45.

94 Ibid., 17: "Et postmodum vidit ut dixit pro venerunt ibi tres custodes nocturni videlicet Hugo Fortis, Johannes Berengarii, et Arnaldus Costa muniti de ensibus et post dixit eidem qualiter erant ita parti et ipsi custodes dixerunt quia in nocte proxime homo occiderat duos ut tres socios suos et tunc dictus Dominus Petrus dixit eis quis hoc fecerat et ipsi tunc responderunt per clerici et deinde interroganit eis si sciebant qui erant nec quo modo vocabantur et ipso dixerunt quod non. Dominus Petrus dixit ipsis custodibus pro irent se bene munitum et si reperiebant aliquem ponerent in domo communi." This murder does not appear in any of the extant criminal records in the archives of Toulouse.

town hall's jail. With this insight provided by Serras, we gain a better sense as to why the night guards conducted their patrol outside of their district, and into one heavily populated with university students: they aspired to encounter a clerk so they could satisfy their own need for revenge. If it was true that a clerk murdered the night guards' companions, and clerical status was identifiable by sight, it greatly weakens the defendants' argument that they did not know that Michael Lemosini was royally protected.

These municipal officers dared to challenge royal authority by singling out a man who symbolized the king's power in order to avenge the death of their friends and neighbors. The men made a performance of their patrol, and walked a path through the neighborhoods of students. They had various types of arms with which to intimidate the scholars, and bided their time to choose their victim. Once they captured Michael Lemosini, they could drag him about the city streets in victory. In some way, they had vindicated their fallen friends by punishing a scholar, any scholar. But they also knew to present their defense in a way which would emphasize that they were fulfilling a civic duty; perhaps they had achieved this goal in their minds. All of the men came from various respectable backgrounds, from a capitol to a grocer, and all shared equal blame for the arrest and abuse of the royally protected individual. This case does not share the same drama or intrigue as other town and gown rows of the fourteenth century, where scholars were left for dead or driven from the communities. But the extensive details involved in the year-long investigation into the matter suggests how serious the royal and municipal authorities were in trying to battle for who had authority in Toulouse. The capitols and their guards played a direct role in subverting royal power through self-serving actions while fulfilling the obligations of their office while in the streets of Toulouse, and in their encounters with the Toulousains and royal representatives.

Conclusion

In many ways, the trial of Garnerius unfolded as a typical crime story with conflicting accusation and defense. But beyond trying to establish Garnerius' guilt or innocence, testimony on both sides of the case reveals much more about the broader social and political tensions between the citizens, the capitols and the municipal officers of Toulouse. It is hard for me to believe that the capitols and their officers stood by idly as their fellow citizens attacked and killed a man under comital safeguard.

Instead, Garnerius' explicit testimony suggests that the municipal authority took advantage of the crowd's passion and frustration in order to fulfill a desire to punish the messenger. Throughout this chapter, I have focused upon the middling role of the sergeants and night guards in the relationship between the capitols and the public of Toulouse. The policing agents interacted with the urban inhabitants on a daily basis, and represented the power and authority of the city government. But whereas many men upheld the obligations of their office by arresting malefactors and by fulfilling the orders of the capitols, just as many sergeants found opportunity to exploit their position of authority. Within these exchanges and negotiations of law and order between the officers and the Toulousains, one common factor is that it all transpired within the public realm. The royal messenger's body had to be carried around the in streets in celebration so that everyone present that afternoon witnessed that justice had been served on the behalf of the city of Toulouse.

CHAPTER FIVE

THE POWER TO PUNISH IN MEDIEVAL TOULOUSE

In October 1283, King Philip III of France attempted to resolve the conflict surrounding the criminal jurisdiction of Toulouse. Earlier that year, the capitols had complained to the king that royal representatives continued to infringe upon their judicial liberties, and sought clarification about the distribution of responsibilities and authority in the municipal organization. As a response to these concerns, Philip mandated that the capitols had the right to preside over all trials concerning crimes committed in the city and surrounding territory of Toulouse in the name of the king, thus establishing the local officials as the first source of justice for the citizens. A royal official sat in on the trials, he continued, but purely as an observer. The capitols interrogated defendants and witnesses, handled lawyers, and rendered their verdicts. But the final step in the criminal process, actually punishing the convicted criminal, had to be approved by the royal vicar or his representative.[1] For centuries, the citizens of Toulouse had turned to their capitols for satisfaction in criminal transgressions. As early as 1226, the citizens had gathered at the town hall to protest the murder of two young men, demanding that the elected officials protect them and achieve justice for the victims by ridding the city of convicted murders, robbers, and corrupt individuals through spectacular executions and banishments.[2] But with the proclamation in 1283, King Philip theoretically shifted the power to punish out of the hands of the capitols and into the vicar's, thus placing his royal representative at the top of the local judicial hierarchy. This transition did not go smoothly. Fifty years later, the capitols continued to respond to their constituents' demands for justice by disciplining criminals in their traditional ways, ignoring the vicar, and essentially resisting the influence of the king in Toulouse's judicial process.

In medieval France, the right to punish criminals gave legitimacy to political administrations, both royal and municipal. Toulouse's capitols

[1] AMT-AA 3:4, and duplicated in registers AA 4:1, AA 5:30, AA 53:27.

[2] Chapter 1 begins with this case, listed in register AMT-AA 2:83, fol. 107v–fol. 111v. For a discussion of the notions of crime and punishment in the eleventh and twelfth centuries in Toulouse, see Wolff, *Histoire de Toulouse*, 94–103. Mundy, *Liberty and Political Power in Toulouse*, 93–121.

held on to this privilege well into the fourteenth century, in direct defiance of the king's proclamations, for several reasons. The public nature of criminal punishments allowed Toulouse's population to be involved in the civic rituals of law and order. The spectacle not only assured the constituents that their local officials fulfilled the obligations of their office, but it also provided the people with the ritual elements of punishments they demanded for justice. In addition, the capitols aspired to subvert royal authority and dominance in the city, and to maintain autonomy and resistance to the royal vicar and his guards who had intruded upon their jurisdictional territory. Throughout this study, the capitols have emerged frequently as figures tangential to the scandals and popular protests which erupted in the city. In the extant legal records and disputes from the thirteenth and fourteenth century, the capitols are depicted as fighting to distance themselves from the actions of the mobs against the outside authority, and trying to establish themselves as complacent and loyal subjects to the king as a matter of self-preservation. This chapter realigns the capitols on the side of their public, binding them in culpability and their desire to preserve a sense of civic autonomy. Municipal and royal leaders fought to secure the power to punish criminals because the process demonstrated authority to the city's inhabitants through horrific spectacle, performed in the living and working space of Toulouse. Rather public punishments bound the citizens (as spectators) with their officials (as enforcers) in the restoration of law and order within the community.

Recent historians have worked to situate medieval punishment within the developments of Roman law. Corporal and capital penalties became more institutionalized in the twelfth century with the centralization of royal authority, and the codification of criminal law.[3] Feudal lords dispensed most justice in the Middle Ages throughout the continent, but with the spread of urbanization, local civic authorities created more rigorous penal system for offenders disrupting the already unstable civic population.[4] By the thirteenth century, the accusatory process that had handled the impulses of personal vengeance between two parties had been replaced by the inquisitorial process. The state, embodied by trained judges and officials of the law, acted on behalf of the public order in matters of conflict, seeking vengeance and satisfaction through monetary or

---

[3] Berman, *Law and Revolution*, 476–477. Peter Spierenburg, *The Spectacle of Suffering: Executions and the Evolution of Repression, from a Preindustrial Metropolis to the European Experience* (Cambridge: Cambridge University Press, 1984), 9.

[4] Berman, *Law and Revolution*, 307–332.

corporal punishment. In other words, justice in criminal affairs came from above; authorities no longer simply mediated the complaints between feuding parties, but officials took the initiative to set out and investigate criminal activity, interrogate witnesses, and oversee the enactment of punishments. Throughout France, the inquisitorial process allowed officials to use methods such as torture in order to challenge defendants' testimony, and bestowed upon the state the right to inflict pain upon the body of convicted criminals.[5] Toulouse stands as a city which fought ardently with their counts and later the king in order to secure their power over judicial practices, believing that this authority to pass judgment over its inhabitants was one of their most valuable privileges.[6] Corporal punishment in the Middle Ages was not part of archaic and barbaric customs, but developed along with the standardization and centralization of the state's authority.

Due to the nature of the archival sources, it is difficult to assess how frequently municipal authorities publicly punished criminals. Most of the statistical evidence from medieval France indicates that the number of people actually executed was relatively low in relationship to the number of people charged with crimes. Between 1387 and 1400, for example, the Parisian Parlement heard more than two hundred cases, of which only four ended in capital punishment.[7] In Arras, the municipal government very infrequently ordered corporal punishment, mutilation and capital executions, with the city averaging only one death sentence a year in the fifteenth century.[8] Jacques Chiffoleau found that the administration of fifteenth-century Avignon preferred to punish criminals with a prescribed set of financial fines, although papal justice had an arsenal of spectacular chastisements at its disposal.[9] Outside of France this seems to be the case as well. David Nicholas has also shown that execution for crime did not occur very often in fourteenth-century Ghent. He argues that the bailiff of the city commissioned the death sentence in less than ten percent of cases each year, and in fact preferred banishment to the death sentence.[10]

---

[5] Esther Cohen, "Symbols of Culpability and the Universal Language of Justice: The Ritual of Public Executions in Late Medieval Europe," *History of European Ideas* 11 (1989): 407–416.

[6] Gardner, "Negotiating Lordship," 350.

[7] Gauvard, *De grace especial*, 897.

[8] Muchembled, *Les Temps des supplices*, 57.

[9] Chiffoleau, *Les Justices du pape*, 211–242.

[10] Nicholas, "Crime and Punishment in Fourteenth-Century Ghent," 328–329.

Historians of Toulouse do not have the luxury of extensive data concerning the exact number of executions from the fourteenth century. One of the vicars, Eustachius Fabri, kept an expense report for the year 1321 to 1322 that provides some clue as to how often the Toulousains witnessed criminals punished. In that year, the municipal trumpeter, Guillelmus Johannes, played his trumpet and announced the crime of one hundred and thirty-nine individuals who either ran the town or stood shackled in the window of the town hall. Of those criminals, Fabri noted, forty-one were then sentenced to death.[11] According to this figure, the local administration executed nearly thirty per cent of the people convicted of a serious crime. The numbers of criminals put to death and how often prisoners ran the town or stood exposed and bound are staggering for a one year period. Unfortunately, there is no other archival evidence to substantiate this entry in the vicar's expense report or provide any explanation as to why this number would be so high. But the importance of executions and punishments in the medieval urban milieu resides not in the frequency, but in the public, ritual meaning behind the events.

Esther Cohen believes that medieval authorities and chroniclers created a "visual trick" through the spectacular executions in medieval cities. Even though the death sentences may not have occurred regularly, she argues, the painstaking processions to the gallows and blood-shed of the prisoner left a lasting impression upon spectators, leading them to recall the particularity and individuality of each execution.[12] With a single decapitation or mutilation, a municipal government could make a statement both about its power, and intolerance for particular crimes that could endure for decades. Historians have debated, however, exactly how to unpack the notion of public punishment as ritual drama. Spierenburg argues that executions were a combination of religious and secular elements, which were intended to provide the criminal numerous opportunities to confess, to repent, and to be reconciled with God before death.[13] A passive crowd stood by as witness to the solemn procession, as priests and clergy accompanied the convict to the scaffold. But Claude Gauvard

---

[11] *CR*, no. 1071, 70: "Guillelmo Johannis, tubicinatori, pro 139 personis per ipsum tubicinatis dum currebat per villam Tholose, vel stabant in fenestra domus communis Tholose, pro excessibus per eos commissis, de quibus 41 persone receperunt mortem, 3 d. tol. pro quilibet: 69 s. 6 d. t."

[12] Cohen, "To Die a Criminal," 300. Robert Mills continues this discussion in *Suspended Animation: Pain, Pleasure and Punishment in Medieval Culture* (London: Reaktion Books, 2005), 16–17.

[13] Spierenburg, *The Spectacle of Suffering*, 46–52, 61–63.

insists that medieval spectators were actively engaged in the whole process (which she believes was lacking in any spiritual tone), and the viewers were prepared to intervene in certain circumstances. If an executioner failed to offer a clean blow with his axe, or a rope broke before a criminal was successfully hanged, the audience could take it as a sign of God's mercy. In both interpretations, administrations placed careful consideration in the preparation of any execution or punishment, in order to appease the public and to advance their judicial or social agenda.

That being said, authorities chose their criminals with discretion. For example, in Paris, outsiders and transients suffered the majority of the executions involving torture, amputations, or bodily remains left display.[14] The most common profile of the executed criminal was a young lower class male, unsettled and unmarried.[15] The Parisian authorities assigned lesser monetary sentences to local inhabitants who had financial and social ties to the community, unless the crime was treason against the king or especially heinous in its nature.[16] These studies imply that if royal or municipal governments chose to demonstrate their authority through the spectacles of punishment, someone who resided on the fringes of the general public became the most viable candidate, perhaps because there would be no popular protest against the execution. In Toulouse, however, the capitols chose to publicly punish prisoners who had committed crimes which resonated with the public in some way. The men and women executed or ritually chastised had disturbed the balance of order within Toulouse, and only through their punishment could it be restored.

The punishment of criminals played a significant role in the everyday life of medieval Toulouse, and this could serve as the reason why the capitols clung so desperately to the right to administer the full range of justice

---

14 Rodrigue Lavoie "Les statistiques criminelles et le visage du justicier: justice royale et justice seigneuriale en Provence au Moyen Âge," *Provence historique* 115 (1979): 15, 18.

15 The administration of early modern Amsterdam also favored this demographic of convicted criminals. Spierenberg, *The Spectacle of Suffering*, 153–165. The criminal trials found in *Les Registres criminelle du Châtelet de Paris* from 1389–1392 suggest a strong connection between crime and the marginalized poor in the royal capitol. Historians who have depended heavily upon this source have been able to provide insight into urban poverty in the fourteenth century. See, for example, Bronislaw Geremek's *The Margins of Society in Late Medieval Paris*, and Jacqueline Misraki, "Criminalité et pauvreté en France à l'époque de la guerre de Cent ans," *Études sur l'histoire de la pauvreté (Moyen âge-XVIe siècle)*, edited by Michelle Mollat, vol. 2 (Paris: Publications de la Sorbonne, 1974), 536–546.

16 Rodrigue Lavoie, "Justice, criminalité et peine de mort en France au moyen âge: essai de typologie et de régionalisation," *Le Sentiment de la mort au moyen âge: Études présentées au Cinquième colloque de l'institut d'études médiévales de l'Université de Montréal*, ed. by Claude Sutto (Montreal: L'Aurore, 1979), 54.

in defiance of the royal vicar. Public punishments were a common element in the daily activity and spatial layout of the city, because the condemned prisoners were not simply transients, but instead, people within the urban social fabric. Therefore, the capitols and the public resented the royal intrusion upon their traditions and rituals of justice, and frequently denied the vicar input in the punitive process. To put it even more simply, the capitols chastised prisoners frequently and in the most populated areas of the city, and the influx of royal and ecclesiastical officials into the city became a direct competition for the capitols' authority to punish criminals, thus limiting their ability to provide the public with spectacular punishments. The capitols had to find new ways in which to hold onto the power of their office, while also satisfying the people's desire to witness the ritual of retribution enacted upon the prisoner's flesh. It is this relationship with their constituents which led to two jurisdictional disputes between the royal vicar and the capitols concerning the execution of three criminals in 1332. In these examples, the Toulousains' demand for justice drove the capitols to organize and perform two very public and dramatic sentences, completely defying the royal vicar's authority, and sparking political controversies which climbed through the legal hierarchy all the way to the king's court. Although the capitols asserted their loyalty to the throne in their letters and pleas to the king, this chapter will argue that the elected officials orchestrated the public punishments in order to demonstrate to the people that their traditions of justice and retribution were still protected, and that royal authority could still be resisted in the streets of their city. Punishment, in other words, served the capitols as the most communal and familiar way to unite with their constituents and maintain a sense of civic autonomy in the fourteenth century.

Punishment as Spectacle in Toulouse

The capitols conducted trials concerning criminal activity that transpired in the open view of the urban inhabitants. Feuds between families were common knowledge among the neighborhood's gossips, and many physical attacks that were reported to the city officials took place in the busy taverns or city streets. Even disputes that erupted inside private homes eventually spilled out into the public eye when the shouts for help awoke the people living next door. If an individual did not personally witness the offense, the municipal trumpeters' official proclamations ensured that the crime was common knowledge. For many of these wrongdoings, restitution had to be public as well. In some cases, victims demanded vindication through public chastisement, so they turned to their capitols to rectify the situation and provide the victim and their family with satisfaction. Public punishments restored the city's perception of order, and the inhabitants achieved the satisfaction that their neighbors witnessed the criminal suffer. For their part, the capitols proved to the audience that the elected officials, once again, protected the public from malefactors and criminal offenses. This section will introduce the various criminal sentences ordered by the capitols, and situate them in the city space in order to demonstrate that spectacular punishments were ubiquitous in the daily lives of the inhabitants and visitors.

The capitols and the royal vicar of Toulouse did realize that it served the administration best in some occasions to collect financial amends for particular crimes. Most civic administrations relied upon a system of fines because it allowed the government to rectify situations peacefully, profitably and without having to maintain jails to accommodate large numbers of prisoners. In Arras, a city in northern France, the municipal officials imposed over 1,600 fines upon the town's 14,000 inhabitants between the years 1400 to 1436.[17] The Bibliothèque Nationale holds a single page from the fourteenth century court of appeals in Toulouse, which contains a list of offenders, their crimes, and the amount of money they had to pay to their victims and the court.[18] For example, Raymundo de Barta Martino, charged with removing his sword from its sheath and threatening a sergeant, paid twenty *sols tols* to the city.[19] This small excerpt from Toulouse's archival records corresponds with the more complete documents of the surrounding vicariate. Most physical attacks, such as the one perpetrated by Remondo Bouquerii and his mother, who collectively threw stones at another woman, warranted fines of around twenty *sols tols*.[20] But there is no real constancy in the issuing of monetary penalties from this region of the Midi. One man who resisted arrest was charged 66 *sols* 8 *dernier tols*,

---

[17] Muchembled, *Le temps des supplices*, 28, 39, 48, 82.

[18] BN, MS lat. 2355. The register holds "diverse pieces and fragments of documents" from the ninth through to the eighteenth century. On fol. 58r, is affixed a small, tattered, and undated excerpt from Toulouse's court of appeals. An unidentified archivist dated it to the fourteenth century.

[19] Ibid. "Raymundo de Barta Martino pro malitiose abstraxit gladium de vagina cuius servientes pro tol XX sols." For a discussion of money used in Toulouse, see Paul Guilhiermoz, "Notes sur des poids et measures du moyen âge," *Bibliothèque de l'Écoles des Chartes*, 67 (1906): 161–233, 402–441.

[20] *CR*, no. 780, 56: "A Remondo Bouquerii et Gauzia, ejus matre, quia cum lapidibus percusserant quondam mulierem, pro toto: 20 s. t."

a rather hefty amount.[21] In Albi, another defendant had to pay 58 *sols* 9 *dernier tols*, for "violently entering a home with bad intentions."[22] Gaillac's court demanded 16 *sols* 6 *dernier tols* from a man who extinguished a city light, thus creating a danger for the patrol men performing their nightly duties.[23] These payments by the criminals were meant to appease the victims and their families, and also cover court costs such as the notary or the arresting officers' fees.

The royal vicar, we can imagine, preferred collecting financial amends from criminals rather than resorting to the capitols' arsenal of options for corporal punishment. It was expensive to coordinate the more elaborate punishments: executioners needed to be paid, trumpeters had to be commissioned, gallows built, and prisoners had to be detained and fed for a period of time prior to their sentence. For example, in 1323, the vicar reimbursed a bailiff in the vicariate of Toulouse over one hundred *sol tols* for the hanging of three criminals and the removal a fourth man's ear.[24] It is no surprise that the royal vicar condemned the capitols' for the types of customary punishment and torture that prevailed in Toulouse. He was exasperated that, "they condemn criminals to corporal punishment such as running the town, suspension, drowning, standing in shackles wearing a sign (*balandranos*) with depictions of the crime, or even wearing a crown of straw just as they were expulsed."[25] The capitols, however, continued to employ these methods of chastisement because it was a symbol of their offices' authority. These spectacles demonstrated to the public that the capitols had reestablished order to the city, and justice to the victims after the crime had been committed. Over the years, the capitols learned to position these events in the most prominent places of the city, such as widely traveled roads, entrances into the city, or the most populous centers of urban activity, in order to reach a broader audience.

Perhaps one of the most common ways in which the capitols could establish their role in the high justice of the city was through the physical

[21] Ibid., no. 765, 55: "Ab Arnaldo Danielis, dicti loci, quia fuit rebellis cuidam servienti volenti eum capere, pro parte: 66 s. 8 d. t."

[22] Ibid., no. 835, 58: "quia pensatis insidiis intravit violenter domum Amelii Symonis : 58 s. 9 d. t."

[23] Ibid., no. 850, 59: "A Durando Audiberti de Galhiaco, quia lumen extinxit et vulnus fecit tempore quo gentes ville custodiebant villam propter Pastorellos: 16 s. 6 d. t."

[24] Ibid., no. 1990, 140: "Petro Ade, baiulo dicti loci, pro expensis per ipsum factis in exequtione Johannis Petri Mauros, Guillelmi Johannis et Ramondi Caprarii, suis demeritis in furchis justicie dicti loci suspensorum, ac Dominice Furnerie, que amisit aurem pro furto per eam commisso, juxta compotum et litteras dicti judicis : 116 s. 1 d. t."

[25] AMT-FF 59, fol. 52v.

presence of the gallows and pillories. Throughout the thirteenth century, the municipal authority erected both temporary and permanent structures in various sectors of Toulouse. Gallows, wooden frames used for hangings, held a tremendous amount of symbolic authority to the people of the Middle Ages.[26] In fact, the Capetian kings regulated how many bodies of executed criminals each of the gallows could hold throughout the kingdom in order to maintain his dominance over lesser jurisdictions. Dukes' gallows could hang eight criminals at a time, and counts were limited to six. The king's gallows in Paris, however, could suspend the bodies of as many as sixty prisoners at the same time.[27] Criminals condemned to execution at the gallows were not simply hanged until their neck broke. Instead, they suffered the slow process of strangulation, their bodies left on display after death until decay and decomposition freed the various parts of their corpse dangling from the ropes and chains.[28] Most authorities reserved "suspension" for men convicted of murder, treason, arson or violent attacks. Although historians have long believed that female convicts were never hanged because medieval attitudes towards woman found it indecent to leave her body exposed, Esther Cohen argues that fears of the supernatural were a more likely explanation.[29] Officials sentenced women convicted of capital offenses to be either buried alive with her victim, or burned at the stake to destroy her body completely, and to prevent her from returning as an evil spirit.[30] The female convict's body had to be completely destroyed. For example, in Aurrillac, after two women strangled all of their children, they were transported to the *fourches* where executioners burned them to ashes. A young girl from Metz in 1495, who had "taken her child by the feet, struck it against the wall and killed it," then "threw it in the well of the house," suffered a similar fate.[31]

---

[26] By the early modern period, gallows and the executioners held a very different place in the minds of urban authority, the city's inhabitants and guild members. For example, an individual who came into contact willingly with the gallows or the exposed corpses was considered "polluted" and dishonored by the public. See Kathy Stuart, *Defiled Trades and Social Outcasts: Honor and Ritual Pollution in Early Modern Germany* (Cambridge: Cambridge University Press, 1999), 125–128.

[27] Henri Ramet, *Histoire de Toulouse* (Laffitte Reprints: Marseille, 1977), 202. Dean, *Crime in Medieval Europe*, 124–125.

[28] Grand, *Justice criminelle*, 99.

[29] J. Gessler, "Mulier suspensa: à délit égal peine différente?" *Revue Belge de philologie et d'histoire* 18 (1939): 974–988. Cohen refutes Gessler's argument in "Symbols of Culpability and the Universal Language of Justice: The Ritual of Public Executions in Late Medieval Europe," *History of European Ideas*, 11 (1989): 412–413.

[30] Cohen, "Symbols of Culpability," 413.

[31] Gonthier, *Le châtiment du crime*, 164.

By the fourteenth century, the capitols had erected three permanent gallows in Toulouse, each called a *salade*.[32] One was situated outside of the Arnaud Bernard Gate, a second close to the Château Narbonnais, and a less commonly used location was outside of the gate near the Cathedral Saint-Étienne. All three stood at the major crossroads of the region, leading to other cities such as Paris, Fronton, and Narbonne. The capitols positioned these permanent gallows by the most frequented gates of the city, so that anyone entering or leaving Toulouse had a clear idea of the city's power to punish criminals. Thus, the capitols could establish the endurance, stability and power of their office through the permanent gallows positioned at the gates of the city, the bodies of convicted criminals swaying and decaying in the wind to serve as a warning to potential malefactors. This sentiment rings true for other city governments, who intended the display of criminals' bodies on gibbets or spikes to serve as a constant reminder of the punishment. In Dijon, the town council only conceded to remove corpses from the gallows after it was fully persuaded that the bodies contained dangerous contagion and diseases.[33] In 1300, the Italian city of Siena initiated a law that ordered the erection of high gallows made of iron, where the bodies of criminals hanged until they fell apart through decay, so that the sight of punishment would inspire fear in others, and deter future illegal endeavors.[34]

Municipal officials had the option of constructing temporary pillories next to major sites of social interaction in Toulouse, such as churches or bridges, in order to address a more specific audience or neighborhood. Criminals condemned to the pillories were held in wooden boards, similar to stocks. After the municipal trumpeter announced the prisoner's crime to the public, the executioner could whip, brand or amputate the hand, ear, or eyes of the individual. Convicted thieves most often suffered this fate. Petrus Fabri, for example, regent for a city in the surrounding vicariate of Toulouse, assigned six sergeants to find a pauper, suspected of stealing a loaf of bread. Once the regent had secured the thief in a pillory, he cut off the criminal's left hand.[35] In Toulouse proper, the capitols would

---

32 *DRT*, vol. 2, 447. Salies does not offer any explanation as to why these areas were known as a "salade," and it is unknown as to how many bodies these medieval gallows could accommodate. By the eighteenth century, however, expense records reveal that as many as twenty-six criminals could be hanged at the same time.

33 *Correspondance de la mairie de Dijon*, ed. J. Garnier (3 vols., Dijon 1868–1870), I, p. 90. As cited in Dean, *Crime in Medieval Europe*, no. 32, 126.

34 Dean, *Crime in Medieval Europe*, 126.

35 *CR*, no. 1998, 141.

build these pillories close to the most prominent sites of the particular *capitoulat* where the crime had been committed, areas such as the courtyard beside the churches of the Daurade or the Cathedral Saint Étienne, the commercial center of Place du Saint Georges, or the Bazacle Bridge on the Garonne.[36] These temporary pillories and gallows demonstrated to the public that the administration of justice was flexible and pervasive. At any given moment the capitols could commission the erection of a scaffold in any neighborhood, and order the civic trumpeter to summon the people to bear witness to the castigation of an offender. Corporal punishment was not relegated to a remote location away from the daily activities of the people of the city. Instead, it could penetrate the most populous and frequented portions of Toulouse and specific neighborhoods.

In addition to the sites of gallows and pillories, the Garonne River also served the capitols as a centralized site to discipline criminals. In a expense report from the early fourteenth century, Toulouse's capitols and vicar not only had to figure "straps, ropes and shackles to hang and drag murders" into the budget, but also "sacks to submerge robbers."[37] At times, other municipal administrations in France plunged women with bad reputations or a querulous nature into the water.[38] Although Toulouse's archival records do not reveal any occasions when the capitols employed the practice of drowning robbers, the capitols incorporated the river into their public punishment of blasphemers, in a spectacle known as the "cage." In 1330, the capitols described the process in a correspondence with King Phillip VI. For a first offense, the criminal convicted of blasphemy was placed in the stocks. A second occasion warranted imprisonment. The capitols had a couple of options if the individual committed the crime a third time. They could order the criminal's upper lip and tongue pierced with a hot iron. Or, the offender faced the "cage." The executioner placed the offender in an enclosure attached to the arm of an apparatus affixed to the Bazacle Bridge. Then, the cage plunged three times into the Garonne River.[39] The document does not disclose how long the cage remained

[36] Gilles, *Les coutumes de Toulouse*, 188 1n.

[37] *CR*, no. 1070, 70: "Pro guysalhis, cordis et una cathena ad suspenendos et trahendos murtrarios et latrines, et pro gahinis ad ponendum in manibus emanotorum, et pro saccis ad submergendum latrines, et pro duobus magidis ad trahendum 2 murtrarios: 58 s.t."

[38] Jean Marie Carbasse, "La peine en droit français," *Recueil de la Société Jean Bodin*, t. LVI, La Peine, 2e partie, 168.

[39] AMT-FF 111, fol. 3. "Pro tales blasphematores in quadam gabia [?] facta et adfingit in Ponte Badecley Tholose ponentur et in flumine Garonne semel secundo et tertio submergentur." This correspondence between the capitols and the royal seneschal is copied in a register from 1426.

under water with each descent, but we can only imagine the prisoner's panic while trapped helpless in this machine, completely at the mercy of the executioner. The Garonne River itself played a prominent role in the lives of the inhabitants of Toulouse: they had to cross one of its four bridges in order to reach the suburb of Saint Cyprian and its hospital, three prominent and ancient churches lined its right bank, and merchants sailed in and out, connecting the city to the Mediterranean and beyond. In one fatal procession celebrating the vigil of the Ascension in 1281, a portion of the Old Bridge collapsed and killed over two hundred spectators and participants.[40] Any punishments which occurred at the Garonne certainly would draw a large crowd of people who either worked or lived by the river, or individuals who were simply passing by at the moment the spectacle was taking place. Through punishments such as the "cage," the capitols could establish their critical and central role in the life of the city, their spatial and social reach, and their responsiveness to the inhabitants' desire not only for justice, but justice made manifest.

As we have seen frequently throughout this study, Toulouse's town hall served as the focal point in celebrating local authority, and civic autonomy. It housed their courtroom and municipal jail. It has only been recently that historians have come to appreciate the importance of municipal jails. For example, in his study of Italian cities, Guy Geltner has shown that the medieval prison was a very visible and accessible institution in the urban realm.[41] Prisons were not necessarily just a location for holding defendants awaiting trial, but imprisonment served as a punishment in and of itself. In Toulouse, the capitols had a variation of punitive containment known as the *costellum*. In this method, a prisoner would stand bound by an iron collar and chains, exposed in a window of the prison for a variable amount of time. The thirteenth-century commentator of the *coutumes* of Toulouse provides one example of this punishment: one evening, night guards arrested a young apprentice baker, named Guillaume Barrau, for sleeping with his master's wife.[42] The capitols chose to proceed with the trial and sentenced the youth to decapitation, despite warnings

[40] Smith reads that the bridge collapsed as the procession was passing over the bridge, and they fell and drowned into the river. *A History of the University of Toulouse*, 72–73, citing the *Praeclara Francorum facinora*, edited by Catel in *Histoire des comtes de Toulouse*, 146. Lafaille reads that the spectators were on boats under the bridge when it fell upon them and killed them. *Annales de Toulouse*, 9.

[41] G. Geltner, *The Medieval Prison: A Social History* (Princeton, Princeton University Press, 2008).

[42] Gilles, *Les coutumes de Toulouse*, 187–188.

from civic lawyers who argued that, because the he was less than twenty-five years old, the father needed to be present. Barrau quickly appealed his case to the vicar, and the capitols conceded to reducing the sentence to a run of the town, and then confinement in the *costellum* for an unspecified amount of time. The capitols employed a very public means of chastising moral and criminal offenders, and on this occasion, the emphasis was upon the symbolism of the town hall and civic jail. By displaying a criminal in a window of the building, the capitols established the notion that punishment was directly under their power and control, centralized within the city, and available for all of the Toulousains to witness throughout the course of their days.

The most dramatic and ritualistic punishment the municipal authority employed was sentencing criminals and moral offenders to run the town. The capitols created a mobile performance of chastisement where a large amount of space and a variety of people witnessed the municipal authorities' ability to reestablish order and justice to the city. Officers dragged the culpable parties to a designated site in the city, where the civic trumpeter, once again, announced the crimes and sounded his horn, before leading the procession of humiliation throughout the most populous and frequented streets during broad daylight. Variations abounded for the treatment of the defendants and for what crimes warranted this punishment. At times, the criminals had to wear objects which revealed their offenses. In Albi, the city's *prud'hommes* sentenced a pickpocket to run the town, naked to his waist, with the objects he had stolen tied around his neck.[43] On other occasions, executioners whipped the prisoner as he ran the town, inviting the public to join in the taunts and throw objects as well.[44] Customary law dictated that adulterers run nude, and in one illustration from a thirteenth-century Toulouse manuscript, the female defendant leads her lover by a rope tied around his penis.[45] Leah Lydia Otis found several examples of prostitutes and procurers in Languedoc sentenced to this punishment into the fifteenth and sixteenth century.[46] For

---

[43] AMA-FF 7, fol. 1v.

[44] *CR*, no. 3525, 210.

[45] BN, MS lat. 9187, fol. 30v. Jean-Maris Carbasse, "«Currant nudi» Le répression de l'adultère dans le Midi médiéval, XIIe-VXe siècles," *Droit, Histoire et Sexualité*, ed. by Jacques Poumarede and Jean-Pierre Royer (Lille: Achevé d'imprimer, 1987), 83–102. Henri Gilles remarks that *la course* must have been common at the end of the thirteenth century, even though it "soulevera alors les protestations des consuls." This seems to be an effort of Gilles to downplay the capitols' role in any of these customary punishments. *Les coutumes de Toulouse*, 256, 2n.

[46] Otis, *Prostitution in Medieval Languedoc*, 91, 95.

thieves, adulterers and prostitutes, the capitols ordered that they forfeit all of their goods to the city after running the town. The criminals then faced perpetual exile from the city. But for particularly heinous crimes, running was replaced with dragging, and the procession ended in death. In 1290, Albi's consuls sentenced B. Salomonis of Noailles who "carnally knew a certain cow," to be tied to the tail of a horse, dragged throughout the streets of the city, decapitated and then burned.[47] In other instances of bestiality, the animal was burned with the fornicator. In 1463, a man in Dijon, charged with an indecent relationship with both a cow and a mare was burned with the two animals until they were reduced to ashes.[48] In the circumstance of running the town, the sound of the trumpeter's horn signaled to the people of Toulouse that a public offender was passing through their streets. Standing in their doorways, either armed with garbage to be thrown or just passing judgment, spectators knew that the capitols had caught and reprimanded a danger to their society.

Convicted criminals followed a specific path through Toulouse, although the trumpeter certainly had the discretion to lead the procession through side streets when occasion warranted. Traditionally, the convict began the spectacle at the Arnaud Bernard Gate, then ran through the city streets, and ended the route upon a grassy section of land in front of the Château Narbonnais. Today, this course can be walked in less then twenty minutes at a leisurely pace. The duration of the event, however, was not as significant as the space covered. The path crossed before major landmarks and also cut through the major social groups of the city: the religious figures and university students who lived in the region of Saint Sernin, the municipal administrators around the town hall, the commercial section closer to the Garonne River, and finally the region surrounding the château, where the lawyers and royal officials were installed. The path joined the sites symbolic to the history of Toulouse, unifying past and present in a deliberate show of civic solidarity.

The inhabitants of Toulouse witnessed several varieties of processions through the years, in which the participants wore specific dress into to accentuate their status and the function of the spectacle. Liturgical processions corresponded with principal religious feast days and the celebrations of Toulouse's sacred figures, such as Saint Sernin (November 30) and

---

47 AMA-FF 7, fol. 1v: "qui, ut dicebatur, carnaliter cum quadam vacca se immiscebat."

48 Gonthier, *Le châtiment du crime au Moyen Âge*, 163. For a discussion of the perceptions of bestiality, see Jonas Liliequist, "Peasants against Nature: Crossing the Boundaries between Man and Animal in Seventeenth- and Eighteenth-Century Sweden," *Journal of the History of Sexuality* 1 (1991): 393–423.

Saint Éxupère (June 14). The events were performed in smaller districts, conducted by the local clergy, forming protective circles around neighborhood parish churches. Royal entries into the city of Toulouse were the only formal processions which overlapped with the punitive route in the Middle Ages and early modern period.[49] In January, 1324, King Charles IV entered the town; Philippe VI in the beginning of 1336.[50] Most royal paths in the later fourteenth century included the cathedral, and the Château Narbonnais, a symbol of royal power ever since the death of Alphonse of Poitiers in 1271.[51] The capitols received the king outside of the Arnaud Bernard Gate in a calculated move to try and orchestrate the event. They entered on horse ahead of the king and his men, so that even though this ritual was a way for the king to assert royal authority, the capitols still held a place of distinction in the eyes of their public.[52] In both phenomena, criminals running the city and the king entering through the Arnaud Bernard Gate, the capitols aspired to demonstrate the power and control they had over the city as a whole, linking together the once divided *cité* and *bourg*, showing that Toulouse stood united under the elected officials.

By sentencing a criminal to run the town, the capitols laid claim and authority to the space they believed their office protected. But for some offenses, this sentence alone did not satisfy the capitols' requirements for justice. Many prisoners faced banishment from the city of Toulouse after

---

49 François Bordes, "Une perception de l'espace urbain: cortèges officiels et processions générales à Toulouse du XIVe au XVIe siècle," *Mémoires de la société archéologique du midi de la France*, vol. LXIV (2004): 147.

50 Chronicler Guillaume Bardin offers a highly romanticized and somewhat dubious description of a royal procession from 1303. *HGL*, X, col. 15. Discussed in Lafaille, *Annales de Toulouse*, 25–35. Most modern historians do not address this event, largely because Bardin claims this procession marks the first installation of a Parlement in Toulouse, an event which did not occur until the fifteenth century. André Viala, *Le Parlement de Toulouse et l'administration royale laïque (1420–1525, environ)*, vol. 1 (Albi: Imprimerie-Reliure des Orphelins-Apprentis, 1953).

51 The earliest details found in the archives concerning these entrances begin with Charles VI's procession of November 29, 1389. See, Bordes, "Cortèges officiels et processions générales," 135–153. For the importance of processions in general, Elizabeth A.R. Brown and Nancy Freeman Regalado, "*La grant feste*: Philip the Fair's Celebration of the Knighting of His Sons in Paris at Pentecost of 1313," *City and Spectacle in Medieval Europe*, eds. Barbara A. Hanawalt and Kathryn L. Reyerson (Minneapolis: University of Minnesota Press, 1994), 56–86. Jean-Pierre Leguay, *La rue au Moyen Âge* (Rennes: Ouest-France, 1984), 189–196.

52 Ibid., 152–153. Lorraine Attreed, "The Politics of Welcome: Ceremonies and Constitutional Development in Later Medieval English Towns," *City and Spectacle*, 208–231. For a discussion concerning the importance of ritual processions solidifying social bonds and social integration in England, see Mervyn James, "Ritual, Drama and Social Body in the Late Medieval English Town," *Past and Present* 3 (February, 1983): 3–29.

running the town, forever condemned to exile. This sentence served as the best and only way to rid the society of a dangerous member without the severity of killing him or her.[53] In other regions of France, the duration of banishment varied from a couple of months to a life sentence; if exiled for life, criminals forfeited all of their possessions to the government. In Paris, the king could pardon the banished person if he felt as though restitution had been achieved, and allowed the criminal a second chance in society. City governments in the Midi, such as Auvillar and Cahors, proclaimed that if a citizen killed a banished person who had infiltrated the city before the end of his sentence, they considered the murder an excusable offense.[54] Other administrations forgave the transgression with a monetary fine, or even allowed the criminal to buy their way out of exile. For example, Guillelmo Poncii Molinerii, banished for stealing wheat, fulfilled his sentence by living outside of Toulouse for one year, and for paying the fine of sixty-five *sols tols*.[55] In most instances, municipal authority banned offenders to unknown destinations, setting the criminal loose into distant territories. Archival records from Toulouse in 1332, however, provide one occasion on which the capitols sentenced a woman, Johaneta de Santolo, charged with "certain crimes" later identified as thefts, to run the town, to forfeit all of her goods, and to live in the city of Moissac (*Moýsiaco*), a small town about eighty-three kilometers from Toulouse.[56] The city would have been easily accessible to Toulouse by the Garonne River, but it is unclear why the capitols designated this specific location. Moissac was under the vicariate of Toulouse, and the capitols frequently sent officers to the city to engage in official business. In fact, municipal sergeant Arnaldus Franciscus encountered Johaneta in this location while on duty, and supposedly tricked her into believing that he had the authority to lift her banishment, and lured her back into Toulouse. The capitols regarded banishment as a way to control and regulate both the space of the city, and its population. Arnaldus Franciscus subverted and challenged this power by sneaking Johaneta back into the civic realm.

By the fourteenth century, the citizens of Toulouse witnessed a series of customary punishments enacted in the streets of the city and within the confines of their town hall. Victims and their families came to expect the

53 Dean, *Crime in Medieval Europe*, 129.

54 Jean-Marie Carbasse, *Histoire du droit pénal et de la justice criminelle* (Paris: Presses Universitaires de France, 2000), 263–266.

55 *CR*, no. 3522, 210.

56 AMT-FF 57, 155.

capitols to administer public justice so that their neighbors and fellow townsmen understood that civic order had been restored. Whereas the majority of criminals paid monetary compensation to their victims or to the city, the capitols chose certain offenders to serve as an example to the community, suffering the consequences of their actions through public humiliation, banishment, or a horrific death. In each case, the capitols managed to satisfy their public, and establish boundaries between proper and improper behavior. The capitols' did not punish criminals in one fixed, marginal location in Toulouse. Instead, they had a variety of very mobile and flexible options to draw from, which could be situated in specific locations, addressing different portions of the city. The pervasive nature of punishments served as a powerful symbol of the capitols' authority over the people and space of Toulouse, and also allowed the public to be a part of the justice system.

The Competition for the Prisoner's Body

At the beginning of the thirteenth century, the lawmakers and administrators of Toulouse were well versed in the rhetoric and practice of criminal punishment. The earliest extant statutes from the city discussed variations of corporal penalties, and the capitols continually challenged their counts for the right to administer justice for the people of the city. The evidence suggests that money was not always the motivating factor for the capitols and the citizens to seek justice for victims and their families. Instead, what we find is that the more outside authority, such as the king or the Dominican inquisitors, threatened to impose their own notions of discipline upon the people of the city, the capitols protested and tried to find ways to subvert these efforts, either openly and aggressively, or through more subtle ways. The customary punishments of Toulouse rose from the practices and traditions of the region, and became codified within the memories and expectations of the people demanding justice for criminal offenses. During the political and religious changes which evolved throughout the thirteenth century, the right to pass judgment and publicly punish criminals became an issue that the Toulousains entrusted to their capitols. By the fourteenth century, the victims and their families turned to the elected officials to protect them from malefactors roaming their streets, and to continue the traditional punishments that demonstrated to the people of Toulouse that justice had been achieved through public spectacle.

The Albigensian Crusade introduced royal crusaders and officers to their first taste of how the Toulousains handled enemies who had penetrated their city walls. Not surprisingly, the northern chroniclers painted a very scathing portrait of their enemies in the south. Authors who witnessed the battles, such as Peter of Les Vaux de Cerney, personally knew the crusading leader Simon de Montfort, and had little sympathy for the men, women and children caught in the crossfire of the battles raging around the Midi.[57] In his *Historia albigensis*, the people of Toulouse in particular emerged as a group of ruthless figures, determined to ward off the royal soldiers who hoped to conqueror their city. One of the most striking components of Peter's text is his description of the Toulousains' treatment of the crusaders caught as prisoners within the city limits. When trying to justify the harsh reparations which came about after the crusades, he recalled:

> When they succeeded in capturing any of our men, they would lead them through the streets of Toulouse with bags round their necks and their hands bound, inviting anyone they met to place one or more coins in the bags, so that the captors could make a profit. Then the executioners put out the eyes of some of their prisoners, and cut out the tongues of others. Others they dragged behind their horses, and left them for the dogs and crows. Others again they cut into pieces, which they catapulted with a trebuchet into our ranks. Others were burnt or hanged. An acolyte from Toulouse Bernard Escrivan…[was] buried alive up to his shoulders, with his hands bound; then they hurled stones and fired arrows at him, as if he were a target set up for archers, and finally heaped fire on him. His roasted remains were left for the dogs.[58]

This account from 1218 no doubt served the author's agenda of vilifying his southern foes, but it also provides some insight to the traditions of punishment in Toulouse, and of course, the city's beloved trebuchet. To begin with, prisoners were paraded around the neighborhoods, their captors preferring to share a spectacle with the people of the city rather than seek a more profitable ransom from their royal enemies. The executioners left the bodies mutilated, or exposed in various locations, in order to serve as a warning to others and a reminder of any small triumph to the Toulousains.

As soon as the royal crusaders conquered Toulouse, obvious changes began to take place with the influx of royal and ecclesiastical figures vying

[57] Yves Dossat, *Paix de Dieu et guerre sainte en Languedoc au XIIIe siècle*, Cahiers de Fanjeaux, vol. 4 (Toulouse, Édouard Privat, 1969), 223.

[58] Peter of Les Vaux-de-Cernay, *The History of the Albigensian Crusade*, ed. and trans. by W.A. Sibly and M.D. Sibly (Woodbridge, Suffolk: The Boydell Press, 1998), 274.

to assert their authority and punish criminals as well. The city felt the repercussions of the defeat with the early demands of the peace treaty in 1229. The king demanded that twenty prominent male citizens be sent as hostages to Paris until the time that he was satisfied that all of the walls of the city and any other of the surrounding impeding structures had been removed from the area.[59] The Dominican inquisitors and the royal officers who aided the friars also punished heretics by tearing down and demolishing their homes. For the inhabitants of Toulouse, it must have been dramatic spectacle to witness their neighbors houses dismantled brick by brick. These demolitions were meant to demonstrate to the community that the heretic was no longer worthy to live among them, but it also shattered to the pride and majesty of the city itself.[60] The towered homes of Toulouse had always been a source of pride for the leaders, and these new punishments by the king and inquisitors threatened the very prestige and endurance of the once walled Roman city.

To make matters worse, these new outside officials began to secure the right to seize and imprison suspected criminals or heretics, and the people of Toulouse became increasingly vulnerable to the torture and whim of the Dominicans and their officers. The friars depended upon royal officials to torture suspected heretics, either in the monastery of the Jacobins, known in the documents as the "house of the Preachers," or at the prison located in the Château Narbonnais. For example, in 1274, the royal seneschal of Toulouse, Eustachius de Beaumarchais, tortured a suspected heretic in order to learn the location of suspects in the region.[61] And even though most studies have shown that the burning of heretics was an uncommon phenomenon in Toulouse, the spectacle impacted the residents of the city. In his vita included in the *Golden Legend*, Saint Dominic himself, "once convicted a number of heretics, and they were condemned to be burned alive. Looking over them, he saw a certain man, whose name was Raymond, and said to the executioners: 'Save that man, do not let him be burned with the rest.' Then he turned to Raymond and said to him kindly: 'I know, my son, I know that one day, even though it may be years away, you will be a good man and a saint!' Raymond was freed, therefore, and persisted in heresy for twenty years. Then he was converted and entered the Order of Preachers, led an admirable life, and died a happy

59 Printed in *HGL*, vol. 8, col. 892–893.

60 Mundy, *The Repression of Catharism*, 65–66. Given, *Inquisition*, 74–75.

61 BN, MS lat. fonds Doat, v. 25, fol. 78r: "fuit captus et questionatus per dominum Eustachium senescallum Tholose, quia non revelaverat ei ubi erant heretici."

death."[62] The other heretics, however, were not so lucky and presumably were promptly executed. Shortly thereafter, the infamous Bernard Gui examined nine hundred and thirty suspected heretics in five hundred trials. Of those found guilty of practicing Catharism or participating in other non-orthodox behavior, Gui sentenced only forty-two to death at the stake, while three hundred and seven went to prison, and one hundred and forty three wore crosses designating their crime to the public.[63] But still, we can imagine that citizens vividly remembered the details of these incidents. When providing testimony to the Dominican inquisitors, one inhabitant of Toulouse, Guillelma, the wife of a lumber merchant who lived on the island of Tunicii, recalled the burning of a clerk in early March, 1274. On that day, she had gathered with five other neighbors down the street from her home and witnessed the event. She learned from the other spectators that the clerk was condemned to death for arguing with the inquisitors.[64] Even though the people of Toulouse were not always the victims in the inquisitors' pursuit of heretics, they still served as witnesses to the death sentences which occurred before the cathedral of Saint Étienne, or even in specific neighborhoods like the island of Tunicii. The inquisitors and the royal officers who carried out their sentences against the suspected heretics were very much a threatening presence in the daily activity of the city, and in the memory of its inhabitants.

Royal and church officials only began to plant the roots of their authority in the city of Toulouse in the early thirteenth century. In 1234, the capitols still had enough power to become involved in the regulation of the punishment being performed by these outside authorities.[65] The Toulousains complained to their elected leaders that the inquisitors, sent into the city by the pope and sanctioned by the king, showed no discrimination in choosing the victims of their excessive punishments and torture. A chronicler sympathetic to the south explained that one of the inquisitors, Guillaume Arnaldi, was not only content to persecute the living for heresy, but also "exhumed and shamefully removed the bodies [of heretics] from the city cemetery, in the presence of the vicar and the population, their bones and putrid bodies dragged through the city, named

62 Jacobus de Voragine, *The Golden Legend*, vol. II, 52.

63 Jean-Marie Carbasse, *La peine de mort* (Paris: Presses Universitaires de France, 2002), 46.

64 BN, MS lat. fonds Doat, vol. 25; fols. 41v-42v.

65 Henri Gourdon de Genouillac, *Histoire du capitoulat et des capitouls de Toulouse* (Paris, 1879; Marseille: Laffitte Reprints, 1974), 6. Citations are to the Laffitte edition.

and condemned by the voice of the town crier."[66] After the inquisitors finished this spectacle they burned the remains of the corpses. The capitols appealed to the both the pope and the Dominican tribunal, and they protested the violation of the tombs. The ecclesiastical officers, the capitols complained, were an aggressive group, who imprisoned suspected heretics without the option of an appeal to the either the capitols or count, and who violated the sanctity of a cemetery. When the seizure and execution of the people of Toulouse did not stop, the capitols took it upon themselves to protect the people of their city. One evening, both the capitols and a crowd of inhabitants united in an attack against the Dominicans, hurling rocks at their home, and shouting insults and threats to the friars inside.[67] Eventually, the protestors penetrated the house and sleeping quarters of the friars. The mob pulled them out of the house, and tied some to a horse and prodded others with knives to escort them from the city. After the fact, one of the capitols said, "It is much better for us to drive them out than to kill them."[68] In this instance, the capitols responded to their peoples' need to protect them, and the combined effort between the two groups expelled the outsiders from the city. Again, the relationship between the capitols and the people shared a mutual interest and support in these large demonstrations of protest. The archbishop soon reinstated the Dominicans in Toulouse, and the competition for the seizure and detainment of suspected malefactors continued to intensify between the capitols, ecclesiastical and royal authorities.

One of the best ways to demonstrate how differently each of the three groups regarded criminals is through the treatment of inmates in the prisons. From a practical and theoretical perspective, the right to imprison criminals by the thirteenth century gave a certain amount of legitimacy to political administrations, from the king to regional counts to city councils.[69] We may assume that the late medieval population internalized this connection between authority and prisons to some extent: in the English uprisings of 1381, for example, protestors targeted both royal and privately

---

[66] Guillaume Pelhisson, *Chronique (1229–1244) suivie du récit des troubles d'Albi (1234)*, ed. by Jean Duvernoy (Paris: CNRS Éditions, 1994), 96. "Et quidam alii per sententiam condempnati sunt, et de cimiteriis ville a dictis Fratribus, presente vicario et populo, extumulati et ignominiose eiecti, et ossa eorm et corpora fetentia per villam tracta, et voce tibicinatoris per vicos proclamata et nominata dicentis: «Qui aytal fara, aytal perira.»"

[67] Ibid., 52.

[68] Ibid., 82.

[69] Jean Dunbabin, *Captivity and Imprisonment in Medieval Europe, 1000–1300*. Medieval Culture and Society (Houndmills, Basingstoke, Hampshire and New York: Palgrave Macmillan, 2002), 46–47.

owned gaols as part of their agenda. Their release of prisoners was a symbolic means of destroying the old world order and creating a new one.[70] Again, the capitols' municipal detainment center was centrally located in the town hall. The jailer who oversaw the facility lived in the building with his family, feeding and monitoring the detainees at all times. The jailer even attended sessions in the capitols' court for certain trials and sentences.[71] In order to release a prisoner, the jailer had to receive a proper letter with a seal from the vicar or the capitols, which suggests that the office was a part of the institutionalized bureaucracy. During the early fourteenth century, we know the office was passed down from father to son in at least one instance, maybe because the boy was raised in the jail and knew enough to step into the position. In 1322, the capitols passed the responsibilities of the prison to Raymundus Bonhomme, the son of the exiting jailor.[72] As part of the ceremony accepting the office, Raymundus received the keys of the prison, and also those of the town hall and the capitols' court. Along with being entrusted with access to the entire building, he pledged an oath of fidelity to the city, and vowed to maintain discretion and integrity with regards to the prisoners. While part of the office required that he monitor the interaction of detainees with their visitors, the capitols also insisted that he feed them satisfactory amounts of bread and water, and maintain the "tradition" that the prisoners eat at a table. The municipal jail then served as a central component of the community at large, which maintained a sense of tradition and continuity with the past, and in the open and civilized nature of the treatment of the detainees.

There are two distinctive features about Toulouse's municipal prison, as best demonstrated with a comparison to other secular jails of Europe. The first is the possibility that the municipal jailer was a position passed down from father to son. We have no way of knowing how long the family of Raymundus Bonhomme held the office in Toulouse, but if this was a hereditary, kept and passed down in one family, it might elevate the status and prestige of the post. At the Fleet prison in London, a singular family

70 Anthony Musson, trans. and ed., *Crime, Law and Society in the Later Middle Ages*. Medieval Sources Series (Manchester and New York: Manchester University Press, 2009), 53.

71 AMT-FF 57, 18. Raymundus Bonhomme was listed present as the city's "*carcerarius*" at the death sentence of Aimery Berenger in 1332.

72 AMT-AA 3: 246. March 5, 1322. This is the same Raymundus Bonhomme in the records from 1332, listed in the above note, and in the case of Arnaldus Franciscus, AMT-FF 57, 159, and in the jurisdictional dispute in register AMT-FF 59.

held the position of warden for over five hundred years. Like Toulouse, Fleet was in close proximity to the central administration, and the office was one that carried a certain amount of weight. The Fleet warden also oversaw Westminster palace, he received a house with a garden, and was a city salaried official. By most accounts, the dignity of the familial office meant that the Fleet warden was more civil and humane than his British counterparts, as was evidenced by a lack of riots or inmate complaints. By contrast, the sergeants who staffed the notorious Newgate prison only received a salary from the system of fines and fees levied upon the inmates, but they were responsible for overseeing the most hardened and violent criminals of England. The king held the warden of Newgate personally and financially responsible if an inmate escaped, and levied a fine of 100s. for each prisoner who got away.[73] As a result, sergeants sometimes placed prisoners in the depths of the prison's dungeons to suffer in horrible conditions. The second significant feature of Toulouse's warden was the capitols' insistence that he feed his inmates proper rations, and that he allow them to eat at a table. At most other locations, the jailer had no responsibility whatsoever to feed his prisoners. Instead, the food and provisions came through a system of payments (resulting in wealthier inmates experiencing better accommodations), or through a distribution of charitable donations. At prisons like the Châtelet in Paris, inmates paid an entrance fee and an exit fee, and they had to pay for their food and their bed. The Châtelet was even divided into fourteen prisons that separated inmates according to their rank, and provided them with the goods that they could afford.[74] Those who could spend six *derniers* slept on a pallet, or bundle of straw, and those who could only afford one *dernier* spent the night in the cold dank dungeon.[75] Jailers had the temptation to intercept alms and donations for their own purposes, but this action could bring about serious repercussions for the offender. The jailer of the Châtelet was responsible for negotiating charitable contributions from the Parisians to make sure that the poor inmates had enough available bread. The baker's guilds always made sure that a portion of their goods made it to the Châtelet, and private donors gave financial contributions to benefit the prisoners as well. The jailer had to make careful records of all of these donations,

[73] Bassett, "Newgate Prison," 234.

[74] Louis Batiffol, "Le Châtelet de Paris vers 1400," *Revue historique* 61–63 (1896–97), 47–49.

[75] Geremek, *The Margins of Society in Late Medieval Paris*, 18.

because if any of the money was misused, he could be arrested by the royal government for theft, for which the punishment was hanging.[76] Although the evidence from Toulouse is far from conclusive, it certainly alludes to a strong possibility that the municipal jailer was meant to be an integral and respectable part of the capitols' administration.

The other jails of Toulouse, the royal jail in the Château Narbonnais and the ecclesiastical prisons, had very different methods of holding prisoners in isolation from the general public, and also competed for primacy and the right to hold inmates. In cities like Lyon, for example, Nicole Gonthier has found a pronounced tension between the royal prison and that of the archbishop in the fourteenth and fifteenth centuries, as both sides complained about the conditions of their rival jails in jurisdictional arguments.[77] The major issue in Toulouse, though, was the fact that whereas royal officers and clerks could only be held in their respective prisons, the city's residents could be arrested and held in the Château Narbonnais when royal officials saw opportunities to profit financially from the overlapping jurisdiction in the city. If royal officers arrested a citizen of Toulouse caught in the process of a suspicious act, or they simply heard of the suspicions of criminal activity, the sergeants could imprison the citizen in the royal jail. For example, in 1332, Arnaldus de Santo Martino was arrested by royal sergeants because several bandits, held in the royal prison awaiting punishment, implicated him it their thefts. But he was later remanded to the capitols, transferred to the jail in the town hall so that he could stand trial for the accusations against him.[78] This, however, provided an opportunity for the vicar and his royal jailers to extort money from the prisoners, and they only released them into the custody of the capitols if they paid a certain fine. In 1313, King Philip IV threatened the royal jailer, under the penalty of dismissal from his post, that he could no longer claim fees from prisoners from the moment when the capitols demanded extradition to their court.[79] This issue came up again one year later, causing the seneschal to reprimand the vicar and his men in charge of the prison at the Château Narbonnais. In this instance, the royal jailer demanded that the each prisoner brought into custody pay a sum of twelve *deniers Toulousains*, three *deniers* for simply entering the jail, and

---

76 Batiffol, "Le Châtelet de Paris," 54.

77 Nicole Gonthier, "Prisons et prisonniers à Lyon aux XIVe et XVe siècles," *Mémoires de la société pour l'histoire du droit et des institutions des anciens pays bourguignons, comtois, et romands* 39 (1982), 15–30.

78 AMT-FF 57, p. 143.

79 AMT-AA 3:152. May 11, 1313.

nine *deniers* for the duration of imprisonment.[80] These fees, which contradicted agreements of jurisdiction between the capitols and vicar, and the conduct of the jailer in general, alarmed the seneschal, and suggested the real lenience of the vicar in overseeing the conduct of his men at the Château.

These oversights and exploitations resulted in an overhaul of the regulations of the royal prison to ensure that the prisoner only paid the jail's fines if found guilty by the capitols. In 1327, Jean Folenfant, vicar of the Château Narbonnais, was caught again demanding financial penalties from prisoners known to be innocent.[81] Among the complaints of the capitols, which prompted the reactions of the king and seneschal, was the concern that the royal jailer did not feed the prisoners adequate amounts of bread and water, and that they did not eat their food at a table with the jailer. We know that jailer Johanni de Barra of the Château Narbonnais in 1322, spent enough money for bread for the imprisoned poor, along with the other necessary "shackles and keys" to run a prison for the year for a budget of roughly 67 *livres*.[82] But the capitols' concern that prisoners were not treated properly by the royal jailer suggests that there was a much different attitude regarding inmates between the two sets of officials. The royal authorities had a detachment from the prisoners in their custody. There seemed to be a rapid turnover in the men who held the office, and the guilt or innocence of the prisoners seemed secondary to the opportunity for profits and fines. Seemingly, royal jailers did not have the same interest in creating a communal atmosphere for the prisoners who were awaiting their fate in court.

Eventually, the ecclesiastical authorities and the Dominican inquisitors learned they achieved greater success in achieving confessions and conversions from suspected heretics through imprisonment, rather than torture. By the fourteenth century, they had several prisons in Toulouse, which served a very distinct purpose of isolating and containing accused heretics and criminal clerks. Canon laws forbid ecclesiastical judges from

80 AMT-AA 3:158. June 18, 1314. This was a mandate of Jean de Mauquenchy, seneschal of Toulouse and Albi, to the vicar of Toulouse.

81 AMT-AA 3:256. July 12, 1327.

82 *CR*, no. 2005, p. 142: "Johanni de Barra, jaulerio castri Narbone Tholose, pro pane plurium pauperum incarceratorum pro toto presenti anno in dicto castro detentorum, compedibus, riblonibus, manotis ferries reparadnis clavibus, serraturis neccessariis pro dictis carceribus et ipsis curandis et pluribus aliis pro dictis prisioniariis neccessariis, juxta compotum cum vicario Tholose factum, partes cum partibus retroacapitum presentis compoti: 67 l. 6 s. t."

shedding blood, so the inquisitors were particularly interested in using incarceration as a punitive function.[83] The Dominican inquisitors had two prisons to house suspected and convicted heretics: one at the basilica of Saint Sernin, and one in the Cathedral Saint- Étienne. Under the direction of Bernard Gui, suspected heretics could also be held in the *mur* of the Château Narbonnais. Conditions in the *mur* could vary from a relatively lenient environment of general confinement in which the suspected criminals had space to wander and interact, or it could be a *murum strictum* in which the prisoner was confined and shackled in a private cell.[84] The king supported most of the prisoners held in the *mur* because he profited from the confiscation of their property if they were condemned. James Given has shown that during any week these prisons held an average of 171 prisoners, including children, during the period of May 6, 1255 and February 6, 1256.[85] In 1321, the king allocated funds for sixty-six men and women who had been sentenced to imprisonment for twenty-eight days in the *mur* of Toulouse.[86] Dominican inquisitors preferred to imprison heretics so they could not corrupt others, and they hoped that inmates might confess their "corrupt thoughts" in a weakened state of food and sleep deprivation. It served the inquisition to isolate suspected heretics from the social networks which provided them moral support and the opportunity to go into hiding.

There was still great protest from the population of Southern France against the actions of the inquisitors well into the fourteenth century. And the officials overseeing the prisons of heretics became easy targets for all of the regional animosity towards outside authority. One of the most dramatic examples took place in the nearby city of Albi, as the citizens launched an all out uprising against the much hated bishop and inquisitor, Bernard de Castanet who oversaw the local prison. The accusers sent appeals to the king and the pope, and claimed that Bernard imprisoned citizens in horrific conditions, without adequate food or water, and that he arbitrarily tortured his inmates. They charged that he ordered the arrest

---

83 The earliest use of isolation as a punishment was employed by monasteries. See Pugh, *Imprisonment in Medieval England*, 374–83.

84 The term *mur* is a common designation of inquisitorial prisons, borrowed from the monastic usage of a punitive confinement in monasteries. Edward Peters, "Prison before the Prison: The Ancient and Medieval Worlds," *The Oxford History of the Prison: The Practice of Punishment in Western Society*, ed. by Norval Morris and David J. Rothman (New York: Oxford University Press, 1998," 28–29.

85 Given, *Inquisition and Medieval Society*, 79.

86 *CR*, no. 1340, 84.

and the imprisonment of certain women he found sexually appealing. He could then summon the females to his palace whenever he desired, and some witnesses claimed that when the women did not return to the prison population, he deposed of the bodies in a suspicious manner.[87] In one allegation, Bernard kept an innocent woman named Marquesia in jail to serve as a sex slave for a number of years before releasing her. Although there has been historical debate surrounding the validity of these accusations, the fact remains that the citizens of Albi demanded royal intervention into the affairs of the inquisitorial prison, and the conduct of Bernard de Castanet served as the impetus for that call to action. The denunciation was a political tool: it was a way in which the citizens of Albi sought protection from the inquisitors, and by extension, could establish the hierarchy of justice and order in the local prisons.

Overwhelmingly, beyond these claims of corruption and abuse, both the royal and ecclesiastical administrations of Toulouse preferred to punish criminals and defendants through imprisonment and series of financial amends. These methods served their intentions to secure confessions from suspects, and to increase the profits of their office. But it isolated the urban public from the judicial process, and prohibited them from witnessing the forms of justice. Whereas the capitols maintained a process of punishments that were generally very open for the Toulousains to observe and to understand that law and order had been restored, both the royal and ecclesiastical employed methods which marginalized the punitive process in the daily lives of the inhabitants of the city.

As the power of royal and ecclesiastical authority grew side by side in the city, the capitols eventually conceded to the king's codification of their customary law codes. In one manuscript of the royally approved *coutumes* of Toulouse from 1296, a series of illustrations provide one example of the capitols' subtle subversion of the king's authority, by displaying an artist's perspective of the city's traditions of public punishments.[88] A capitol, believed to be Petrus de Solio, commissioned the manuscript.[89] The unknown artist included images of customary punishment to serve as a reminder and to guide to his patron as to the traditional authority to

[87] Megan Cassidy-Welch, "Testimonies from a Fourteenth-Century Prison: Rumor, Evidence and Truth in the Midi," *French History* 16 (2002), 3–27.

[88] BN, man. lat. 9187. The text and commentary are printed in Henri Gilles, *Les Coutumes de Toulouse (1286) et leur Premier Commentaire (1296)* (Toulouse: Imprimerie Maurice Espic, 1969).

[89] Gilles, *Les Coutumes*, 58.

punish once held by the leaders of an independent Toulouse.[90] The artist depicts criminals with passive postures and tormented facial expressions, revealing their anguish at the hands of the executioner. Conversely, those rendering the sentences often show indifference to their wards, symbolizing the contained order of the state in relationship to the impassioned chaotic nature of the convicts.[91] Each page depicts another criminal's suffering, from a murderer buried alive with his victim to one unfortunate man about to be castrated by a long blade.[92] The most obscure image is a representation of the Justinian Code's punishment for parricide, which has no regional tradition whatsoever. In the illustration, a shirtless criminal carries a sack and leads a procession of four guard armed individually with a serpent, a cock, a monkey and a dog. Upon reaching a body of water, according to the Code, an officer tied the convict in the bag with all of the animals and threw him in to drown.[93] The text and commentary surrounding these images do not discuss criminal prosecution or punishment at all.

The authorities in Toulouse developed their own ways to punish criminals. Royal officers found it was more effective and profitable to demand financial amends from criminals who entered their prison, whereas the ecclesiastical leaders chose to imprison and isolate suspected and convicted heretics inside of the *murs*. But the capitols and their constituents

---

90 L'Engle's article, "Justice in the Margins," is the first to examine the images collectively. Marie-Laure Le Bail's "Le droit et l'image: sur un cas d'essorillage," focuses upon fol. 28v, in which an executioner is severing the ear of a criminal. *Médiévales* 9 (1985): 103–117. Jean-Marie Carbasse's article, "*Currant Nudi*: la repression de l'adultère dans le Midi médiéval (XIIe–XVe siècles)," references fol. 30v., the "adulterers," and the image graces the cover of the essay collection, *Droit, Histoire & Sexualité*. Several of the images have been published individually in a variety of works concerning medieval crime and punishment, although rarely does the corresponding text examine the history of Toulouse. This includes, but is certainly not limited to: fol. 32r., a scene of decapitation and the amputation of a hand is reproduced on the cover of Chiffoleau's *Les justices du pape*; the "adulterers" reproduced in Claude Gaignebet and Jean-Dominique Lajoux, *Art profane et religion populaire au Moyen Âge* (Paris: Presses Universitaires de France, 1985), 53; the "adulterers" and fol. 24r, the branding/blinding of a criminal and the dismemberment of a corpse, are found in Roger Merle, *Les grandes affaires criminelles de Toulouse* (Toulouse: Édouard Privat, 1978), 33. Nicole Gonthier includes fol. 29v, the whipping of a criminal and amputation of a hand; fol. 30r, a picture of the stocks and a townsman throwing eggs at the wrongdoer; and fol. 34v, the boiling of a criminal in a cauldron in *Le châtiment du crime au Moyen Âge, XIIe–XVIe siècles* (Rennes: Presses Universitaire de Rennes, 1998), 97. The castration scene, fol. 32v, is reproduced in R. Howard Bloch, *Etymologies and Genealogies: A Literary Anthropology of the French Middle Ages* (Chicago: The University of Chicago Press, 1983), 142.

91 Le Bail, "Le droit et l'image," 109.

92 BN, MS lat. 9187, fol. 23v., and fol. 32v respectively. L'Engle argues that castration was used for rapists or sodomites. "Justice in the Margins," 145. Gonthier claims that castration was used for adultery or any sex outside of marriage. *Cris de Haine*, 189.

93 BN, MS lat. 9187, fol. 34r.

had a long history of customary punishments, which were very public and physical in their nature. As the king's men became more active in their participation in the judicial process, the capitols began to lose their power to administer the punishments like the ones found preserved in the manuscript discussed above. It became increasingly important for the capitols to guard their tradition of punishments in order to demonstrate their power to the people of the city. When they did punish criminals, the capitols made a conscious decision to make the spectacle as pervasive as possible. By using different districts of the city, the capitols did not merely tuck the criminals away, but they had to make sure that they reached a wide audience. By the fourteenth century, the capitols found that they were unwilling to concede particular criminals to the vicar for fear that they would lose the opportunity to satisfy the public's demand for swift justice. And so one of the last sites upon which they could challenge royal authority and demonstrate it to the public in general was through orchestrating their own public punishments without the involvement of the royal vicar.

1332: The Jurisdictional Battle for the Power to Punish

When King Philip changed the jurisdictional policy of Toulouse in 1283, all of the capitols' criminal sentences had to be approved by the royal vicar or his representative. With the restructuring of the court system, defendants could also appeal to the vicar to reconsider the capitols' verdicts, and continue through the legal hierarchy all the way to the king's court in Paris. With these appeals, the victims and their families would have to wait months, or even years, to receive satisfaction, as opposed to the rapid resolution of disputes contained within the local arena.[94] Fifty years later in 1332, the capitols tried two very controversial criminal cases that incited them to violate this royal mandate: they organized very public punishments without involving the royal vicar. In these two situations, which occurred within months of each other, the capitols were not willing to risk losing control of the offenders by placing them within the royal judicial system and court hierarchy. Instead, they quickly and decisively punished the two criminals before any royal official could become involved in the

[94] Lavoie, "Justice, criminalité et peine de mort," 48. Lavoie discovered that the majority of criminals who received the death sentence were executed the same day they were found guilty. In most cases, the entire trial, deliberation and penalty phase took no more than eight days when appeals were not considered.

process. The first case involved a squire of a university student, named Aimery Berenger, who attacked and disfigured a capitol. The capitols tried, convicted, and publicly executed Berenger within days after the assault took place, and denied all of his requests for appeals or the involvement of the vicar.[95] In the second case, the capitols forced a single mother named Berengaria Vitalis to undergo a ritual punishment called a *rege ribaldum*, again without the vicar's knowledge or consent. The court found her guilty of selling her daughter's virginity to a young man.[96] I want to suggest that the very nature of these particular crimes compelled the Toulousains to demand public punishments from their elected officials, so that they could witness first-hand that justice and order had been restored to the city streets. For their part, the capitols found an opportunity not only to satisfy their constituents' cry for restitution, but also to restore some of the prestige and legitimacy of their office by undermining the authority of the royal vicar. Even though several of the capitols pled ignorance when the king became aware of their transgressions, it is clear that many of them deliberately commissioned and participated in the punishments in order to prove to the public that not all of Toulouse's customs and traditions could be usurped by the northern, royal authority.

This section begins with the details of the Aimery Berenger's offense, because I contend that the people and capitols of Toulouse were so enraged by this crime they were emboldened to subvert royal authority and dramatically execute the squire, regardless of the consequences. While the king was in Paris just learning of the city's violation of his ordinance, the elected officials back in Toulouse publicly chastised another prisoner, Berengaria Vitalis, just a few months later. Almost every aspect of Aimery Berenger's case sparked the public and capitols' need for revenge

---

[95] The original notarial manuscript from the trial and the capitols' verdict against Aimery Berenger is AMT-FF 57, pp. 1–30. The entire case is copied by a different notary's hand in register AMT-FF 58. Fragments of the case have been transcribed in a variety of locations. An abbreviated version of the accusation and some of the witness testimony is copied in AMT-AA 6, fol. 23. The archivist Roschach summarized this document in French in his *Inventaire de M. Roschach*, 107. Fournier published Roschach's version of the trial, and several letters between the King, archbishop of Toulouse, and the capitols from the Vatican archives in, *Les statuts et privilèges des universités françaises*, vol. 1, nos. 563–589. A royal letter from 1335 is also in *HGL*, X, col. 749, no. 291. All of my discussion and evidence is drawn from register AMT-FF 57.

[96] The inquest into the execution of Berengaria Vitalis and convicted thief, Guillelmus de Portello, are recorded in register AMT-FF 59. Although I have searched extensively for an accurate translation of *rege ribaldum*, none has proven satisfactory. Dr. François Bordes, director of the Municipal Archives of Toulouse, suggested that it was an expression akin to "charivari," or a regional expression for any ritual punishment.

against the squire. Easter evening of 1332, capitol Franciscus de Gaure and several of his officers set out to patrol his *capitoulat* of Saint Rome, which included neighborhoods surrounding the town hall. As they passed by a tavern located on a side street, the municipal troop came upon Aimery Berenger and several of his friends, drunk and causing a commotion in the street with local women.[97] The fact that individuals were overindulging on a holy day was cause enough for the capitol and his men to pause in their patrol. But to make matters worse, Aimery Berenger and his gang were carrying illegal arms, identified in the records as a variety of weapons such as swords, lead instruments, daggers and shields.[98] So far, the fairly routine encounter between the night guards and the rowdy tavern crowd had taken a sinister twist.

According to witness testimony, Franciscus de Gaure identified himself as a capitol to the group, thus proclaiming his authority to seize the illegal weapons, arrest them and take them to the town hall. From all accounts, de Guare not only verbally clarified his status and office, but he was also wearing the "clothes of the capitols."[99] From a visual perspective and through his proclamation, the rowdy group of men could not mistake de Guare's status as the highest ranking officer of Toulouse. Aimery Berenger, however, chose to offer a few choice insults and led his men into a brawl with a rallying against the municipal officials.[100] The scuffle and blows that followed left Franciscus de Gaure without his lip, nose and several teeth, perpetually disfigured in the face. Medical experts later confirmed that although the wounds themselves were not necessarily fatal, de Gaure could only communicate through writing. This whole exchange took place in one of the most populous district of Toulouse, and surely there would have been people drawn to this commotion who witnessed a capitol and municipal patrol under attack. But perhaps more significantly, Franciscus de Gaure lived in this very neighborhood which he represented as a capitol.[101] He followed in the footsteps of his father who had held the same

---

[97] AMT-FF 57, 4: "cum quibusdam mulieribus."

[98] Ibid., 1.

[99] Ibid.: "et vestes dicti capitulatus defferendo dixit eis ego ut capitularius tholose." For a discussion of the sumptuary characteristics of the capitols attire, see Jean-Paul Buffelan, *La noblesse des capitouls de Toulouse* (St Gaudens: L'Adret, 1986), 133–134.

[100] AMT-FF 57, 2. In the archival records, Aimery Berenger says "amlor amlor firetz firezt," a rally cry for fights. Other printed sources, including Fournier, list a variety of other insults and cheeky exchanges that are not in the archival manuscript or court testimony.

[101] It should be remembered that the night guards consulted Franciscus de Gaure later that year during an attack of a father and son in that same neighborhood. AMT-FF 57, 207.

office on multiple occasions throughout the early decades of the fourteenth century.[102] Residents of the street, therefore, observed one of their well established neighbors and chosen elected official fall at the hands of an outsider, who was only in the city because of his tangential affiliation with the university.

Just as they had done on numerous other occasions of criminal misconduct, the people and capitols of Toulouse sought immediate and aggressive retribution for this crime. The notary for the case observed that "the enormity of the crime caused a great commotion for the public who live in Toulouse who can scarcely believe these deeds."[103] It is not surprising then, several night guards and two hundred armed townsmen showed up hours after the confrontation at the household of university students where Berenger lived, arrested him and the students, and escorted them all to the jail at the town hall.[104] If the capitols had been following the legal protocol as established by the king, they should have paused with their lawyers at this moment and defined the legal status of Aimery Berenger. As a squire to a university student, did Berenger enjoy the same legal protection of the students, who were considered clerks? Because there was no precedent in Toulouse, the capitols should have handed Aimery Berenger over to the royal vicar who would then decide the squire's fate and proper criminal jurisdiction. But the capitols and their officers had no intention of surrendering Berenger to ecclesiastical or royal authorities. They considered the issue, but then made great pains to have their justification recorded. After they released the university students from their custody, the trial of the squire began the next morning, without the presence of the vicar or a royal procurer, as thousands of townspeople merged upon the town hall anxiously waiting to see justice for capitol Franciscus de Gaure. On the second day of the trial, after the capitols heard the testimony of medical experts and witnesses, the notary recorded Aimery Berenger's

---

[102] In Lafaille's *Annales*, Franciscus de Gaure the Elder held the office for the *capitolat* of Saint Rome in 1331, 1322, 1317, and 1307.

[103] AMT-FF 57, 3: "et enormitate dictorum criminum et magno tumultu populi qui erant in tholosa qui vix credare posset actus." p. 8 also mentions the "magno tumultu populi."

[104] *HGL*, 10, 38–39. "Quidam cives, qui illuc accurrerant, eum in suam domum et lectum transtulerunt. Hoc scandalosum facinus magnas turbas per totam civitatem excitavit. Hora nona de nocte capitulares cum CC hominibus armatis apprehenderunt nobilem Aymericum Berengarium, scholasticum, culpabilem vulneris inflicti, et eum in carceren obscurum conjecerunt; quaestioni applicatus fuit, confessus est crimen et ad decapitationem condemnatus."

confession,[105] and noted the squire was wearing lay clothing and did not have a clerical tonsure. Again, the capitols deliberately noted that Berenger was not in clerical garb to support their claims of jurisdiction. The third day, the capitols announced their verdict of guilt before an audience in the town hall, and issued an immediate death sentence. In a very swift and decisive fashion, the municipal officials were poised to reclaim a portion of their city's traditions and autonomy through a spectacular and very public execution of Aimery Berenger.

The capitols assigned a punishment meant to accomplish several symbolic functions at various sites in the city, while incorporating different audiences into the event. First, they commanded that municipal officers escort Aimery Berenger to the Arnaud Bernard Gate, from which the squire would be forced to run through the streets of the *bourg* to the home of Franciscus de Gaure that was situated close to the town hall.[106] The civic trumpeter announced the prisoner's condemnation to the public as the procession passed by the basilica Saint Sernin, and gathered an audience of predominantly university affiliates who lived in this region of Toulouse. With this path, the capitols followed the traditional punishments of running the town, while perhaps also hoping to make an impression of their power upon the royally protected scholarly community. When they reached Franciscus de Gaure's home, an executioner cut off Berenger's right hand, the limb which had committed the grave offense to the public and the capitol. Again, spectators would be summoned to this amputation, localizing the restitution within the neighborhood for de Gaure, his family and the residents who witnessed the assault. For the third stage of the criminal sentence, municipal officers tied Aimery Berenger to the tail of a horse, which dragged him to a field before the Château Narbonnais. The squire probably lost consciousness after the limb had been removed, which spared him the pain of being hauled, bloody and handless, through the dirt and stone roads of the city, tied to a horse no doubt agitated by the extra load and surrounded by the noise of an angry crowd. At the château, the greatest symbol of royal power in Toulouse, an executioner cut off the squire's head, and left both head and body on display, as a warning to others who dared defy the capitols' status and authority, and a sign to the

105 AMT-FF 57, 8. The king would later hear charges that the capitols applied torture to Aimery Berenger in order to secure his confession, but the archival records do not mention this.

106 Ibid., 18.

public that vengeance and justice had been achieved. The complete action of the sentence probably lasted no more than an hour. But at each stage of the event, the capitols raised the level of Berenger's humiliation and suffering to a heightened intensity, reinforcing to the public that their office had the legitimate power to achieve justice, without the interference of outside authority.

The friends and family of Aimery Berenger quickly alerted the royal vicar and archbishop of Toulouse to this matter. For a few months, while the vicar gathered evidence and drafted complaints to the king, the capitols and their officers perhaps enjoyed a period of triumph because it seemed as though they had managed to remove royal involvement from their judicial structure and system of punishments without facing any consequences. It was in this phase of assuredness that the capitols and their officers attempted to organize a second public punishment without the vicar. In order to piece together this second case, I draw from two separate archival sources. The first is the criminal register from 1332, in which the capitols heard charges against a young man, Johannes de Manso, accused of kidnapping and raping a young virgin named Mastaroza.[107] While in the municipal archives of Toulouse, I came upon a second register (mistakenly attributed by the archivist to the Aimery Berenger case) which held the transcripts from the royal seneschal's inquest into a jurisdictional dispute between the royal vicar and capitols. In this document, the vicar protested that the capitols commissioned an unauthorized punishment of a woman named Berengaria Vitalis, believed to have sold her daughter's virginity, the same Mastaroza mentioned above, for "money and other goods" to Johannes de Manso.[108] Once again, the capitols commissioned a public punishment which pushed them further away from the side of loyal royal subjects, and closer to that of the people of Toulouse. In the case of Aimery Berenger, the capitols and their officers conducted a very deliberate trial and sentence which successfully excluded the vicar's involvement, and gave them a small sense of victory and resistance. But months later, as the royal and ecclesiastical response to the squire's execution began to grow, the capitols hurried to coordinate Berengaria's punishment in order to hold on to this semblance of autonomy for the people of Toulouse. This second attempt to defy of royal authority began with a

---

107 Ibid., 59–60.

108 AMT-FF 59, fol. 39v. Both cases of Johannes de Manso and Guillelmus de Portello were heard before the capitols' court on June 10. The *rege ribaldum* took place on the Feast of Saints Peter and Paul, June 29 in 1332.

coordinated ritual punishment, and eventually disintegrated into a chaos when the capitols and their officers could no longer control the actions and emotions of the spectators.

In early June, 1332, the capitols' criminal notary recorded very explicit charges of rape against Johannes de Manso, son of Lord Helio de Manso. The accusations claimed that over several days and evenings Johannes de Manso lured both Mastaroza and her mother, Berengaria Vitalis, into a relationship of trust with "false words" and "false promises of friendship."[109] On one afternoon, Mastaroza invited Johannes into her home and he raped her, holding her by the neck and stifling her screams for help by covering her mouth with clothes lying nearby. Johannes then left, only to return later that night to "extract Mastaroza violently from her house" in order to hold her captive in his home a few blocks away. In the capitols' criminal register, Berengaria Vitalis was identified as a single mother. Mastaroza's father, Bernardus of Castranova, lived in the neighborhood of Bolbonne, a few blocks from where mother and daughter lived by the church of Saint Saveur.[110] Several "friends and relatives," probably including Berengaria, confronted Johannes de Manso, and demanded her release from his home. These same concerned individuals stood before the capitols in their court and demanded vengeance in this misdeed.

Two weeks later, the municipal sergeants arrested and imprisoned Berengaria Vitalis in the town hall for prostituting her daughter. There are no extant court records which reveal the investigative process into Berengaria's culpability. Instead, we can only assume that the capitols' had secured the necessary evidence to warrant a ritualistic punishment that denied the royal vicar any role in Berengaria's case or appeals. In the end, we only know the details of the punishment and the latter half of Mastaroza's story because it was the second time in two months that the capitols and their officers had publicly undermined the vicar. In the seneschal's inquest into the jurisdictional dispute between the municipal officials and the vicar, three capitols, several of their sergeants, trumpeter Guillelmus Johannes, and the municipal jailer, Raymundus Bonhomme all stood accused of conspiring against royal authority.

In late June, 1332, nearly twenty days after the capitols first heard the charges against Johannes de Manso, municipal officers extracted two criminals from the town hall and forced them to perform a ritual

109 AMT-FF 57, 59.

110 This area is close to the Cathedral Saint Étienne.

punishment. Guillelmus Portello, convicted of theft, was sentenced to run the town, forfeit all of his goods to the city, and then go into exile. Berengaria Vitalis, convicted of selling her daughter for sexual purposes to Johannes de Manso, would suffer the same punitive fate, but the capitols included an extra touch. She would also wear a crown of straw (*garlanda de palea*) upon her head. On the day in question, each of the men who would be defendants in the seneschal's trial played a different role in the orchestration of the punishment. According to the later charges, three capitols, Petrus Rubey, Raymundus de Santo Paulo, and Vitalis Durandi all gathered at the town hall, and convinced the jailer to release the prisoners into their custody.[111] The municipal jailer, Raymundus Bonhomme, who lived with his family at the town hall in order to survey and feed the prisoners, claimed in his defense testimony that the capitols provided him with the proper documentation necessary to transfer the criminals into their custody for punishment.[112] In other words, either the capitols forged the royal vicar's seal of approval on the letter and duped the jailer, or Raymundus Bonhomme simply knew how to save himself from losing his home and livelihood. Regardless, the capitols and several officers gathered the prisoners and bound them in shackles, placed the crown of straw upon Berengaria's head, and began to lead them by a rope towards the Arnaud Bernard Gate. The first step of bypassing royal approval and intervention in the execution of the punishment had been accomplished.

From this point, other municipal officers steadily joined in the *rege ribaldum*, becoming implicated in the case either consciously or innocently. Johannes de Agenesio, a sergeant for the capitols, testified that on that late June afternoon, he was drinking with friends in a bar near the town hall. Looking outside, he identified several of his colleagues leading a man and a woman towards the Arnaud Bernard Gate. He realized instantly that they were about to run the town because of the way the couple were bound and shackled. He continued drinking for a while, until he and his friends decided to proceed towards the gate as well.[113] Meanwhile, trumpeter Guillelmus Johannes claimed that two or three sergeants of the

---

[111] AMT-FF 59, fol. 11r. All three of the capitols were elected from *capitolats* situated on the right bank of the Garonne: the Daurade, St. Pierre des Cuisines and Pont Vieux respectively. Presumably, all lived a short distance from each other, and thus were able to collaborate and plan this ordeal. Berengaria Vitalis and her daughter lived in the capitolat of Saint Étienne. Their elected official, capitol Raymundus Rosel, was not involved in the punishment.

[112] Ibid., fol. 50r.

[113] Ibid., fol. 8r.

capitols approached him as he was passing through the neighborhood of Arnaud Bernard. He recalled that the officers held the man and a woman by a cord "in the way like they were criminals."[114] One of the sergeants handed him a parchment (*cartus*) which listed the offenses and punishments for the two prisoners, and instructed the trumpeter to read the announcement immediately, sound his horn, and begin the punitive procession. When pressed during interrogation to identify the officers and the signature or seal on the mandate, whether it was a capitol or the royal vicar, the trumpeter claimed to not recall. By the time municipal sergeant Johannes de Agenesio and his drinking companions arrived at the north end of town, the procession had begun and they were a "great multitude of people following and whipping [the prisoners]." Guillelmus Johannes led the crowd, playing his trumpet and calling out the crimes to the spectators, condemning them "on behalf of our lord the king."[115] Even though the capitols and their officers claimed to be acting with best intentions as servants of the king, the royal representative in the city, the vicar, remained excluded from the entire process.

By the time the procession reached the lawn of the Château Narbonnais, the participants had reached a fevered, almost riotous state of emotion. Matheus de Bosto, another sergeant of the capitols, stood with a local merchant before the château that afternoon, when the sound of a trumpet and the loud commotion of a crowd descended upon him, interrupting the conversation. He described a woman wearing a crown of straw, bound in chains, who preceded the wave of people. Officers promptly directed her to a scaffold that stood before the château. After other guards escorted the thief, Guillelmus Portello, out of the adjacent city gate, officers turned their attention to Berengaria Vitalis, still shackled and secured on the platform. Witnesses recounted that several capitols made rousing speeches to the throngs of people surrounding the spectacle, inviting their cries of disdain and judgment against Mastaroza's mother. After this had gone on for some time, someone approached Berengaria with a candle, and set the crown of straw on fire. From all accounts, this last action (committed by an unidentified participant of the crowd) was completely spontaneous and took the municipal officers by surprise. One capitol even rushed to get water from the Garonne River to put out the flames.[116] Clearly, the fine line

114 Ibid., fol. 13v.
115 Ibid., fol. 8r: "ex parte domini nostri Regis."
116 Ibid., fol. 20r.

between ritual justice and mob violence had been blurred. The capitols intended this crown of straw to humiliate Berengaria as she ran through the town, so that all could see she had committed a sexual crime. The crowd's fervor drove that punishment one step further by setting the crown of straw on fire, leaving permanent scars to her face and ruining her hair; she carried a sign of her misdeed for the rest of her life. Beyond this specific example, burning a crown of straw emerges frequently in the execution of heretics. Joan of Arc was reported to have worn one, as was the sixteenth-century Spanish philosopher and physician Michael Servetus (1511–1553), condemned by the Inquisition as a heretic, and sentenced to burn at the stake. At his execution, the Inquisitors placed a crown of straw upon his head that had been doused in sulfur to intensify his suffering.[117] At the beginning of this punishment of Berengaria, it appeared as though the capitols and the people of Toulouse had a common goal of achieving justice for young Mastaroza. But in the end, things spiraled out of control, as the mob's interests may have overlapped with the municipal officials, but they were not congruent.

In the two punishments discussed in this section, the capitols and their municipal officers responded to the public's demand for justice. After Aimery Berenger assaulted a capitol, hundreds of men gathered their own weapons and assisted the night guards in arresting him in his home. To a lesser extant, the friends and relatives of Mastaroza appealed to the capitols to find some sort of aid for the young girl, who was either victimized by a neighbor or her own mother. The capitols found in these cases an opportunity to assert the autonomy of their office by ignoring the royal vicar, and coordinating their own resolution to the crimes. According to the law, Aimery Berenger should have been immediately released to the vicar so that he could determine who had proper jurisdiction over the squire and the vicar or one of his representatives should have approved the punishment. But the nature of his crime was such an affront to the capitols and people of Toulouse, the municipal officials were unwilling to surrender him to outside authority. Instead, the capitols commissioned a symbolic and elaborate punishment, which accentuated their reclamation of their traditions and autonomy. The capitols intended the *rege ribaldum* of Berengaria Vitalis to serve as a statement of their power, and their efforts to protect the citizens of Toulouse. The capitols hurried through the enactment of both punishments so that they received the gratification of

117 Gonthier, *Le châtiment du crime*, 163.

satisfying their constituents, and their own desire to demonstrate their power to administer justice. They performed these deeds publicly, and audaciously, ending the ritual literally on the doorstep of the largest symbol of royal authority in the city, the Château Narbonnais. In the end, the capitols and several of their officers faced the consequences in the royal court for bypassing the authority of the vicar by denying his participation in the execution, or the appeals process. [118] But for a period of time, the capitols enjoyed their defiance of outside authority through these very public punishments, and the people of Toulouse witnessed justice and order restored to their community.

Conclusion

The people who lived and worked in the city of Toulouse witnessed public executions and saw criminals being punished through exposure or running the town fairly regularly. The sound of the trumpet, the proclamations of the offense, the smell and sight of corpses rotting on the gallows all reminded them that their officers were busy at work to rid their streets of malefactors, and to achieve justice for victims and their families. Thus punishment had a presence and meaning in the daily rituals of the Toulousains. The power to administer this punishment was a privilege the capitols were determined not to lose, even if it meant directly opposing royal mandates. The jurisdictional disputes concerning the sentencing of Aimery Berenger, and Berangaria Vitalis reveal the lengths to which the capitols would go in order to secure this right, largely because they understood the importance it served as a symbol of authority to the general public. Municipal authority performed the administration of justice for several reasons. In one respect, it confirmed their centralized authority. Governments could write laws, and preside over criminal cases, but punishment was the realm in which the people of the city could see the power of their officials in action. Secondly, the public of Toulouse did not always have the patience or tolerance for the judicial process. At times they demanded immediate gratification, and expected their elected officials to fulfill this request by punishing particularly heinous crimes. After the Albigensian Crusade, it proved difficult for the capitols and their public to surrender this power to punish to royal officials. The king's men appeared to be unwelcome outsiders to the municipal organization, and

[118] AMT-FF 59, fol. 49r.

punishment, then, became a site of political contestation. The king, however, was too powerful to allow the capitols' subversion of his officers' authority to last too long. In the end, the king's centralized government, armed with trained lawyers and loyal sergeants, suppressed these attempts at resistance, and Toulouse became further integrated into the Capetain Kingdom.

CONCLUSION

The execution of Aimery Berenger became a turning point in the history of medieval Toulouse, largely because King Philip VI's harsh reaction altered the entire composition of the municipal administration and financially devastated the city. Despite the protests of the capitols, who insisted that they did not know that Berenger was under royal safeguard, King Philip believed that the municipal administration had acted in bad faith, and had deliberately ignored his proclamation protecting university scholars and the squires of noble families.[1] In August, 1334, King Philip ordered his officers to seize the property and goods of eleven capitols while his royal vicar and seneschal conducted an investigation into the matter. The capitols were then arrested and sent to a royal jail in Paris. The twelfth capitol joined his former colleagues a few months later.[2] This order removed the municipal officials from the public's sight in Toulouse and rendered them inconsequential to the daily social processes of the city. In July 1335, as the twelve capitols sat in prison, the king and Parlement handed down a severe judgment against the whole city for Berenger's execution in July, 1335. The Parlement declared that through his association with the university and its students, Aimery Berenger should have been considered a "noble stranger," and a clerk in tonsure.[3] Since he was under royal safeguard, the capitols had no legal right to conduct a trial and to punish the squire. The capitols who served the city in 1332, and who played a pivotal role in the lives of the Toulousains, were promptly sentenced to death in Paris. The king realized that their punishment had to play out for the rest of the municipal officers and people of Toulouse in the living and working space of the city.

In his first step to regain control of Toulouse, King Philip VI ordered armed guards to take possession of the town hall, and to stand outside of the building so that the citizens who passed by saw the intimidating spectacle of royal force from October 27, 1335, to the following January.[4] This municipal building, which had served the citizens and its capitols as the

1 *Statuts*, vol. I, no. 576, 532.
2 Ibid., nos. 573–574, 526.
3 Ibid., no. 576, 532. "Nobilem forensem, clericum in tonsura et habitu clericali."
4 Ibid., no. 579, 533.

symbolic link to its glorious past, was now under direct watch of the royal officers. Philip also reduced the number of elected capitols from twelve to eight, thus limiting the possibility for the municipal officials to conspire against royal power, and to gather the support of their constituents.[5] This same mandate stipulated that the city could only have a limited number of sergeants and men who formed the night guard. The city and the newly elected capitols faced heavy financial repercussions as well. The citizens had to pay higher taxes, which prompted a more aggressive survey of taxable immoveable and moveable goods in the city beginning in 1335.[6] The municipal government had to erect a chapel in the city for the repose of Aimery Berenger's soul, and had to distribute 4,000 *livres* among his friends and relatives.[7] When the city began to fall short on its payments, the king revoked Toulouse's corporate privileges, and royal officials confiscated all municipal property. But the king and his royal representatives recognized the importance of symbolically using space to reinforce the notion that Toulouse was, now, a royal city. Thus, the king ordered that people of Toulouse perform a ritual reversal of Berenger's execution, which involved a solemn funeral procession throughout the streets of the city.

At the king's command, the municipal officials of Toulouse gathered what was left of the squire's body that had been exposed to the elements for years in front of the Château Narbonnais. These reversals, or "unhangings," of a wrongfully convicted criminal were not unusual in Paris, especially in conflicts between clerks and secular authority. I referenced earlier an incident in 1304, where the king punished a provost who had hanged an innocent student by commanding the official cut down the corpse (which had been suspended for some months), and kiss it on the mouth.[8] In a second case, another provost executed a student without first granting him a trial. The University of Paris complained to the king, and the clerk's body was taken off of the gibbet and marched back into the city. The provost, found guilty of wrongfully condemning the clerk, had to march in front of the clerk's body and proclaim his wrong doing to the whole city

---

5 AMT-AA 3, 228, February 1336.

6 AMT-AA 6, 51. In February of 1336, the capitols and citizens negotiated an agreement with the king to set up a payment plan to cover the total sum of 50,000 *livres tournois*, to restore some of the municipal privileges.

7 Fournier, *Les statuts*, no. 576, 532.

8 *Chartularium universitatis parisiensis: sub auspiciis Consilii Generalis Facultatum Parisiensium, ex diversis bibliothecis tabulariisque collegit et cum authenticis chartis contulit Henricus Denifle auxiliante Aemilio Chatelain* vol. II (Bruxelles, Culture et Civilisation, 1964), 116, no. 650.

and spectators, asking for their prayers, and stopping at every crossroad.[9] In Toulouse, the king did more than punish a careless provost. He punished the entire city, from the officers to the citizens. The highest ranking public officials led the march, and the remaining citizens followed them two by two. They paraded through the streets carrying Aimery Berenger's remains in a casket, and chanted, "O all of you, inhabitants of Toulouse, both men and women, beg God for the well-being of the Aimery Berenger's soul, who against law and justice was cruelly martyred and decapitated."[10] The participants stopped by the bishop's residence to ask for his forgiveness before the ceremony concluded with Berenger's Christian burial in the cemetery of the Daurade.[11] The king's employment of urban space and its inhabitants, the same arena which had served the people of Toulouse so effectively in shaping their local politics, reasserted the understanding that Toulouse was under royal control and law.[12]

As the Aimery Berenger controversy was reaching a resolution between the king and local officials in Toulouse, the region faced issues more pressing than debates concerning judicial precedence. Languedoc suffered from crop failures as early as 1334, and once the Black Death swept through in 1348, it became increasingly difficult for people to find sustenance.[13] But the greatest threat to Toulouse and Languedoc began in 1340, with the renewed fighting of the Hundred Years War in the nearby region of Guyenne. The English troops became more entrenched in the area and loomed closer to Toulouse, and the capitols and its inhabitants realized that they needed the king and his military protection.[14] At this moment, an outside threat in the form of the English pushed the transition of the Toulousains fully into the royal kingdom. The king sent correspondence to the capitols praising them for their strength and loyalty in the wake of the military threats. For the first time since the Albigensian Crusade, the king

[9] Discussed in Cohen, "'To Die a Criminal,'" 291–292.

[10] Fournier, *Les Statuts*, no. 575, 527. "Aula major dicte domus compavimentum totius domus capitularis palestratum per fuit. Die Martis, hora quarta, clamatores defunctorum per omnes carrerias civitatis et burgi clamaverunt: 'O vos omnes, habitatores Tholose, tam homines quam femine, Deum rogate pro salute anime Aymerici Berengarii, qui contra jus et justitiam per vos crudeliter martyrisatus fuit et per borellum decapitatus.'"

[11] Gourdon de Genouillac, *Histoire du capitoulat*, 24.

[12] Gauvard, "Pendre et dépendre," 206–207, 209. Cohen, *The Crossroads of Justice*, 133.

[13] R.L. Lavigne, "La Peste Noire et la commune de Toulouse; le témoignage du livre des matricules des notaries," *Annales du Midi* 83 (1971): 413–417. Wolff, *Histoire de Toulouse*, 184–185.

[14] Jonathan Sumption, *The Hundred Years War I: Trial by Battle* (Philadelphia: University of Pennsylvania Press, 1990), 455–488.

allowed the capitols and the citizens the right to rebuild their fortifications and the ancient city walls. The capitols commissioned artisans and raised taxes to pay for the necessary materials; the archbishop even sent a letter to the clerks that commanded they pay their share for the repairs.[15] This common enemy of the English and the realties of war allowed the capitols, the citizens, the ecclesiastical affiliates and the king to unite for the welfare of the city space.

But let us return to the beginning of this story and to the local forum of Toulouse in the late thirteenth and early fourteenth century. In this period of political transition into the royal kingdom, the relationship between municipal officers and urban residents was negotiated through symbolic uses of various urban spaces. Each location throughout Toulouse carried a different meaning for the urban residents and their administration. The various neighborhoods served as micro-communities, where disputes between citizens over status and honor could lead to longstanding grudges and outbreaks of violence. Even the town hall represented the endurance and centrality of the local administration in the lives of the Toulousains, and became a common location for popular protests and other gatherings of citizens. Within this urban environment, the capitols and their sergeants interacted with the people in the streets and in their courtroom, as they all struggled to maintain an orderly community through the performance of justice. This nuanced relationship between the municipal officers and the citizens played out in the public sphere, until the presence and authority of the royal officers complicated the political and jurisdictional landscape. This work has explored how the capitols and their officers collaborated with, and sometimes manipulated, the public in order to subvert royal sovereignty through demonstrations which incorporated the city space.

The criminal records and jurisdictional disputes reveal that the Toulousains – citizens and capitols alike – resisted royal sovereignty well into the fourteenth century, largely due to their mutual (although not always congruent) understanding of crime, punishment, and justice. Ever since the Raymondine counts controlled the city, the people of Toulouse turned to their elected officials to protect them from malefactors, and to render justice to the victims through various punishments and reparations within the community. Once the royal vicar began to impede upon this cooperative process of law and order between the municipal

---

15 The bishop's letter is found in AMT-layettes II, 47, dated 1356. The register of the payment distribution and the list of commissioned workers are recorded in AMT-EE 32, 1355.

authority and the Toulousains, the capitols devised means of subverting the king's sovereignty by ignoring mandates concerning jurisdiction. The public spectacles of protest which unfolded in the forum of the civic squares and thoroughfares were sparked by the clashes between local inhabitants and representatives of royal power in Toulouse. When the capitols feared that the perpetrator may go unpunished due to the legal loopholes of royal protection and privilege, they coordinated events which incorporated the city space and spectators in order to reclaim their autonomy from the French administration.

The French people are often stereotyped for their habit of spilling into the streets in riotous protest at the slightest provocation. But in the fourteenth century, much as today, the participants of these events who clashed with authority figures and filled the public spaces in demonstrations of protest, were not necessarily mindless delinquents. Instead, the men and women of Toulouse considered and approached their public space as a forum of political negotiation with the municipal officials. If the citizens were disgruntled with the capitols' actions, or inactivity, they did not hesitate to flock to the town hall and demand that their concerns be addressed. The lives of the Toulousains played out in the plain view of their neighbors, including personal conflicts, grudges, and even the violent attacks. When the capitols sought justice for the victims, this too needed to involve the public, so that acceptable behavior was regulated and defined through a reciprocal exchanges and interactions between the administration and the people. If the local governments did not evolve to accommodate new social, economic or demographics demands, thousands of protesters filled the city space to help shape the new policies of the city.

* * *

By the beginning of the fourteenth century, Toulouse's administrators put forth a concerted effort to assure the rest of France that the city was a royal, orthodox, and now, safe city. The evils of the Cathar heresy that had penetrated the once great capitol of Languedoc had been expelled and eliminated by the power of royal crusaders. Those who had fallen to heresy either converted to Christianity at the hands of the Dominican inquisitors, or suffered the consequences. In fact, more voices started to echo the sentiment of Jean de Garland from 1230 that started this book: Toulouse was a city as full of stability, food, wine and pleasantries. By 1319, Petrus de Martiris of the abbey of Saint Sernin, insisted that Toulouse had progressed to a place first amongst the great cities of the western world, because it was a city irrigated by "both the fountains of law and of divinity," and its fame was "brilliant as a star shining on the entire world."[16] Four years later, the scholars of Toulouse who longed to revive the traditions of the region's troubadours began an international poetry competition, known as the *Jeux Floraux* (Floral Games) in 1323. The contest celebrated the region's traditional language of Occitan, the splendor of Toulouse and the hospitality of its people.[17] It provided an occasion for the capitols to host an elaborate feast for distinguished guests and their officers. This event contributed to the impression that the city was an environment thriving with literature and prosperity.[18] The intellectuals who lived through the political and religious turmoil of the thirteenth and fourteenth centuries, in other words, were eager to accentuate and to reestablish the city's glory.

Despite all of the posturing of these medieval poets and scholars, we now understand the harsh reality of living in Toulouse in this same era. Decomposing bodies of criminals hanged from the gallows, violent attacks erupted in taverns, and at any given moment, the municipal trumpeter could announce a prisoner was about to run the streets of the city. Today, the inhabitants of Languedoc are more likely to celebrate and embrace this tumultuous history by visiting torture museums that document the Cathars' story through terrific instruments of pain and suffering. In many respects, these modern tourist attractions serve the same function as the capitols' town hall in the Middle Ages. Both are a testament to Languedoc's resistance to outside authority. The torture museums suggest that the Cathars only conceded to the demands of church officials after suffering unspeakable pain at the hands of the Dominican friars and royal officers. The medieval town hall contained the trebuchet that killed Simon de

---

[16] Étienne de Gan, *De fundationibus tempore loco et nominee Tholose et Rome, Anglie, Britanie, Narbonie et Parisius*, AMT-AA 5: 1, cited in Smith *The University of Toulouse*, 76. "Inter urbis magnificas, nostra et vestra civitas Tholosa affatim preconiis digna velut sidus nucans, cultu decorata divino, fonte utriusue juris et divina irrigata, numerosa populi caterva ac mercibus opulenta radios honoris ex hac fameque frangranciam spargit et mittit per orbem." Étienne de Gan cited Petrus de Martiris in a fifteenth-century history of Toulouse, dedicated to the archbishop of Toulouse, Bernard de Rouseque (1451–1474).

[17] Lafaille reprinted several of the early invitations to poets to participate in the events, as well as several of their works, all of which glorified Toulouse as the force behind the preservation of troubadour traditions. *Annales de Toulouse*, 61–63, and *Preuves*, 64–84. See also François Gélis, *Histoire critique des Jeux floraux : depuis leur origine jusqu'à leur transformation en Académie (1323–1694)* (Geneva: Slatkine, 1981).

[18] François Bordes, "Pouvoir municipal et gastronomie au XVe siècle: les festins des capitouls de Toulouse," *Du bien manger et du bien vivre à travers les âges et les terroirs* (*Actes du LIVe congrès d'études régionales de la Fédération historique du Sud-Ouest* (*Brantôme, 19–20 mai 2001*), (Pessac: Maison des Sciences de l'Homme d'Aquitaine, 2002), 95–116.

Montfort in the Albigensian Crusade. This military apparatus reminded the Toulousains that they fought bravely and determinedly to protect the autonomy of their city from the royal crusaders. In the fourteenth century, the Toulousains struggled to achieve a balance between preserving the customs of Languedoc and accommodating the political and social demands of being part of France. But in the Middle Ages, as today, the people of Toulouse played an active role in shaping the city's political and social future.

SELECTED BIBLIOGRAPHY

I. *Archival Sources*

Archives municipales d'Albi

Albi, France

FF7 (1297–1411) Diverse Jurisdictional Conflicts between Albi's Consules and Royal Vicar

Archives municipales de Moissac

Moissac, Frace

FF1 (1301–1308) Register of the City Consules' criminal sentences

Archives municipals de Toulouse

Toulouse, France

AA1 (1141–1279) Cartulary of the *Bourg*
AA2 (1141–1279) Cartulary of the *Cité*
AA3 (1141–1556) *Livre blanc*, cartulary of Bernard de Sainte-Eulalie (1295)
AA4 (1192–1322) Fourteenth century cartulary
AA5 (1152–1539) *Livre blanc*, cartulary of Jean Balard (1540)
AA6 (1152–1560) Cartulary of Jean Balard (1560)
AA34 (1273–1730) Diverse acts of the Capetian kings
AA35 (1273–1730) Diverse acts of the Capetian kings
AA56 (1341) Copy of an ordinance by Robert de Charny, knight, and councilor of the king, citing various reformations in Toulouse.

BB269–273 *Douze Livres de Toulouse 1295–1675*

FF57 Criminal Trials of the Capitols, 1332
FF58 Trial of Aimery Berenger, 1332
FF59 Inquest into the Jurisdiction of the Capitols, 1332
FF60 Inquest into the conduct of the Capitols against a university scholar, 1336
FF61 Bernard de Marignac Affair, 1394
FF62 Affair of Clare de Portet, 1428–1444.
FF111 Process before the Senechal against Jean Dupuy, inquisitor at Toulouse concerning a blasphemer. Copy certified by Pierre de Comminges, royal notary of Toulouse, 1426.
FF 616 Register of the *guet*'s rounds, June 16, 1539 to August 28, 1542.

Series II, Cartons 1–100

Bibliothèque municipale de Toulouse

Toulouse, France

MS 874, Dominican cartulary of diverse documents from thirteenth and fourteenth centuries

Archives départmentales de la Haute-Garonne

Toulouse, France

1 G 345 Cartulary of the Archbishop (1286–1327)
1 G 346 Cartulary of the Archbishop (1286–1327)
1 G 347 Cartulary of the Archbishop (1279–1438)
4 G 39 Fonds of cathedral chapter of Saint Etienne (1339)

Bibliothèque nationale

Paris, France

MS Lat. 9187, Customary Law of Toulouse (1286) with Commentary (1296)
MS Lat. 2355, N.A., fol. 58, Financial Inventory of the Toulouse's court of appeals, 14th Century
MS Lat. 11848, Bernard Gui's Acts of Toulouse's Inquisition (1307–1323)

II. *Archival Catalogues and References*

Dumas de Rauly, Charles and Alfred Gandilhon. *Inventaire-sommaire des archives communales et Hospitalières de Moissac*. Montauban: Imprimerie et Lithographie Forestie, 1906–1907.

Jolibois, Emile. *Inventaires-sommaires des archives communales antérieurs à 1790 (Albi)*. Paris: Imprimerie et Librairie Administratives de Paul DuPont, 1869.

Roschach, Ernest. *Ville de Toulouse – Inventaire des Archives Communales antérieurs à 1790*, vol. 1 (only 1 completed) Séries AA, nos. 1–60, Toulouse: Édouard Privat, 1891.

Saint-Blanquat, Odon de. *Inventaire des archives antérieurs à 1790 (Ville de Toulouse)*. Toulouse: Graphoprint, 2 vols., 1976–1977.

Salies, Pierre. *Dictionnaire des rues de Toulouse: voies publiques, quartiers, lieux-dits, enseignes, organisation urbaine*, 2 vols. Toulouse: Éditions Milan, 1989.

III. *Printed Primary Sources*

Berger, Élie, ed. *Layettes du trésor des chartes*, vol. IV. Paris: Plon-Nourrit, 1902.

Denifle, Henri. *Les universités françaises au moyen- âge; avis à M. Marcel Fournier, éditeur des Statuts et privilèges des universités françaises; avec les documents inédits*. Paris: Émile Bouillon, Éditeur, 1892.

Dossat, Yves. *Saisimentum Comitatus Tholosani*. Paris: Bibliothèque Nationale, 1966.

Douais, Célestin ed. *Documents pour servir à l'histoire de l'inquisition dans le Languedoc*. Paris: H. Champion, 1977.

Fournier, Marcel. *Les statuts et privilèges des universités françaises, depuis leur fondation jusqu'en 1789*, vol. 1 Aalen, Italy: Scientia Verlag, 1970

Gadave, René. *Les documents sur l'histoire de l'université de Toulouse et spécialement de sa faculté de droit civil et canonique (1229–1789)*. Toulouse: Imprimerie et Librarie Édouard Privat, 1910.

Gilles, Henri. *Coutumes de Toulouse (1286) et leur premier commentaire (1296)*. Toulouse: Imprimerie Maurice ESPIC, 1969.

Jean Le Fèvre, *Chronique de Jean Le Fèvre, Seigneur de Saint-Remy*, ed. François Morand. Paris: Librairie Renouard, 1876, vol. I.

Journal d'un Bourgeois de Paris sous Charles VI et Charles VII, ed. André Mary. Paris: H. Jonquières, 1929.

Limouzin-Lamothe, Roger. *La commune de Toulouse et les sources de son histoire, 1120–1249*. Paris and Toulouse, 1932.

Maillard, François ed. *Comptes royaux (1314–1328)*. Paris: Imprimerie nationale, 1961.

Meijers, Eduard Maurits. *Responsa doctorum tholosanorum*. Haarlem: H.D. Tjeenk Willink & Zoon, n.v., 1938.

Molinier, Auguste. *Correspondance administrative d'Alphonse de Poitiers*. 2vols. Paris: Imprimerie Nationale, 1894 and 1900.

Mulholland, Sister Mary Ambrose BVM. *Early Guild Records of Toulouse*. New York: Columbia University Press, 1941.

Pales-Gobilliard, Annette. *Le Livre des sentences de l'inquisiteur Bernard Gui (1308- 1323)*, 2 vols. Paris: CNRS Éditions, 2002.

Peter of les Vaux-de-Cernay. *The History of the Albigensian Crusade. Peter of les Vaux- de-Cernay's Historia Albigensis*. Translated by W.A. Sibly and M.D. Sibly. Woodbridge, Suffolk: The Boydell Press, 1998.

Peter of les Vaux-de-Cernay. *Petri Vallium Sarnaii monachi Hystoria albigensis*, ed. Pascal Guébin and Ernest Lyon. vol. 1. Paris, Champion, 1926–1939. Van Limborch, Philipp. *Historia inquisitionis, cui subjungitur Liber sententiarum inquisitionis Tholosanae ab anno Christi MCCCVII ad annum MCCCXXIII*. Amsterdam: Apud H. Wetstenium, 1692.

William of Puylaurens. *The Chronicle of The Albigensian Crusade and Its Aftermath*. Translated by W.A. Sibly and M.D. Sibly. Woodbridge, Suffolk: The Boydell Press, 2003.

William of Tudela and an Anonymous Successor. *The Song of the Cathars: A History of the Albigensian Crusade*. Translated by Janet Shirley. Brookfield, Vermont: Ashgate Publishing Company, 1996.

IV. *Secondary Sources*

Attreed, Lorraine. "The Politics of Welcome: Ceremonies and Constitutional Development in Later Medieval English Towns." In *City and Spectacle in Medieval Europe*, edited by Barbara A. Hanawalt and Kathryn L. Reyerson, 208–231. Minneapolis: University of Minnesota Press, 1994.

Baldwin, John W. *The Government of Philip Augustus: Foundations of French Royal Power in the Middle Ages*. Berkeley: The University of California Press, 1986.

Balzaretti, Ross. "'These are things that men do, not women': The Social Regulation of Female Violence in Langobard Italy." In *Violence and Society in Early Medieval West*, edited by Guy Halsall, 175–192. Woodbridge, Suffolk: The Boydell Press, 1998.

Bartlett, Robert. *The Hanged Man: A Story of Miracle, Memory, and Colonialism in the Middle Ages*. Princeton: Princeton University Press, 2004.

Berman, Harold J. *Law and Revolution: The Formation of the Western Legal Tradition*. Cambridge, Massachusetts: Harvard University Press, 1983.

Biraben, Jean-Nöel. "La population de Toulouse au XIVe et XVe siècles." *Journal des Savants* (1964): 285–300.

Bordes, François. "Pouvoir municipal et gastronomie au XVe siècle: les festins des capitouls de Toulouse." In *Du bien manger et du bien vivre à travers les âges et les terroirs (Actes du LIVe congrès d'études régionales de la Fédération historique du Sud-Ouest (Brantôme, 19–20 mai 2001)*, 95–116. Pessac: Maison des Sciences de l'Homme d'Aquitaine, 2002.

——. "Une perception de l'espace urbain: cortèges officials et processions générales à Toulouse du XIVe au XVI siècle." *Mémoires de la sociététe archéologique du midi de la France* vol. 66 (2004): 135–153.

——. "Vêtements et fonctions municipales à Toulouse" (XIIIe-XVe siècle): du text à l'image." *Vêture et pouvoir* (2003): 125–136.

Boyer, Georges. "Remarques sur l'administration de Toulouse au temps d'Alphonse de Poiters." In *Mélanges I: Mélanges d'histoire du droit occidentale*, 198–209. Paris: Sirey, 1962.
Boutaric, Edgard. *La France sous Philip le Bel – Étude sur les institutions politiques et administratifs du Moyen âge.* Paris: Henri Plon, 1861.
Bowsky, William M. "The Medieval Commune and Internal Violence: Police Power and Public Safety in Siena, 1287–1355." *The American Historical Review* 73 no. 1 (October, 1967): 1–17.
Brundage, James A. *Law, Sex, and Christian Society in Medieval Europe.* Chicago: University of Chicago Press, 1987.
——. *Medieval Canon Law.* London and New York: Longman, 1995.
Buffelan, Jean-Paul. *La noblesse des capitouls de Toulouse.* St. Gaudens: L'Adret, 1986.
Cabau, Patrice. "Les évêques de Toulouse (IVe-XIVe siècles) et les lieux de leur Sepulture." *Mémoires de la Société Archéologique du Midi de la France*, 59 (1999): 123–162.
Carbasse, Jean-Marie. "«Currant nudi» Le répression de l'adultère dans le Midi médiéval, XIIe-VXe siècles." In *Droit, Histoire et Sexualité*, edited by Jacques Poumarede and Jean-Pierre Royer, 83–102. Lille: Achevé d'imprimer, 1987.
——. *Histoire du droit pénal et de la justice criminelle.* Paris: Presses Universitaires de France, 2000.
——. "La peine en droit français des origines au XVIIe siècle." In *La peine*, 157–172. vol. 2. Bruxelles: DeBoeck, 1991.
Catel, Guillaume. *Histoire des comtes de Toulouse, avec quelque traitez et chroniques anciennes, concernans la mesme histoire.* Toulouse: P. Bosc, 1623.
Certeau, Michel de. *The Practice of Everyday Life*, translated by Steven Rendall. Berkeley: The University of California Press, 1984.
Chague, Marie-Martin. "Conribution à l'étude du recrutement des agents royaux en Languedoc aux XIVe et XVe siècles." In *France du Nord et France du Midi: Contacts et influences réciproques*, 359–378. vol. 1. Toulouse: Actes du 96e Congrès National des Sociétés Savantes, 1971.
Chalande, Jules. *Histoire Monumentale de l'Hôtel de Ville de Toulouse.* Toulouse: Imprimerie St. Cyprien, 1922.
Chiffoleau, Jacques. *Les justices du pape: délinquance et criminalité dans la région d'Avignon au XIV siècle.* Paris: Publications de la Sorbonne, 1984.
——. "La violence au quotidien: Avignon au XIV siècle d'après les registres de la cour temporelle." *Mélanges de l'École française de Rome: Moyen Âge au Temps Modernes* 92 (1980): 325–371.
Cohen, Esther. "'To Die a Criminal for Public Good:' The Execution Ritual in Late Medieval Paris." In *Law, Customs, and Social Fabric in Medieval Europe*, 280–304.
——. "Patterns of Crime in Fourteenth-Century Paris." *French Historical Studies* 11 (Spring, 1980): 307–327.
——. "Symbols of Culpability and the Universal Language of Justice: The Ritual of Public Executions in Late Medieval Europe." *History of European Ideas*, 11 (1989): 407–416.
Coppolani, Jean. *Toulouse: Étude de géographie urbaine.* Toulouse: Imprimerie Edouard Privat, 1951.
Coulet, Noël. "Quelques aspects du milieu médical en Provence au bas Moyen-Âge." In *Vie priveé et ordre public à la fin du moyen- âge: Études sur Manosque, la Provence et le Piémont (1250–1450)*, edited by Michel Hébert, 119–138. Aix-en-Provence: Université de Provence Service des Publications, 1987.
Courtemanche, Andrée. "The Judge, The Doctor, and the Prisoner: Medical Expertise in Manosquin Judicial Rituals at the end of the Fourteenth Century." In *Medieval and Early Modern Ritual: Formalized Behavior in Europe, China, and Japan*, edited by Joëlle Rollo-Koster, 105–123. Boston: Brill, 2002.
Cox, J. Charles. *The Sanctuaries and Sanctuary Seekers in Mediaeval England.* London: G. Allen and Sons, 1911.
Crawford, Catherine. "Medicine and the Law." In *Companion Encyclopedia of the History of Medicine*, edited by W.F. Bynum and Roy Porter, 1622–1624. London: Routledge, 1993.

Davis, Natalie Zemon. *Fiction in the Archives: Pardon Tales and their Tellers in Sixteenth-Century France.* Stanford, California: Stanford University Press, 1987.
Davis, Robert C. *The War of the Fists: Popular Culture and Public Violence in Late Renaissance Venice.* New York: Oxford University Press, 1994.
Dean, Trevor. *Crime in Medieval Europe, 1200–1550.* London: Pearson Education, 2001.
De Ridder-Symoens, Hilde. "Rich Men, Poor Men: Social Stratification and Social Representation at the University (13th-16th Centuries)." In *Showing Status: Representations of Social Positions in the Late Middle Ages*, edited by Wim Blockmans and Antheun Janse, 159–175. Turnhout, Belgium: Brepols, 1999.
Dossat, Yves. *Paix de Dieu et guerre sainte en Languedoc au XIIIe siècle*, Cahiers de Fanjeaux, vol. 4. Toulouse, Édouard Privat, 1969.
Du Mège, Alexandre. *Histoire des institutions religieuses, politiques, judiciaires et littéraires de la Ville de Toulouse.* Toulouse: Imprimerie de Laurent Chapelle, 1844.
Ellul, Jacques. *Histoire des Institutions, vol. 3: Le Moyen Âge.* Paris: Presses Universitaires de France, 1962.
Fédou, René. "Les sergents à Lyon aux XIVe et XVe siècles: une institution, un type social." In *Bulletin Philogique et Historique (jusqu'à 1610)*, 283–292. Paris: Bibliothèque Nationale, 1967.
Foucault, Michel. *Discipline and Punish: The Birth of the Prison.* Translated by Alan Sheridan. New York: Vintage Books, 1979.
Garapon, Antoine. *Bien juger: Essai sur le rituel judiciaire.* Paris: Odile Jacob, 1997.
Gardner, Christopher. "Negotiating Lordship: Efforts of the Consulat of Toulouse to Retain Autonomy under Capetian Rule (ca. 1229–1315)." Ph.D. dissertation, Johns Hopkins University, 2002.
Gauvard, Claude. "*De grace espécial: crime, état et société en France à la fin du Moyen Age.* 2 vols. Paris: Publications de la Sorbonne, 1991.
——. "La criminalité parisienne à la fin du Moyen Âge: une criminalité ordinaire?" In *Villes, bonnes villes, cités et capitales: Études d'histoire urbaine (XIIe-XVIIIe siècle) offertes à Bernard Chevalier*, edited by Monique Bourin, 361–370. Caen: Paradigme, 1993.
——."Fear of Crime in Late Medieval France." In *Medieval Crime and Social Control*, edited by Barbara A. Hanawalt and David Wallace, 1–48. Minneapolis: University of Minnesota Press, 1999.
——."Les officiers royaux et l'opinion politique en France à la fin de Moyen Âge." In *Histoire comparée de l'Administration (IVe-XVIIIe siècles)*, 583–593. Munich: Artemis, 1980.
——. "Pendre et dépendre à la fin du Moyen Âge: les exigences d'un ritual judiciaire." In *Riti e rituali nella società medievali*, edited by Jacques Chiffoleau, Lauro Martines, and A. Paravicini Bagliani, 191–214. Spoleto: Centro italiano di studi sull'alto medioevo, 1994.
Genouillac, Henri Gourdon de. *Histoire du capitoulat et des capitouls de Toulouse.* Marseille: Laffitte Reprints, 1974.
Geremek, Bronislav. *The Margins of Society in Late Medieval Paris*, translated by Jean Birrell. Cambridge: Cambridge University Press, 1987.
Gessler, J. "*Mulier suspensa*: à délit égal peine différente?" *Revue Belge de philologie et d'histoire* 18 (1939): 974–988.
Gilles, Henri. "Une cause d'injures à Toulouse à la fin du XIIIe siècle." *Annales de la faculté de droit et des sciences économiques de Toulouse* 17 (1969): 121–144.
——. "L'Enseignement du droit en Languedoc au XIIIe siècle." In *Les Universités du Languedoc au XIIIe siècle*, 205–229. Toulouse: Privat, 1970.
Given, James B. *Inquisition and Medieval Society: Power, Discipline and Resistance in Languedoc.* Ithaca: Cornell University Press, 1997.
——. *Society and Homicide in Thirteenth Century England.* Stanford: Stanford University Press, 1977.
——. *State and Society in Medieval Europe: Gwynedd and Languedoc under Outside Rule.* Ithaca: Cornell University Press, 1990.
Gonthier, Nicole. *Cris de haines et rites d'unité: la violence dans les villes, XIIIe-XVIe siècle.* Turnhout: Brepols, 1992.

——. *Le châtiment du crime au moyen âge, XIIe-XVIe siècles.* Rennes: Presses Universitaire de Rennes, 1998.
——. *Délinquance, justice et société dans le lyonnais médiévale: de la fin du XIIIe siècle au début du XVIe siècle.* Paris: AP éditions Arguments: 1993.
Gosselin, Ronald. "Honneur et Violence à Manosque (1240–1260)." In *Vie priveé et ordre public à la fin du moyen- âge: Études sur Manosque, la Provence et le Piémont (1250–1450)*, edited by Michel Hébert, 45–63. Aix-en-Provence: Université de Provence Service des Publications, 1987.
Green, Thomas A. *Verdict according to Conscience: Perspectives on the English Criminal Trial Jury, 1200–1800.* Chicago: University of Chicago Press, 1985.
Groebner, Valentin. *Defaced: The Visual Culture of Violence in the Late Middle Ages.* Trans. Pamela Selwyn. New York: Zone Books, 2004.
——. "Losing Face, Saving Face: Noses and Honor in the Late Medieval Town." *History Workshop Journal* 40 (1995): 1–15.
Guenée, Bernard. *Tribunaux et gens de justice dans le bailliage de Senlis à la fin du Moyen Âge (vers 1380-vers 1550).* Paris: En dépôt à la Société d'éditions Les Belles Lettres, 1963.
Guilhiermoz, Paul. "Notes sur des poids et measures du moyen âge." *Bibliothèque des écoles des chartes*, 67 (1906): 161–233.
Hallam, Elizabeth M. *Capetian France, 987–1328.* New York: Longman, 2001.
Hammer, Carl I. "Patterns of Homicide in a Medieval University Town: Fourteenth-Century Oxford." *Past and Present* 78 (1978): 3–23.
Hanawalt, Barbara A. *Crime and Conflict in English Communities, 1300–1348.* Cambridge: Harvard University Press, 1979.
——. "The Female Felon in Fourteenth Century England." In *Women in Medieval Society*, edited by Susan Mosher Stuard, 125–140. Philadelphia: The University of Pennsylvania Press, 1976.
——. *'Of Good and Ill Repute:' Gender and Social Control in Medieval England.* Oxford: Oxford University Press, 1998.
——. "Violent Death in Fourteenth and Early Fifteenth-Century England," *Comparative Studies in Society and History* 18 (1976): 297–320.
Hébert, Michel. "*Voce preconia*: note sur les criées publiques en Provence." In *milieux naturels, espaces sociaux: études offertes à Robert Delort*, edited by Élisabeth Mornet and Franco Morenzoni, 689–701. Paris: Publications de la Sorbonne, 1997.
Higounet, M. "Le peuplement de Toulouse au XII siècle." *Annales du Midi.* Toulouse: Édouard Privat, 1943. 489–498.
Huizinga, Johan. *The Autumn of the Middle Ages*, trans. Rodney J. Payton and Ulrich Mammitzsch. Chicago: The University of Chicago Press, 1996.
James, Mervyn. "Ritual, Drama and Social Body in the Late Medieval English Town." *Past and Present* 3 (February, 1983): 3–29.
Jarousseau, Géraud. "Le guet, l'arrière-guet et la garde en Poitou pendant la Guerre de Cent Ans." *Bulletin de la Société des Antiquaires de l'Ouest* 8 (1965): 159–202.
Laffaile, Germain de. *Annales de la ville de Toulouse depuis la réunion de la compté de Toulouse à la couronne*, 2 vols. Toulouse: Guillaume-Louis Colomyez, 1687–1701.
Laribière, Geneviève. "Le mariage à Toulouse aux XIVe et XVe siècles." *Annales du Midi* 79 (1967): 335–361.
Lavigne, R.L. "La Peste Noire et la commune de Toulouse; le témoignage du livre des matricules des notaries." *Annales du Midi* 83 (1971): 413–417.
Lavoie, Rodrigue. "Les statistiques criminelles et le visage du justicier: justice royale et justice seigneuriale en Provence au Moyen Âge." *Provence historique* 115 (1979): 3–20.
——. "Justice, criminalité et peine de mort en France au moyen âge: essai de typologie et de regionalization." In *Le Sentiment de la mort au moyen âge: Études présentées au Cinquième colloque de l'institut d'études médiévales de l'Université de Montréal*, edited by Claude Sutto, 33–55. Montreal: L'Aurore, 1979.

Le Bail, Marie-Laure. "Le droit et l'image: sur un cas d'essorillage." *Médiévales* 9 (1985): 103–117.

Le Goff, Jacques. "La ville médiévale et le temps." In *Villes, bonnes villes, cités et capitals: Études d'histoire urbaine (XIIe-XVIIIe siècle) offertes à Bernard Chevalier*, edited by Monique Bourin, 325–332. Caen: Paradigme, 1993.

Leguay, Jean-Pierre. *La rue au moyen âge*. Rennes: Ouest-France, 1984.

L'Engle, Susan. "Justice in the Margins: Punishment in Medieval Toulouse." *Viator: Medieval and Renaissance Studies* 33 (2002): 133–165.

Liliequist, Jonas. "Peasants against Nature: Crossing the Boundaries between Man and Animal in Seventeenth- and Eighteenth-Century Sweden." *Journal of the History of Sexuality* 1 (1991): 393–423.

Martin-Chabot, E. "La tradition capitoline à Toulouse à la fin du XIIIe siècle." *Annales du Midi*, 29–30 (1917–1918): 345–354.

Merle, Roger. *Les grandes affaires criminelles de Toulouse.* Toulouse: Édouard Privat, 1978.

Mills, Robert. *Suspended Animation: Pain, Pleasure and Punishment in Medieval Culture.* London: Reaktion Books, 2005.

Mirot, Léon. *Les insurrections urbaines au début du règne de Charles VI (1380–1383): Leur causes, leurs consequences.* Paris: Albert Fontemoing, Éditeur, 1906.

Misraki, Jacqueline. "Criminalité et pauvreté en France à l'époque de la Guerre de Cent Ans." In *Études sur l'histoire de la pauvreté (Moyen âge- XVIe siècle)*, edited by Michelle Mollat, 536–546. Paris: Publications de la Sorbonne, 1974.

Mulholland, Sister Mary Ambrose. "Statutes on Clothmaking: Toulouse, 1227." In *Essays in Medieval Life and Thought, Presented in Honor of Austin Patterson Evans,* edited by John H. Mundy, Richard W. Emery and Benjamin N. Nelson, 167–180. New York: Columbia University Press, 1955.

Mundy, John Hine. "Hospitals and Leprosaries in Twelfth and Early Thirteenth Century Toulouse." In *Essays in Medieval Life and Thought*, 181–205.

——. *Liberty and Political Power in Toulouse, 1050–1230.* New York: Columbia University Press, 1954.

——. *Men and Women at Toulouse in the Age of the Cathars.* Toronto: Pontifical Institute of Mediaeval Studies, 1990.

——. "The Origins of the College of Saint-Raymond at the University of Toulouse." In *Philosphy and Humanism: Renaissance Essays in Honor of Paul Oskar Kristeller*, edited by Edward P. Mahoney, 454–461. New York: Columbia University Press, 1976.

——. *The Repression of Catharism at Toulouse: The Royal Diploma of 1279.* Toronto: Pontifical Institute of Mediaeval Studies, 1985.

——. *Society and Government at Toulouse in the Ages of the Cathars.* Toronto: Pontifical Institute of Mediaeval Studies. 1997.

Nahon, Gérard. "Les juifs dans les domains d'Alfonse de Poitiers, 1241–1271." *Revue des Études Juives* 124 (1966): 157–211.

Nicholas, David. "Crime and Punishment in Fourteenth-Century Ghent." *Revue Belge de Philologie et d'Histoire* 48 (1970): 289–334, 1141–1176.

Otis, Leah Lydia. *Prostitution in Medieval Society: The History of an Urban Institution in Languedoc.* Chicago: The University of Chicago Press, 1985.

Paterson, Linda M. *The World of the Troubadours. Medieval Occitan Society, c.1100–c.1300.* Cambridge: Cambridge University Press, 1993.

Pennington, Kenneth. *The Prince and the Law, 1200–1600: Soveriegnty and Rights in the Western Legal Tradition.* Berkeley and Los Angeles: University of California Press, 1993.

Peters, Edward. *Torture.* New York: Basil Blackwell, Inc., 1985.

——. "Prison before Prison: The Ancient and Medieval Worlds." In *The Oxford History of the Prison: The Practice of Punishment in Western Society*, edited by Norval Morris and David J. Rothman, 3–43. New York: Oxford University Press, 1998.

Prevenier, Walter. "Violence against Women in a Medieval Metropolis: Paris around 1400." In *Law, Custom and the Social Fabric in Medieval Europe*, 263–284.

Prin, Maurice and Jean Rocacher. *Le Château Narbonnais: Le Parlement et le Palais de Justice de Toulouse*. Toulouse: Éditions Privat, 1991.

Pugh, Ralph B. *Imprisonment in Medieval England*. Cambridge: Cambridge University Press, 1968.

Reyerson, Katheryn L. "Flight from Prosecution: The Search for Religious Asylum in Medieval Montpellier." *French Historical Studies* 17, No. 3 (Spring, 1992): 603–626.

Ramet, Henri. *Histoire de Toulouse*. Marseille: Laffitte Reprints, 1977.

Roschach, Ernest. "Comment l'hôtel de ville de Toulouse a pris le nom de Capitole." *Revue de Toulouse* 23 (1866): 445–448.

——. *Les Douze Livres de l'Histoire de Toulouse Chroniques Municipales Manuscrites du Treizieme au Dix-Huitieme Siecle (1295–1787)*. Toulouse: Douladoure-Privat, n.d.

Rossiaud, Jacques. *Medieval Prostitution*. Translated by Lydia G. Cochrane. New York: Blackwell, 1988.

——. "Prostitution, Youth and Society in the Towns of Southeastern France in the Fifteenth Century." In *Deviants and the Abandoned in French Society*, 1–146. Baltimore, MD: The Johns Hopkins University Press, 1978.

Ruggiero, Guido. "The Cooperation of Physicians and the State in the Control of Violence in Renaissance Venice." *Journal of the History of Medicine and Allied Science* 33 (1978): 155–166.

——. "Constructing Civic Morality, Deconstructing the Body: Civic Rituals of Punishment in Renaissance Venice." In *Riti e rituali nelle società medievali*, edited by Jacques Chiffoleau, Lauro Martines, and Agostino Paravinci Bagliani, 175–190. Spoleto: Centro Italiano Di Studi Sull'Alto Medioevo, 1994.

Salies, Pierre. *Études sur le notariat Toulousain au moyen âge*. Albi: Imprimerie-Reliure des Orphelins Apprentis, 1959.

Saige, Gustave. *Les Juifs du Languedoc antérieurement au XIVe siècle*. Paris: Gregg Pub., 1881.

Shatzmiller, Joseph. "Médecins et expertise médicale dans la ville médiévale: Manosque, 1280–1348." In *Vie priveé et ordre public à la fin du moyen- âge*, 105–117.

——. *Médicine et justice en Provence médiévale: documents de Manosque, 1262–1348*. Aix-en-Provence: Publications de l' Université de Provence, 1989.

Silverman, Lisa. *Tortured Subjects: Pain, Truth and the Body in Early Modern France*. Chicago: The University of Chicago Press, 2001.

Smail, Daniel Lord. "Common Violence: Vengeance and Inquisition in Fourteenth-Century Marseille." *Past and Present*, 151 (May, 1996): 28–59.

——. *The Consumption of Justice: Emotions, Publicity, and the Legal Culture in Marseille, 1264–1423*. Ithaca: Cornell University Press, 2003.

——. "Hatred as a Social Institution in Late-Medieval Society." *Speculum* 76, no. 1 (January 2001): 90–126.

Small, Carola M. "Prisoners in the Castellany of Artois in the Early Fourteenth Century," *Histoire sociale – Social History*, vol. XXVI (November 1993): p. 345–372.

Smith, Cyril Eugene. *The University of Toulouse in the Middle Ages: Its Origins and Growth to 1500 A.D.* Milwaukee, Wisconsin: The Marquette University Press, 1958.

Spierenburg, Pieter. *The Spectacle of Suffering: Executions and the Evolution of Repression, from a Preindustrial Metropolis to the European Experience*. Cambridge: Cambridge University Press, 1984.

Strayer, Joseph R. *Les Gens de Justice du Languedoc sous Philippe le Bel*. Toulouse: Association Marc Bloch, 1970.

——. *The Reign of Philip the Fair*. Princeton, N.J.: Princeton University Press, 1980.

Stuart, Kathy. *Defiled Trades and Social Outcasts: Honor and Ritual Pollution in Early Modern Germany*. Cambridge: Cambridge University Press, 1999.

Sumption, Jonathan. *The Albigensian Crusade*. London and Boston: Faber & Faber, 1978.

Tardif, Adolphe François. *Le droit privé au XIIIe siècle d'après les coutumes de Toulouse et Montpellier*. Paris: A. Picard, 1886.

Timbal, Pierre. *Un conflit d'annexion au Moyen Âge: L'application de la coutume de Paris au Pays d'Albigeois*. Toulouse: Privat, 1949.

Toureille Valérie. "Cri de peur et cri de haine: haro sur le voleur. Cri et crime en France à la fin du Moyen Âge." In *Haro! Noël! Oyé! Pratiques du cri au Moyen Âge*, edited by Didier Lett and Nicolas Offenstadt, 169–178. Paris: Publications de la Sorbonne, 2003.

Tlusty, B. Ann. *Bacchus and Civil Order: The Culture of Drink in Early Modern Germany.* Charlottesville: University Press of Virginia, 2001.

——. "Civic Defense and the Right to Bear Arms in the Early Modern German City." *Acta Histriae* 10 (2002): 493–506.

——. "Violence and Urban Identity in Early Modern Augsburg: Communication Strategies Between Authorities and Citizens in the Adjudication of Fights." In *Cultures of Communication from Reformation to Enlightenment: Constructing Publics in the Early Modern German Lands*, ed. James Van Horn Melton, 10–23. Burlington, VT: Ashgate Publishing Company, 2002.

Viala, André. *Le Parlement de Toulouse et l'administration royale laïque (1420–1525, environ)*, vol. 1. Albi: Imprimerie-Reliure des Orphelins-Apprentis, 1953.

Vidal, Jean-Marie. "Menet de Robécourt, commissaire de l'inquisition de Carcassone." *Moyen Âge* 16 (1903): 425–449.

Wakefield, Walter L. *Heresy, Crusade and Inquisition in Southern France*. Berkeley: University of California Press, 1974.

Wolff, Philippe. *Les "estimes" Toulousaines des XIVe et Xve siècles*. Toulouse, Centre National de la Recherche Scientifique, 1956.

——. *Commerces et Marchands de Toulouse (vers 1350–1450)*. Paris: Librairie Pilon, 1954.

——. *Histoire de Toulouse*. Toulouse: Édouard Privat, 1958.

INDEX

Accusatory Procedure 26, 138
Adultery 24, 64, 114, 164n90
Albi 4, 18, 112, 144, 149, 150, 162–163
Albigensian Crusade 1, 3, 5, 12, 23, 40, 51, 109, 129, 154, 175, 179, 183
Alcohol 85, 88, 127, 167
  see also Drinking
Amputation 141, 169
Arras 89, 112, 115, 139, 143
Asylum 17, 31–32, 119–120
Avignon 46, 61, 74, 75, 86, 113, 120, 139

Banishment 24, 118, 137, 139, 151–153
Bardin, Guillelmus 43, 67, 129, 151n50
Bartlett, Robert 10
Berenger, Aimery, squire 8, 49, 59, 67, 166–170, 177–179
Berenger, Petrus, capitol 131, 133
Berman, Harold J. 29
Bestiality 150
Bishop (of Toulouse) 26, 30, 31, 33, 35, 53, 68, 113–114, 170, 179
Black Death 46, 179
Blasphemy 26, 146
Bonhomme, Raymundus, jailer 158, 171–172
Bosto, Bernardus de, lawyer 68, 82–84, 93–94
Bourdieu, Pierre 9–10
bourg (also Bourg) 5, 6, 21–22, 31, 49–50, 53–54, 70, 107, 115, 129, 130, 151, 169
Bowsky, William M. 108
Brewers 61, 85
Bribery 105–106, 110, 117, 119
Bridges (of Toulouse)
  Bazacle Bridge 21, 92, 147–148
  Pontis Veteris 69
Brothel 118
  see also Prostitution
Butchers 48–49, 61

Capetian Kings (specific)
  Louis VII 5
  Philip Augustus 25, 33
  Louis IX 34, 91, 115
  Philip III 36, 137, 165
  Philip IV 28, 31, 38, 107, 160
  Louis X 38
  Charles IV 35, 151
  Philip VI 115, 147, 151, 177
Capitols
  Administrators 1–2, 5–7, 11, 13, 22–23, 52, 56, 125–126, 158
  Election Process 36
  Jurisdiction of 24, 27, 35, 58, 64–66, 73, 89–90, 95
  Privileges of Office 12, 37–41, 50–51, 106–107
  Restrictions Against 25, 29, 30, 31, 36, 49, 124, 177–180
  Role in Undermining Outside Authority 3, 4, 8, 14–15, 17–18, 20, 60, 103–104, 131–134, 141–142, 156–157, 163. 165–176
  Title 39
  Use of Customary Punishments 142–153
capitoulats 13, 22, 49
Carcassone 4, 52, 112, 113
Castration 164
Cathars 1, 4, 18, 19, 24–27, 34, 47, 52, 55, 112–113, 155–157, 161, 162, 181, 182
Certeau, Michel de 11
Château Narbonnais 21, 22, 25, 28, 30, 36, 41, 47, 51, 55, 56, 57, 69, 78, 92, 93, 146, 150, 151, 155, 160–162, 169, 173, 175, 178
Châtelet de Paris 45, 141
Chiffoleau, Jacques 45, 74, 75, 86, 113, 139
cité 5, 21–22, 49, 107, 151
Citizens Arrest 89–90
Citizenship (definition of) 23
Clergy
  Criminal Element 77, 114, 118, 161
  Living Space of Toulouse 68, 70
  Privileges 3, 8, 26, 30, 31, 33, 35, 128, 131, 160, 168, 177, 178
  Role in Ritual Justice 128, 140, 151
  Victims of Violence 59, 133–134, 156
Clothing 24, 51, 53, 56, 86, 90, 91, 93, 132, 167, 171
  see also lay clothing
Cohen, Esther 45, 140, 145
Cohn, Samuel K. 11–12
Conspire
  see Revenge
Costellum 148–149
Counts

Raymondine of Toulouse 12, 18, 20–24, 27, 47, 49, 106, 139, 145, 180
see also Poitiers, Alphonse of
Coutumes de Beauvaisis 89
Coutumes de Toulouse 38, 51, 111, 148, 163–164
Crimes
Deception in 86–87
Historiography of 43–46
Premeditated Public Assaults 82–84, 85–86
see Blasphemy, Homicide, Rape, Theft
custos nocturnos
see Guet, Night Guards

Daurade 22, 24, 26, 50, 54, 67, 70, 111, 147, 179
Decapitation 140, 148, 169
Defamation 75–77, 95
Dijon 115, 146, 150
Doctors
see Medical Experts
Dominicans
Dominic, Saint 155
Inquisition 27, 37, 55, 100, 112–113, 155–156, 161, 162
Officials 1, 3, 6, 12, 14, 20, 30, 34
Protests Against 156–157
Drinking 33, 58, 120, 121, 172, 173
see also Alcohol
Douze Livres 40

"éstimes" 6, 49–50, 53
Excommunication 19, 25, 33, 34
Expulsion
see Banishment

Fabri, Eustachius, vicar 140
Foucault, Michel 9
Franciscus, Arnaldus, sergeant 59, 70, 118–120, 121, 152

Gaillac 144
Garland, Jean de 1–2, 34, 181
Garonne River
As Location of Crime 38, 69, 85, 91–92, 99
Part of City's Topography 17, 20, 21, 22, 47, 48, 50–51, 55, 60, 67, 68, 152
Use in Punishment 31, 147–148, 150, 173
Gates (of Toulouse)
Arnaud Bernard Gate 22, 54, 63, 70, 79, 80, 132, 146, 150, 151, 169, 172–173
Badacley Gate 70, 87, 121
Matabovis Gate 59, 68
Narbonnais Gate 54, 67, 92
Pousonville Gate 22, 54
Villeneuve Gate 22, 54, 88
Gaure, Franciscus de, capitol 67, 124–125, 167–169
Gauvard, Claude 116, 140–141
Geltner, Guy 148
Geremek, Bronislav 61, 114
Ghent
see David Nicholas
Gonthier, Nicole 61, 86, 114, 160
Grocers 62, 68, 81, 99, 130, 132, 134
Groebner, Valentin 91
Grudges 79–80
see also Hatred
Guet 109–111
Gui, Bernard 7, 156, 162
Guilds
Members listed in Toulouse's Criminal Records 61–62
Obligations in Paris 110, 159
Statutes 6, 10, 37, 48, 60, 74

Hanawalt, Barbara A. 10, 44, 64, 81
Hanging 67, 141, 144–147, 154, 160
Reversal of 128, 178
Hammer, Carl I. 44
Hatred 80–81
Heretics 174
see Cathars
Homicide 32, 44, 114
Hostages 51, 155
Hundred Years War 45, 109, 129, 179

Illegal Arms
Excuses for Carrying 78–79
Involvement in Crime 30, 59, 69, 70, 100, 119, 127, 133, 167
Regulation Against 24, 90, 107
Injury
Mortal Wounds 80, 81, 84, 98
Resulting in Deformity 82–84, 91
To the Head 78, 80, 82, 86, 88, 98, 121, 124, 133
see also Mutilation
Inquisition
see Dominicans
Inquisitorial Procedure 138–139
Insults
see Defamation
Inns
see Taverns

Jacobins 55, 155
Jeux Floraux 182

Jews 3–4, 47, 97
Johannes, Guillelmus, trumpeter 140, 171–173

Kidnapping 31, 68, 87, 170

Law
  Canon law 27, 30, 31, 33, 161
  Customary law 5, 24, 29–30, 39, 84, 89, 99, 149, 163
  Roman law 28, 32, 138
Lawyers 7, 9, 32, 52, 55, 57, 64, 66, 81, 96, 130, 149, 168
Lay Clothing 30, 96, 169
L'Engle, Susan 105
Lemosini, Michael, scholar 130–134
Lepers Plot 3–4
Location (of criminal activity from AMT-FF57) 65–71
Lyon 61, 82, 86, 92, 105, 113, 114, 115, 116, 119, 160
Kibre, Pearl 32–33

Manso, Johannes de 62, 68, 170–172
Master
  of Guild 60, 148
  of University 1, 32–36, 50, 59, 126, 127
Medical Experts 9, 59, 87, 97–98, 100, 167, 168
Messengers
  Municipal 2, 9, 32, 59, 95–96, 107, 109, 123
  Of the vicar 103, 104, 117, 126, 135
Moissac 21, 75, 118, 152
Montfort, Simon de 51–52, 109, 154
Montpellier 32
Motivations (for violent attacks) 79–81
Mulholland, Sister Mary Ambrose 60
Mundy, John Hine 6, 25, 53, 54
Mutilation 17, 31, 66, 83, 139–140, 154
  see also Injury

Nicholas, David 44, 75, 80, 97–98, 109, 139
Nicholaý, Guillelmus, doctor 98
Night Guards
  Altercations Involving 69, 167–168
  Arrests Made by 78–79, 148, 174
  Corruption of 104, 106, 116, 121, 123–126, 131–134
  Responsibilities of Office 46, 105, 111–112, 120
  Victim of an Attack 82
  see also guet
Nirenberg, David 3–4
Nomenclature (in Languedoc) 58–59

Notary
  Corruption of 112–113
  Criminal Perpetrator 59, 130
  Involvement in Criminal Proceedings 83, 99
  Official of the Court 2, 9, 11, 29, 50, 52, 55, 58, 77, 80, 95, 98, 123
  Protected official 107
  Victim of assault 120

Oaths
  Of service or loyalty 5, 17, 37, 41, 83, 110, 117, 158
  In Criminal Trials 63, 74, 96, 97
Occupations (of defendants listed in AMT-FF57) 59–62
Otis, Leah Lydia 149

"Parens scientiarum" 34–35
Parlement 28, 20, 31, 32, 36, 56, 57, 107, 114, 120, 139, 177
Peace Treaty of Paris (1229) 1, 19, 25, 34, 129, 155
Physician
  see Medical Experts
Place St. Georges 48, 62, 68, 70, 81, 123, 147
Plague 129
Plot
  see Revenge
Poitiers, Alphonse of 5, 25, 28, 35, 49, 151
Pope (specific)
  Alexander III 33
  Innocent III 18, 25
  Honorius III 34, 52
  Gregory IX 19, 34
  Innocent IV 35
  John XXII 4
  Benedict XII 113
Portello, Guillelmus 68, 87, 172–173
Prison
  Ecclesiastical 53, 55, 161–163
  Municipal 31, 52, 58, 78, 91, 111, 148–149, 157–160
  Royal 55, 115, 160–161
  see Costellum
Procession 12, 92, 112, 140, 148–151, 164, 169, 173, 178
Prostitution 64, 70, 90–92, 94, 113, 118, 121
Protests (in Toulouse) 2, 3, 4, 11–12, 17–18, 32, 45, 46, 52, 66–67, 103, 141, 157, 162, 180
Punishment
  Burned at the stake 156
  The "cage" 147
  Customary Punishment (of Toulouse) 24

Demographic of those punished 141
Fines 143–144
Frequency of Executions 139–140
Gallows/Pillory 24, 145–147
"Running the Town" 149–151
Visual Depiction of customary punishment 163–164
see Banishment, Costellum, Rege Ribaldum

Rallying Cries (inciting violence) 103–104, 125
Rape 24, 26, 68, 86, 110, 114, 121–122, 171
Rege Ribaldum 166, 172, 174
Residency (of defendants in AMT-FF57) 62–63
Revenge 34, 83, 84, 86–88, 93, 104, 124, 130, 134, 166
Ritual
Of Justice 10–11, 74, 92, 94–100
Punishments 138–141, 149–151, 166–175
see Rege Ribaldum

Saint Cyprian (suburb) 64, 69, 90, 91, 148
Saint Étienne (cathedral) 21, 22, 26, 54, 55, 67, 68, 77, 113, 146–147, 156, 162
Saint Sernin (basilica) 21, 26, 39, 47, 49, 52–55, 60, 70, 130–132, 150, 162, 169, 181
Saletas, Stephanus 66, 82–84, 93–94, 99
Santolo, Johaneta de 118, 119, 121, 152
Saturninus, Saint 26, 39–40
Seneschal 4, 5, 28, 35, 38, 66, 107, 126, 130, 131, 155, 160, 161, 170, 171, 172, 177
Sergeants
Attacks Against 116–117
Ecclesiastical 112–114
Inciting Violence 123–125
Municipal 2, 9, 14, 59, 66, 70, 79, 96, 104, 107–108, 111, 112, 152, 171, 173, 178
Royal 12, 26, 29, 55, 112, 112, 114–116, 160
Police Brutality 120–122
Serras, Guillemus, Master 133–134
Shepherds Crusade 3–4
Slander
see Defamation
Smail, Daniel Lord 80
Small, Carola M. 89, 112
Space
Conceptual methodology 9–10
see also Asylum
Squire 8, 49, 56, 59, 67, 129, 166–170, 174, 177, 178

Taverns
As Places of Business 21, 47, 55–57, 71, 110, 113, 114
As Sites of Conflict 33, 65, 78, 84, 85–86, 88, 116, 121, 127, 167, 182
Owners involved in Conflicts 60, 64, 69, 82, 99
Taxation 2, 51, 67, 116, 178, 180
see also les "éstimes"
Theft 31, 43, 44, 45, 56, 57, 61, 64, 69, 82, 87, 118, 119, 152, 160, 172
Threats (of interpersonal violence) 13, 17, 68, 75, 77–78, 79, 81, 82, 83, 88, 91, 124, 157
Torture
As part of Inquisitorial procedure 27, 32, 112, 139, 141, 144, 155, 156, 161
Exemption from 37–38
In Corrupt Acts 4, 31, 40, 121, 162, 182
Town Hall (of Toulouse) 2, 14, 17, 22, 23, 32, 36, 39–40, 47, 51–52, 66, 67, 84, 94, 103–104, 107, 140, 148–149, 158, 168, 172, 179–180
Town Crier 89, 90, 95, 96, 98, 100, 157
Transients 58, 73
Treason 15, 38, 141, 145
Trials (procedures in Toulouse) 96
Trumpeter (of Toulouse) 2, 14, 90, 96, 140, 142, 144, 146, 147, 149, 150, 169, 171, 172, 173, 182
Tudela, William of 51, 109

University
of Paris 1, 33–34, 178
of Orleans 128
of Oxford 44, 127
of Toulouse 12, 28–29, 32–35, 36, 50, 53, 98
Town and Gown Rows 33, 126–134

Vicar
Count's 5, 21, 24, 25, 103, 117
Royal 28, 29, 30, 35, 36, 47, 55, 60, 69, 89, 90, 107, 115, 126, 137, 138, 140, 142–144, 147, 149, 156, 158, 160, 161, 165, 166, 168, 170–175, 180
Villamuro 66, 93
Vitalis, Berengaria 166, 170–175

Weapon (used in criminal activity)
Dagger 78, 86, 167
Knife 78, 85, 92, 157
Roof Tile 88
Staff 78, 80, 85, 99, 103, 121, 132, 133

Stone/Rock 78, 81, 84, 85, 88, 116, 143, 154, 157
Sword 77, 78, 79, 82, 84, 87, 94, 108, 121, 123, 124, 125, 127, 132, 143, 167
Weavers 60, 62, 123–124
Wolff, Philippe 49, 56
Women
As conspirators 93–94
As perpetrators 63–64, 81, 86, 91, 93, 145
As victims 81, 92–93, 120–122, 163
As witnesses 99–100
Religious Orders 54
Slander Committed by 75–77
Execution of 145
see Vitalis, Berengaria

www.ingramcontent.com/pod-product-compliance
Lightning Source LLC
Chambersburg PA
CBHW070003240926
52025CB00004B/30
9789004234642